From Vick-tim to Vick-tory
The Fall and Rise of Michael Vick

by Kenneth N. Robinson, MS

Strategic Book Publishing and Rights Co.

Strategic Book Publishing and Rights Co.
12620 FM 1960, Suite A4-507
Houston, TX 77065
www.sbpra.com

ISBN: 978-1-62516-352-3

Book Design: Suzanne Kelly

Cover artwork provided by Nathaniel Key, www.natekey.com

Dedication

To my wife Tonya, and my daughters Za'imah, Na'ilah, Layla, and Noelle: Thanks for your patience, prayers, and support throughout this arduous process.

A special thanks to my mother Janet, my twin brother Tim, and my aunt Betty ("Low") for being there without fail. To all of my siblings, cousins, aunts, uncles, and paternal grandmother, who believed in me and encouraged me to "Aim High," thank you all.

This book is especially dedicated to the memory of my late maternal grandparents, Sam and Fredell Jarrett, who migrated from Marvell, Arkansas, to Buffalo, New York in 1950.

Acknowledgements

First and foremost, all praises are due to G-d for blessing me with life and a will to better it. Once more, thanks to my entire family, whose unchanging love and support has empowered me to be me. Thanks to Ron and Greg, who taught us the letters of the alphabet by age two—*Look at me now!* To my brother Darvin ("Mugz"), thanks for your unique inspiration.

To my alma mater, Buffalo State, thanks for according me such a quality education. Of course I cannot forget Dr. John H. Song, Professor of Criminal Justice, who encouraged me to become "Master Robinson."

Thanks to the entire Department of Sociology, including Drs. Gary Welborn, Thomas Weinberg, Amitra Wall, Eric Krieg, and Ron Stewart. Thanks to the resourceful Dr. Chuck Newman and the E.H. Butler Library on campus. As well, a special thanks to Bruce Fox and Kaylene Waite of Instructional Resources. To my colleagues and all the students at Buffalo State, whom I have had the good pleasure of serving, you're appreciated much. Big up! To Don Patterson and the Upward Bound Program, those summers have been great. To Darryl "Juice" Carter of STEP (Science Technology Entry Program), thanks for involving me in your meaningful work with high school students. Thanks to the high school students in the Buffalo State Challenge—by the yard can be hard, but inch by inch is a cinch.

Thanks to the media sources who accorded me space for my critical writings. These include: *The Challenger News*, *The Buffalo Criterion*, *The Thinker*, *The Buffalo News Sports Talk Column*, and www.blackathlete.net. A very special acknowledgement is warranted in memory of the late Allen Wilson, a sports writer for the *Buffalo News*. Peace to Brother Roy St. Clair for the support and "Brother Aqil" (RIP), the best writing

v

instructor I ever had. To Downtown USA, always home! Ezelle Williams, thanks for Malcolm's book; I have not looked back. Thanks to the Buffalo & Erie County Public Library, an excellent reservoir for research.

A debt of gratitude is extended to Dr. Reuben A. Buford May, Session Organizer, on the *Sociology of Sport*, who accepted my paper on the Subculture of Violence Theory (Chapter I of this book), which I presented at the American Sociological Association annual meeting in Las Vegas, Nevada, in August 2011. Thanks to Dr. Adrienne N. Milner, sport sociologist, from the University of Alabama at Birmingham, for reviewing this book. Your keen observations and suggestions amounted to a prodigious contribution that I will always appreciate.

To Nathaniel Key, the illustrator of the book cover, you came through in the clutch!

A special thanks to Imam Fajri Ansari for all you've done and the Believers at Masjid Nu'Man. Much appreciation is extended, posthumously, to the life and legacy of Imam W. Deen Mohammed.

I'd be remiss if I didn't acknowledge the subject of this work, NFL quarterback Michael Vick. A lesser human being would have folded under such duress. Thanks for inspiring me to write this book.

Thanks to all of the forbearers who paved the way for an individual like me to have a voice in this society, and the courage to use it.

A heartfelt debt of gratitude is owing to the Strategic Book Publishing and Rights Co. The quality service and professionalism that I experienced made this difficult endeavor much easier.

"A ship at harbor is safe. But that's not what ships are for."

"What is it you want? With your brains you can have it. Knowledge will get it for you."

Cooley High, 1975

Table of Contents

Foreword

Fandom, media, and the National Football League, when operating simultaneously, can produce euphoria and, sadly, shame. In the case of fans, what determines the eventual outcome is winning or losing; in the case of the media, greater sponsorships; and for NFL players, it's their persona on and off the field. In a perfect world this tripartite relationship results in everyone having their pleasures satiated. Fans and the media experience the euphoria of pro football on Sundays, Mondays, and sometimes Thursdays. Unfortunately for many players, the experience of euphoria is likely to vacillate with that of shame, and the latter is more likely to happen off the field.

In this book, Kenneth Robinson addresses the shame that the iconic Michael Vick experienced. Robinson does so in poignant and pointed detail, chronicling the rise, fall, and return of one of the NFL's elite players. Central to Robinson's examination is the influence of Vick's social milieu and racism. Though the general consensus is Vick contributed to his own undoing, Robinson demonstrates how a confluence of factors is indeed the real culprit. In Chapter I, he uses historical and theoretical analyses, to show that Vick's penchant for cruelty to animals was shaped by a parent culture whose ethos for violence is as American as apple pie. Robinson's research reveals, that the parent culture of dog fighting, which influenced Vick, is actually centuries old, and traceable to Ancient Europe. There, it evolved and was transplanted to America in the nineteenth century, becoming a staple of the South. As meaningful as this retro-analysis proves to be, it merely sets the stage for Robinson's theoretical framework, which uses Marvin Wolfgang's Subculture of Violence Theory to explain Vick's involvement in dog fighting. In making this extraordinary connection, the author is dutiful in delineating Wolfgang's central summation, that the violence exhibited by blacks is only partly different from the parent culture of violence. Chapter II discusses race and the retributive reaction of the NFL and its dominant alliance, which include the media, corporate sponsors, and the politics of the state, all of who shaped the league as we know it today, and contributed mightily to Vick's demise. In addressing the issue of race, Robinson examines the inequitable treatment of Vick in comparison to other league miscreants who are white; e.g., head coach Bill Belichick and his Spygate scandal, which the author argues, may have violated federal laws, and quarterback Ben Roethlisberger, who was twice accused of sexual assault, truly a more egregious violation of both the league's and society's moral creed. Robinson's concerns about race as an interceding variable seem plausible since, unlike Vick, neither Belichick nor Roethlisberger were charged with a crime.

Chapter III bears witness to the unenviable habit of the NFL saying one thing in public while doing diametrically the opposite in private. The "thing" Robinson exposes here is the abject hypocrisy permeating the league. In a nutshell, when it comes to cruelty to animals, league policy finds the behavior abhorrent. However, when one examines the NFL's relationship with China, a country with as sordid a record of animal cruelty as there is, one finds disingenuousness par excellence. Using both data and acid discernment to support his exposé, Robinson concludes for each dog killed by Vick, behavior that the league excoriated, China ordered the slaughter of more than 13,000 dogs, behavior the league ostensibly overlooks. It is important that Robinson examines the NFL and its business relationship with China, if for no other reason than to illustrate how the NFL projects and protects its brand while at the same time demonizing the brand of those instrumental in the proliferation of the NFL.

Seemingly, sports and its storied history of opening doors for the underprivileged would escape the venom spewed by the likes of Rush Limbaugh and those of his ilk. Yet we see in Chapter IV Robinson's ability to present a narrative clearly showing the bedfellow arrangement between America's exemplar of evil-speak and its most popular and prosperous sport—NFL football. Moreover, in Chapter IV the opportunism of those so-called bastions of animal protection is revealed, indicating how Vick's misfortune unwittingly increased the fortunes of organizations that ought to be above using sensationalism for gain. Yes, speculation of such behavior emanating from the Humane Society of the United States (HSUS) and PETA (People for the Ethical Treatment of Animals) is correct. Yet, Robinson chides the Humane Society especially, for agreeing to partner with Michael Vick, while on the other hand allowing Rush Limbaugh to record a public service announcement, in which he referred to street-fighters of dogs as "people like Michael Vick". The author's analysis of arrests data by race shows that subsequent to Limbaugh's public recording, the number of blacks arrested for dog fighting increased disproportionately when compared to whites and Hispanics.

Chapter V takes a critical look, in black and white at the differences in treatment by race in the scandals involving quarterbacks Michael Vick and Ben Roethlisberger. Expanding on his analysis introduced in Chapter II, Robinson argues persuasively, that the powerful elites demonized Vick but sanitized Roethlisberger. Specifically, while both may have engaged in unconscionable behavior, Robinson draws on Howard Becker's Sequential Model of Deviant Behavior, to illustrate how "labeling" works in the interests of the white football player, but to the detriment of the black one. This chapter shows how one's acceptance and success as a quarterback in the NFL depends largely upon the media, corporate sponsorship, and the politics of the state. In fact, Robinson's spiel on state political influence in this chapter is riveting. So much so, it could be discussed as "The Continued Significance of Race and Politics in the NFL."

Continuing the position broached in Chapter V, Chapter VI again compares the treatment of Vick, a convicted dog fighter, to the treatment of Floyd Boudreaux, notorious for his dog fighting acumen. This discussion unequivocally indicates a bias in relation to how local, state, and federal officials perceive and treat individuals suspected of dog fighting. Vick, the black defendant, experienced the full force of the law in being convicted on state and federal charges. In stark contrast, Boudreaux, who is white and renowned as the don of dog fighting, was acquitted on state charges and was never charged by the federal government. In this instance, Robinson broaches the delicate subject of selective enforcement by race, an important discussion that needs to be held in America.

For each wrongful comeuppance there is the likelihood of redemption for the aggrieved. As it pertains to Vick's seemingly unjust penalty, his redemption is both absolute and a work in progress. This is made clear in Chapter VII, the final chapter, "Redemption: The Fall and Rise of Michael Vick." This chapter addresses the depths of Vick's fall from grace, with emphasis placed on the toll it took on him, his family, and his finances. But where the rubber hits the road in this chapter is in Robinson's discussion of Vick's comeback, beginning with his release from prison and ending with him not just surpassing the public's expectations of Vick the football player, but also the public's opinion of Vick the man. Buffeted with the author's discussion of Vick's animal rights advocacy, this final chapter is a primer on how to rebuild an image shattered by greed, naiveté, racism, and the lack of compassion. For African-American males, there is a need for greater compassion, rather than none, given the history of institutional defamation, exploitation, incarceration, and oppression.

From Vick-tim to Vick-tory: The Fall and Rise of Michael Vick is more than a book about the rise and fall of an athletic icon. It delves deep into the heart and soul of professional sports, revealing the inequities that exist in a multicultural, multiracial, and class-divided society. Ultimately, it shows how money and power at the highest levels can be used unjustly. It begs the question: Was Michael Vick's fall a consequence of his own doing, or was it par for the course for any black male perceived as going beyond his place in a racially hostile society? That Vick was disgraced during the infancy of the United States' experiment with post-racism lends credence to the latter rather than the former. No matter how far a black man rises in the United States, he is always subject to being brought down both by his own doing or the willful doings of others. What is so appealing about Robinson's narrative is he makes it clear that even if the greatest among black men is brought down, with fortitude and resilience, he can redeem himself and rise again. For that truth, I thank him immensely.

Buffalo, NY
Ron Stewart, Ph.D.
October 2012
SUNY-Buffalo State

Preface

If Michael Vick, who has a tattoo of Superman's insignia on the back of his right hand, is akin to Superman on the football field, then the dog fighting scandal proved to be his kryptonite.

From Vick-tim to Vick-tory: The Fall and Rise of Michael Vick chronicles the odyssey of the NFL's superstar quarterback. This phenomenal football player went from a life of unbridled opulence to being ostracized by the NFL and society. In 2007 he was indicted, pled guilty, and sentenced to nearly two years in federal prison for operating an illegal dog fighting enterprise. In 2009 Vick resumed his NFL career after being released from prison. As deplorable as his dog fighting crimes were, *Vick-tim* addresses several outstanding questions. To wit: Why would Michael Vick risk a very successful and lucrative NFL career over dog fighting? While dogs were certainly abused, mistreated, and killed, was Vick himself somehow a victim in the dog fighting debauchery? How does Marvin Wolfgang's research, which produced the *Subculture of Violence Theory,* help to explain Vick's involvement in dog fighting? What role did the NFL and its dominant allies, such as the media, corporate sponsors, and the politics of the state, play in quickening his downfall? How does *Labeling Theory* offer a plausible explanation for Vick's social demise?

As for Vick somehow being a victim, it is hard to imagine him as such given the tumultuous torture he and his co-defendants inflicted upon innocent dogs. But qualitative research in this book shows that Vick was the apparent victim of a centuries-old, decadent culture of animal combat that made dog fighting as a blood sport popular and even permissible in his eyes. Many found it difficult to explain why he ventured into dog fighting. The prevailing view of the time, propagated by sports reporters, animal rights advocates, and even academia, suggested hip-hop culture was to blame. Yet in 2009 during a revealing interview on CBS's *60 Minutes*, Vick indicated that his involvement in dog fighting was influenced by a "so-called culture." But rather than hip-hop, research in *Vick-tim* shows that this *so-called culture* is inextricably linked to a parent culture of dog fighting, the origins of which go back to 43 AD, when the Romans and Britons clashed using fighting dogs. This parent culture evolved and emerged in America in the nineteenth century. A thorough examination of the history of dog fighting must include its requisite conduct norms of gambling, baiting, and the killing of underperforming dogs. That Vick demonstrated these barbaric behaviors is pivotal when considering Wolfgang's *Subculture of Violence Theory* as a credible explanation for Vick's involvement.

Wolfgang's perspective holds that the violence exhibited by blacks is only partly different from the *parent culture* of violence. In America, one such parent is the United Kennel Club, which in 1817 began fighting the Staffordshire terrier, which became the American pit bull terrier. By the 1930s, the American Pit Bull Terrier Association was staging dog fights with pit bulls throughout the South, where Vick grew up. Such dog fighting cultures and organizations were actually progenitors of Michael Vick's Bad Newz Kennels. All of which gives additional credence to Wolfgang's subculture of violence theory as an explanation for Vick's participation in dog fighting. In addition to this subcultural phenomenon, the book chides the negative influences of popular culture that made Vick a scapegoat for animal cruelty.

The NFL's suspension of the star quarterback for dog fighting is denounced in this book as the height of hypocrisy, especially since the NFL never suspended its business ties to the People's Republic of China, which has a wretched record of animal cruelty, yet is still paid to broadcast league programming. This communist state ordered the indiscriminant massacre of 110,000 dogs from 2006 through 2009, dates that encompass the period when Vick was being vilified. To put this in broader perspective, for every dog that Vick was held responsible for killing (eight), China slaughtered 13,500. A disparity of gross proportions, yet no one asked the NFL to explain such a blatant contradiction. Today the NFL still pays China, which has no laws against animal cruelty. Hence millions of dogs are slaughtered there each year. Many are skinned alive for the illicit international fur trade. Oddly enough, half of all fur coats purchased by unsuspecting Americans are made in China, coming off the backs of dogs and cats, without a remark or rebuke from the league. Still, content analysis in *Vick-tim* shows the electronic and print media never questioned the NFL about this inherent conflict of interest, but condemned Vick incessantly. Corporate sponsors like Nike and Reebok dropped Vick, but like the NFL, continue to do business with China. *Vick-tim* addresses these and other related matters as reflecting the arrogance of power in America's sports culture.

Furthermore, this book observes that the nexus between dog fighting and sports culture in America was in place long before Vick's dog fighting debacle. Today upwards of 300 educational institutions in America—high schools, colleges, and universities—use the fighting bulldog as their mascot, most notably for its symbolic value in sports. The bulldog is the ancestral parent of the pit bull and was first bred in Europe for the express purpose of animal combat. Interestingly enough, one of the most successful teams in NFL history was the Canton Bulldogs of the 1920s. Thus, a significant part of the NFL's football ethos was built upon the culture of dog fighting. *Vick-tim* ushers in such meaningful views to expand our understanding of what happened to Vick and the dogs, and to call attention to the conflicting nature of this social problem in our society. Michael Vick must now wear this problem like an albatross around his neck, as the unwitting face of animal cruelty.

This work also uses "labeling theory" to explain the harm that deviant descriptors can have when attached to someone like Vick. His hometown of Newport News, Virginia, was pejoratively labeled *Bad Newz*. Hence his dog fighting organization was named *Bad Newz Kennels*. In his football career, he was labeled a *black quarterback*, which made him an outsider in the quarterback fraternity. The media dubbed him *dangerous*, given his style of play on the field, which seemed to influence his dangerous conduct off the field. Could such disparaging references have influenced Vick's perception of himself and ultimately his foray into dog fighting, despite the risks to his lucrative career? Noted sociologist W.I. Thomas held that if you believe a situation is real, then it is real in its consequences.

Despite the tumultuous events of the past, Michael Vick returned to the role of a starting NFL quarterback in a stunning reclamation. In 2010 he was voted NFC Offensive Player of the Month, along with other honors, and was a Pro Bowl selection. Vick's remarkable resurrection culminated in the Philadelphia Eagles capturing the NFC East Division crown, and he was named NFL Comeback Player of the Year. In 2011, he became the first NFL player to sign two different contracts, years apart, each worth more than $100 million.

Yet, despite such a heroic resurgence, his road to redemption continues in the shadow of his ill-fated past. *Vick-tim* is the unique account of the fall and rise of Michael Vick that must be told.

CHAPTER I

The Subculture of Violence Theory

An Explanation for Michael Vick's Involvement in Dog Fighting

"There is a direct line from (fighting dogs in) bull baiting at the Smithfield market in London in the early 19ᵗʰ century to dogfighting (involving Michael Vick's Bad Newz Kennels) in Smithfield, Virginia, in the early 21st (century)."

—Edmund Russell, Professor, University of Virginia

(2007, para.14)

In 2007 the sports world was shocked at the stunning revelation that NFL star quarterback Michael Vick of the Atlanta Falcons was involved in an illegal dog fighting operation, notoriously known as "Bad Newz Kennels." The riveting revelations were appalling for several reasons. For one, Vick had become one of the most popular and exciting All-Pro players in the NFL. Secondly, in 2007, he was also the game's highest-paid player with a ten-year, $130 million contract. Moreover, at his peak, Vick was among the most marketable professional athletes, earning upwards of $60 million in corporate endorsements (Bell, 2007). But even more outrageous were the repugnant details of dogs experiencing some of the worst forms of animal cruelty.

There were accounts of female pit bulls, resistant to mating, being forcibly restrained by a rape stand so male dogs could impregnate them. Even worse, dogs that did not perform well in test matchups or in actual combat were killed in the most depraved ways. The horrific methods for killing underperforming dogs included electrocution, drowning, hanging, shooting, and even being slammed to the concrete. While Vick was indeed a licensed dog breeder, his was not a license to commit such debauchery. As gruesome as these details are and as much as they should affect our sensibilities, such particulars should not, however, diminish our social responsibility to explore why it happened. Nor should it obscure the need to address several outstanding questions. To wit: Why would Vick risk a very productive and lucrative NFL career by operating an illegal dog fighting ring? What factors led him to venture into a seedy and shadowy world of animal combat using dogs? What sort of historical and theoretical analyses of dog fighting might better explain Vick's involvement in such a hideous pastime? These and other meaningful queries were never addressed. Instead, the media used sensational subterfuge and graphic accounts of animal abuse to infuriate rather than inform the public. Consequently, such questions were never posed or adequately probed by the mainstream press, scholars in academia, nor by animal rights advocates.

This chapter will serve as a disquisition on variables left unexplored. For example, upon his release from prison in 2009, Vick stated during an interview on CBS's *60 Minutes* that his involvement in dog fighting was influenced by a "so-called culture." This insightful revelation was completely overlooked. The following discussion will examine the meaning of this *so-called culture*, both historically and theoretically, to better understand and explain why Vick became involved in the illegal blood sport. His comments that the police in his neighborhood ignored dog fighting were treated as insignificant by the public, the press, academia, and the courts. However, research in this commentary will show that historically, police officers throughout the South were not only lax in their law enforcement of dog fighting, but were active participants in the blood sport. The latter is significant in shedding light on why Vick thought it was okay to fight dogs, and gives credence to his outcry that police in his community were unconcerned about it. Other important points that the public was left to ponder include the question of whether Vick's celebrity profile and race influenced the federal investigation. Nor was the issue of equal protection of the law by race ever broached over the unequal distribution of punishments for animal cruelty crimes. These important factors will not be ignored in the discourse that follows.

Additionally, this work contends that although Vick was indeed wrong for his actions, still more wrongfully he was punished for centuries of sins associated with dog fighting. Worse than that, a vast and powerful network of media, law enforcement, animal rights groups, federal lawmakers, and the courts contributed to labeling Vick as the face of animal cruelty. This chapter will address the collateral consequences of Vick being singularly seen as the epitome of animal abuse in the eyes of the public. But since he identified a so-called culture as influencing him, the more immediate question becomes, whose behavior was he actually emulating?

The discussion herein will demonstrate that a retrospective analysis on dog fighting is not only beneficial to understanding the longitudinal legacy of the blood sport, but is foundational in uncovering meaningful causes that influenced Vick's involvement in this so-called culture. The in depth historical analysis in this work portends to show that this culture of dog fighting that Vick alluded to has an identifiable *parent culture* that is traceable to ancient Europe. Moreover, the very depraved indifference to animal life that Vick demonstrated toward his dogs was consistent with parallel conduct norms that are centuries old. Such translucent norms associated with dog fighting, which was passed down from Europe, include animal combat, baiting, gambling, and killing underperforming dogs. This broader historical perspective was never given to the public, which was left with the impression that such heinous acts of animal cruelty were somehow unique to Michael Vick. But as this narrative will show, although these conduct norms associated with dog fighting did not begin in the Ridley Place projects where Vick grew up, they wound up there nonetheless.

For the purposes of this discussion, identifying and explaining this "culture", which Vick alluded to, will lead me to explore the preceding parent culture of dog fighting violence, which came to America in the nineteenth century, where it evolved. Examining this historical precedent is central to offering Marvin Wolfgang's *subculture of violence theory* as a reliable explanation for Vick's adaptation to this form of animal combat. As this discussion will highlight, the *subculture of violence theory* holds that the violence exhibited by blacks is only partly different from the parent culture of violence (Wolfgang & Ferracuti, 1967). During the discourse on the Vick dog fighting scandal, there were several references to both a "culture" of dog fighting and the formation of a subsequent "subculture." I will analyze, define, and discuss both of these concepts, later in the chapter. But before doing so, a recapitulation of Vick's reference to a "so-called culture" is pivotal to developing this meaningful discussion.

As noted, shortly after being released from prison in 2009, Vick indicated in an interview with James Brown on CBS's *60 Minutes* that his involvement in dog fighting was influenced by a *so-called culture*. This rather significant and thought-provoking disclosure has gone unattended to, until now.

So-Called Culture

In 2007, ESPN's *Outside the Lines* aired a segment on the emerging Vick investigation. Among those interviewed was John Goodwin, deputy manager of the Animal Cruelty Campaign of the Humane Society of the United States (HSUS). During the interview, Goodwin used the term *subculture* in describing the involvement of Vick and other professional athletes in dog fighting (Naqi, 2007). Mark Plowden, spokesman for the Attorney General of South Carolina, which had created a dog fighting task force in 2004, also made reference to dog fighting subcultures in America (Burke, 2007). These comments from Goodwin, Plowden, and Vick shed light on the subculture of dog fighting. Their comments also give reason for exploring the parent culture, which Wolfgang's violence theory illuminates, in explaining Vick's involvement in this decadent blood sport. A historical review of dog fighting's evolution will help for several reasons. On the one hand, since Michael Vick has pledged to educate the community about dog fighting as a social problem, he could benefit from a broader understanding of its history and his own adaptation to this criminogenic vice. Secondly, the more properly informed the public is about dog fighting as a social problem, the greater the chances of stemming the growth of this criminally deviant behavior. Additionally, this chapter will reveal what has been hidden in plain sight; that is, the link between dog fighting and America's sports culture was there long before Michael Vick's scandal. There is widespread hypocrisy in our culture. Upwards of 300 high schools, colleges, and universities use the fighting bulldog as their mascot. The bulldog was bred for the express purpose of animal combat in England. Its descendant, the pit bull, became a fixture in dog fighting matches in America from the nineteenth century to the present. Dog fighting organizations like the United Kennel Club (UKC) were actively involved in sanctioning dog fights, complete with referees (Gibson, 2005). Research in this book shows that organizations like the UKC and the American Pit Bull Terrier Association[1] hosted dog fights across interstate lines and continued to do so well into the twentieth century, thereby making them progenitors of Vick's Bad Newz Kennels. Not even Michael Vick could have understood the vastness of this so-called culture that he identified in his 2009 interview on *60 Minutes*. As much as the Vick scandal received an inordinate amount of public attention, it did not open up a Pandora's box of discourse on the tradition of this aberrant spectacle, or on the various forms of animal cruelty that are in many ways more widespread and harmful in our society. This chapter will address these significant voids in the public discourse.

A review of these various forms of animal cruelty will raise pertinent questions about selective enforcement by race, and the

---

1 State of Alabama archives, letter from American Humane Society to Gov. of Alabama, January 20, 1934.

bigger question of equal protection of the law, given the unequal distribution of punishments for different forms of animal cruelty. Currently, all fifty states and Congress punish dog fighting as felonious; by contrast, other acts of animal cruelty, such as hoarding, neglect, abuse, and bestiality are not uniformly punished as felonious. These differential punishments underscore rampant structural inequities deeply embedded in the American criminal justice system. Such stark inequities compel me to reexamine the Vick dog fighting debacle. This more comprehensive review will enlighten the public and provide suggestions for policy implications.

Why the Renewed Focus on the Vick Dog Fighting Scandal?

The importance of this renewed focus on Vick is especially warranted given the missed opportunities by the mainstream media, academia, animal rights organizations, and state officials. These important institutions should have used the Vick case to educate the public about dog fighting as a social problem in America, both historically and presently.

The mainstream media's coverage was especially troublesome. For one, the pathological perspective of the scandal, which was outlined by sports reporters, distorted the issue. Lost in the sensational subterfuge was the fact that Vick's dog fighting case was not a sports story, but instead a story of a sports figure with a legal dilemma. This is not to suggest that sports reporters were not supposed to cover it, but their virulent views seemed to set the tone for the general media's biased and bullying coverage of Vick during his downfall. The other concern with sports reporters leading the discussion is the documented history of black athletes being raised to superman status when they please us with their athletic prowess, only to be thrown to the ground when they fail to satisfy media appetites for sports glory. On the other hand, blacks attempting to play quarterback in the NFL are often portrayed in the media, as a gross deviation from the normalcy of whites at the position. Consequently,

6

they have been treated as unfit to play the coveted role in the NFL. The negative notion of a *black quarterback*, accompanied by their purported lack of leadership and intelligence, has been perpetuated by the sports reporting media historically. Not so surprisingly, as this work will show, after his criminal probe and conviction a number of sports reporters suggested Vick not be allowed to return to the NFL, and certainly not as a quarterback. But rather than focus entirely on his NFL life, which is what occurred in the aftermath of the investigation, a more balanced perspective would have probed for social factors in Vick's personal life which may have influenced his involvement in dog fighting. Vick's upbringing in the Ridley projects does not go far enough to explain his involvement in dog fighting.

On the other hand, if the public were as concerned about dogs as the social reaction suggested, there should have been concerned inquiries, such as: Why did it happen? How widespread is the problem of dog fighting in the United States? What other forms of animal cruelty should we be concerned about? But because the media portrayed it simply as a scandal, the coverage was smitten with sensationalism that fueled greater public animus. Consequently, Americans were enraged but no more enlightened about this facet of animal cruelty. Most came away from the Michael Vick narrative with the view of him as an antagonist in the strict sense, when he may have been part protagonist as well. Rather than leading the discussion, the mainstream media followed the lead of sports reporters and animal rights organizations like the Humane Society of the United States and PETA (People for The Ethical of Animals). The mass hysteria caused by these entities quickened Vick's demise and contributed to the view of him as the face of animal cruelty. Concomitantly, a skewed discourse followed. Dog fighting and animal cruelty became synonymous with street fighters of dogs, thereby placing an inordinate amount of attention on inner-city blacks, using Michael Vick as Exhibit A.

As a consequence of these so-called advocates failing to expand the scope of the discussion to include a history of dog fighting, commentary on the blood sport was plagued by racialism.

7

Consequently, dog fighting, which has always been celebrated and practiced by white males in rural Southern communities, was now seen as a problem of urban, inner-city blacks. As a result of animal rights advocates revving up the public's anger, which the media acquiesced to, academicians became a part of the audience, and the politics of the state responded with retribution. In light of the vitriolic venom spewed at Vick and inner-city blacks, every state in America made dog fighting a felony, as did the federal government. Given this emergent profile of the dog fighter, which cast inner-city blacks as the sum of animal cruelty, selective enforcement of the law by race seemed to follow. Research throughout this book shows that subsequent to Michael Vick's Surry County home being raided by police, the number of African-Americans arrested for dog fighting increased at an alarming rate.

According to an analysis of arrest data on dog fighting[2], in the five years following Vick's home being raided on April 25, 2007, African-Americans accounted for seventy-four percent of all arrests for dog fighting (306 of 415). This percentage, which amounted to a nineteen percent increase over the five years prior to the raid, was more than three times higher than whites, who accounted for twenty-three percent of all dog fighting arrests; a decrease of fourteen percent during the same period. Latinos, who are more likely to be arrested for cockfighting, were a mere three percent of defendants arrested for dog fighting; a five percent decrease from the five years prior to the raid of Vick's place. As this data shows, in the five years that preceded Vick's property being raided and in the five years that followed, African-Americans were the only group whose percentage of arrests for dog fighting increased. Even more revealing, comparative analyses in Chart 1.1 shows that in the five years preceding Vick's criminal probe and conviction, and in the five years that followed, the number of blacks arrested for dog fighting more than tripled from sixty-four to 306. On the other hand, the number of whites

---

2 The analysis examined upwards of 643 criminal arrests for "Fighting" animals by race between 2002-2012 using data deduced from www.pet-abuse.com. Only those cases where photos of the defendants were available (i.e. mug shots or still pictures) are included to more accurately determine race or ethnicity.

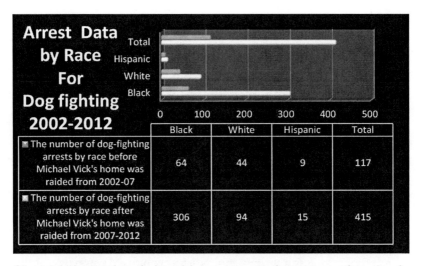

	Black	White	Hispanic	Total
▣ The number of dog-fighting arrests by race before Michael Vick's home was raided from 2002-07	64	44	9	117
▣ The number of dog-fighting arrests by race after Michael Vick's home was raided from 2007-2012	306	94	15	415

Chart 1-1: Arrest data deduced from www.pet-abuse.com using search term "Fighting." The data shows dog fighting arrests by race before and after Michael Vick's home in Surry County, Virginia was raided by State police on April 25, 2007. Only cases with photos of defendants were counted.

arrested for dog fighting increased only slightly during the same period, from forty-four to ninety-four. Such disparities contributed mightily to the view that Michael Vick's dog fighting scandal became a new chapter in American racialism.

In light of these data and the questionable events surrounding Vick's legal case, including the impact of informal and formal social sanctions, newer concerns are emerging over selective enforcement and differential treatment by race in the American criminal justice system. Incidents of animal cruelty in America such as abuse, neglect, hoarding, and the sordid act of bestiality are more often committed by deviant whites rather than deviant blacks. Yet, such indices of animal abuse, evokes little or no public outcry. The polarizing responses of animal rights advocates only perpetuated the distorted view that blacks like Michael Vick were the prototypes of animal cruelty. That African-Americans harbor such concerns about this matter, even in retrospect, should not be misinterpreted as an attempt to play the race card. Instead, this work portends to expose it as having been dealt during the Michael Vick dog fighting scandal.

The heightened exhortations of "Sack Michael Vick," perpetuated by demonstrators and media pundits alike, most of whom were white, prompted African-Americans to interject the issue of race. Among the dissenters were civil rights groups like the NAACP of Atlanta, which wondered aloud if the press coverage infringed upon Vick's rights to due process. While the media failed to spur more intellectual dialogue, the reluctance of academia to offer more illuminating views on dog fighting is notable and quite frankly inexcusable. Where was the attempt to probe for social factors that were no doubt influential in Vick's dog fighting debacle? Vick's exposure to dog fighting in the Ridley projects, which the media and animal rights groups harped on, was not the only factor involved. Moreover, the silence on the part of academicians from colleges and universities was especially unsettling given the number of institutions who use the bulldog as their school's mascot. Of course, as noted, the bulldog is the ancestral progenitor of the pit bull terrier, which Michael Vick used for dog fighting. Moreover, high schools, colleges, and universities use the bulldog as the amulet of their institutions because of its legend as a ferocious fighter earned in animal combat. It is worth reiterating that the bulldog, which is heralded as an icon in sports culture in the West, was bred for the expressed purpose of taking down bulls in some of the earliest forms of dog fighting.

This latter point was edified by Edmund Russell of the University of Virginia. Russell (2007) proved to be a rarity in departing from the prevailing idleness of intellectual thought, which plagued the discussion of Vick's dog fighting disaster. Instead, he provided an informative perspective on the history of the blood sport of dog fighting in Europe, with particular attention accorded to the bulldog. Kalof and Taylor (2007) of Michigan State expanded the scope of the discussion with a meaningful account of dog fighting's historical evolution. On the other hand, that other academicians failed to weigh in with such broader views was surprising, especially at prestigious institutions of higher learning such as Yale University, the University of Georgia, Butler University, and Georgetown University. These institutions, among others, identify with the fighting bulldog as their mascot. Moreover, the NFL is not guiltless in using sports to perpetuate the practice of dog fighting. Among the first and foremost powerhouses in the NFL was the Canton Bulldogs. The *Bulldogs* were NFL champions in 1922 and 1923, when they won twenty-five straight games, a record that still stands today. Furthermore, in light of the Bulldogs' initial success, and NFL football being founded there, Canton, Ohio, is home to the Pro Football Hall of Fame. Yet no sports reporter or journalist spoke of the cruel and twisted irony of the NFL condemning Vick for his involvement in dog fighting, while one of its original teams was nicknamed the Bulldogs. Like other sports teams, Canton chose the bulldog for its identity and notoriety developed through animal combat. Why is it important to make this extraordinary connection between institutions using the bulldog as a mascot and Vick's involvement in dog fighting? Once more, this association underscores the fact that the nexus between sports culture and dog fighting precedes the Michael Vick dog fighting scandal. Secondly, because the pit bull is a descendant of the bulldog, it helps to bolster the view that a preceding parent culture of dog fighting, which has been celebrated in America historically, influenced a subculture of violence that captivated Vick.

These discussion points are noteworthy and should have been hashed out. The failure of the media, academia, animal rights groups, and even the politics of the state to bring out these historical artifacts cast Vick's behavior as inimitable. If the public at large is as alarmed about dogs being harmed, as their response to Vick indicated, then they deserve to be better informed about the extent of this social problem and its extensive history. The absence of a wider discussion simply perpetuates the media's misappropriated attempt to make Vick the link between sports culture and dog fighting. Even worse, Vick and other so-called street fighters of dogs, most of whom are black males from urban communities, became the faces of animal cruelty. Concomitantly, due to this information vacuum and the failure of academia in America to more broadly state otherwise, a reliable social theory never emerged. A social perspective like the subculture of violence theory provides a convincing counter-view to explain the rise in popularity of dog fighting and Vick's ultimate demise.

In light of such noticeable shortcomings in the public dialogue, the following section will include a retrospective analysis of dog fighting that goes back to Europe in 5 BC and Rome in 43 AD. Moreover, this review will show how dog fighting as a sports spectacle evolved over centuries where it continued to spread throughout Europe before coming to America in the nineteenth century. When the fighting Staffordshire terrier arrived in America in 1817, blacks were still slaves. Thus their initial exposure to the blood sport of dog fighting occurred as a plantation game, like chicken fighting, cock fighting, racing, boxing, etc. These historical reflections support the argument that Vick's dog fighting deeds were influenced by a *parent culture* that spans centuries. Establishing the longitudinal existence of this *parent culture* will be pivotal to presenting the *subculture of violence theory* as a plausible rationalization for Vick's involvement in dog fighting as a criminogenic enterprise.

Social Theory

The *subculture of violence* perspective stems from the branch of *social learning* theories. It holds, among other points of view, that the violence exhibited by blacks is only partly different from the *parent culture* of violence (Wolfgang & Ferracuti, p.100). Unbeknownst to Vick and others, this parent culture and its accompanying *conduct norms*, of breeding, training, gambling, baiting, and killing underperforming dogs, spans the globe. Vick's exposure to dog fighting, which first occurred when he was eight, evolved over the course of his life to include the above mentioned norms, but as a subcultural phenomenon. These conduct norms have characterized the blood sport for hundreds of years and became standardized through organizations, such as the United Kennel Club of the nineteenth century and the American Pit

Bull Terrier Association of the twentieth century. As noted, these organizations, which sprang up throughout America and helped to popularize dog fighting as a blood sport, were forbearers of Michael Vick's Bad Newz Kennels. But before offering historical and theoretical explanations for Vick's downfall, it will be helpful to review the events that led to it.

The Fall of Michael Vick

In April 2007, the NFL hosted its annual draft in New York City's Radio City Music Hall amid swirling allegations that superstar quarterback Michael Vick of the Atlanta Falcons was involved in an illegal dog fighting operation. NFL Commissioner Roger Goodell had asked Vick if the allegations were true, which Vick flatly denied. Goodell gave Vick the benefit of the doubt and allowed him to participate in the ceremonies as planned. Vick, his former head coach Frank Beamer of Virginia Tech, and two other alumni, DeAngelo Hall and Bruce Smith, were scheduled to represent the university following the tragic April 16 shootings on campus. In 2001, Vick, just out of Virginia Tech University, was the first overall pick of the Falcons. Now six years later, as he stepped to the podium amid unseemly accusations of dog fighting, he was derisively booed by fans. The reason fans booed was an obvious reaction to the growing media reports that he was involved in an illegal dog fighting ring. Before the draft would conclude, a cloud of suspicion shrouded Vick and a storm of controversy ensued. Public sentiment turned decisively against him. While Vick said the right things publicly and privately to allay the concerns of Atlanta Falcons owner Arthur Blank and Commissioner Goodell, the truth about the accusations would come to light. The world would come to know the NFL's most versatile, exciting, and highest-paid football player operated Bad Newz Kennels, a criminogenic dog fighting enterprise hidden in the backwoods of his home state of Virginia. The public response to the gruesome accounts of animal cruelty alleged to have been committed by Vick and his comrades echoed throughout the country, resulting in calls for him to be permanently banned from the NFL. By contrast, a staggering number of NFL players have done far worse in abusing human victims. Such criminal acts from other NFL players have included charges of sexual assault, assault and battery, murder for hire, drug possession, vehicular manslaughter, and domestic abuse. In June of 2013, Aaron Hernandez, tight end of the New England Patriots, was charged with first degree murder in the execution style killing of another man in North Attleborough, Massachusetts. He was also a person of interest in a double-homicide, in Boston, when two men were killed in a drive-by shooting in 2012. Yet the level of public interest and outrage over Vick's mistreatment of dogs struck a chord of anger over cruelty to *animals*, the likes of which were previously unseen in this country. Despite that, Vick was not the first professional athlete to be charged with dog fighting.

ESPN's *Outside The Lines* (Naqi, 2007) reported that then-NBA forward Qyntel Woods and NFL running back LeShon Johnson were both charged for participating in dog fighting. Yet these incidents did not elicit the same level of public acrimony as Vick's. Incidentally, both Woods and Johnson pled guilty in 2005 to their crimes. While Woods received a reduced charge of animal abuse, Johnson was convicted on three related charges of dog fighting, yet neither was sent to prison. Despite the unconscionable acts of depravity committed against the dogs by Vick, there was a strong sense that the rancorous reaction of the public was beyond their concern over animal cruelty. Moreover, many protesters indicated they were not really dog lovers. They were simply hopping on the bandwagon.

Not since the O.J. Simpson case had a professional athlete been so publicly vilified. Nor was there a greater expression of unrestrained vitriol. In the wake of the dog fighting details going public, Vick easily became the most hated person in America, not just in the world of sports. With the public clamoring at a fever pitch, which included threats of lynching, the NFL and its alliance of the media, corporate sponsors, and the politics of the state all lined up against Vick. Consequently, the investigation of the star quarterback took a turn for the worse.

Vick's Property is Raided

On [3]April 25, 2007, Michael Vick's property at 1915 Moonlight Road in Smithfield, Virginia, in Surry County, was raided by law enforcement authorities. Although Vick was a licensed dog breeder, police believed they found evidence of a breeding and dog fighting operation. Authorities found as many as fifty-four pit bulls, and a number of them showed signs of injuries consistent with the results of dog fights. There were medical supplies for treating injured animals, including syringes, and car axles buried in the ground to bound dogs with heavy chains. This latter measure prevented dogs from choking, an important consideration given their value as fighting dogs with thousands of dollars at stake. Vick later claimed that although the property was indeed his, he spent very little time there. While [4]Gerald G. Poindexter, the Surry County Commonwealth's Attorney, plotted his course of action in milling over evidence gathered from the April 25 raid, the federal government took an interest in the probe with unannounced intentions to become the lead law enforcement agency in the investigation. Incidentally, the NFL voluntarily sent members of its security department, unsolicited, to assist the federal probe at Vick's property (*NFL Security offers to help*, n.d.). Still, Poindexter wondered aloud why the federal government had taken such extraordinary interest in the Vick case and openly questioned whether race and the quarterback's celebrity were factors. As noted, several lower-profile professional athletes had been charged for their involvement in dog fighting, yet the federal government did not get involved. Then on May 3, 2007, the federal government revealed just how serious they were in landing an indictment against Vick, when [5]President George W. Bush signed an amendment to the Animal Welfare Act (AWA), making it a felony to engage in dog fighting.

---

3 United States of America v. Purnell Peace, Quanis Phillips, Tony Taylor, and Michael Vick, 2007, U.S. District Court for the Eastern Division of Virginia.
4 http://usatoday.printthis.clickability.com/pt/cpt?action=Local.
5 Congressional Research Service: Animal Welfare Act: Background and Selected Legislation, Geoffrey Becker, May 8, 2009.

Kenneth N. Robinson, MS

Race to Get Vick

Although Poindexter had indicated that parallel investigations would be conducted in the Vick probe, by June federal investigators announced plans to execute a sealed search warrant on his property. It was now clear who was the lead agency investigating the allegations against the star quarterback. On the strength of President Bush signing the Animal Fighting Prohibition Enforcement Act of 2007 (the amended AWA), which guaranteed felony charges for dog fighting, on July 17, 2007, Michael Vick and three co-defendants, Tony Taylor, Quanis Philips, and Purnell Peace, were indicted on federal charges. The charges outlined were: "Conspiracy to Travel in Interstate Commerce in Aid of Unlawful Activities and to Sponsor a Dog in an Animal Fighting Venture."[6] Vick could have argued in court that his property where the dogs and medical supplies were found was a by-product of his role as a licensed breeder, just as dog fighting legend Floyd Boudreaux did in 2008. What was different from Boudreaux's case was that Vick's co-defendants agreed to testify against him.

It was in 2005 when Boudreaux, a licensed dog breeder who is white and renowned as the *don* of dog fighting, was charged, along with his son Guy, with forty-eight counts of dog fighting in the state of Louisiana. The police raid of his property uncovered an abundance of evidence suggesting a dog fighting operation, including fifty pit bulls, illegal steroids, computer records, videos, treadmills, chains used to latch dogs, and a sawed-off shotgun. The plethora of dog fighting evidence notwithstanding, Boudreaux argued in court that he was simply a dog breeder. Yet his reputation as a dog fighter was so legendary that he had been reportedly featured in dog fighting magazines. Legend has it that he once traded one of his famous fighting dogs for a house. Another defendant in a dog fighting case had a photo of himself posing with Boudreaux. Incidentally, Louisiana state laws allow prosecutors to use inferable evidence like magazines, pictures,

6 United States of America v. Michael Vick, et.al. July 17, 2007. Conspiracy to Travel in Interstate Commerce in Aid of Unlawful Activities and to Sponsor a Dog in an Animal Fighting Venture. Eastern District of Virginia.

videos, and other artifacts as evidence to establish culpability in dog fighting cases. Despite the latitude of such state laws and a cache of incriminating artifacts typically associated with dog fighting, he and his son were acquitted on all charges in October 2008. At the time, Michael Vick was in the fourth quarter of his prison sentence. The Boudreauxs' case seemed to benefit from the convictions of Vick and his co-defendants. In the wake of the NFL star's criminal investigation, the blood sport became a problem associated with street fighters in urban communities, most of whom are black.

That such ideation contributed to the acquittal of the Boudreauxs seems especially plausible since he and his son are white males from the rural South. Additionally, there is evidence that following Vick's property being raided and the inordinate amount of law enforcement focus on street fighters, the rate of African-Americans arrested for dog fighting increased alarmingly. All of which, once more, raises relevant questions of selective enforcement by race. An analysis of data on dog fighting arrests by race,[7] deduced from www.pet-abuse.com, shows that in the five years that preceded Vick's dog fighting dilemma versus the five years that followed, the number of African-Americans arrested increased nearly five-fold. Furthermore, in the five years that followed Vick's home being raided, the number of blacks arrested for dog fighting outnumbered that of whites by a ratio of three to one. Even more revealing of selective enforcement by race, Chart 1.2 shows, in the five years that preceded the raid in 2007, African-Americans were fifty-five percent of all defendants charged for dog fighting. But in the five years that followed, the number of African-Americans arrested increased to seventy-four percent—a surge of nineteen percentage points. In stunning contrast, over the same period, the number of white defendants charged with dog fighting

---

7 The data analysis from www.pet-abuse.com looked only at animal fighting cases where mug shots or other still photos of defendants were available to more accurately determine race. The sample included defendants whose arrest data was documented from incidents occurring in the five years before Michael Vick's property was raided on April 25, 2007 and the five years which followed.

17

decreased by fourteen percentage points from thirty-seven percent in the five years prior, to twenty-three percent in the five years that followed. Interestingly enough, Hispanics also saw their arrest rates for dog fighting decrease from eight percent to three percent. This further suggests that Michael Vick became the face of dog fighting and African-Americans became primary targets.

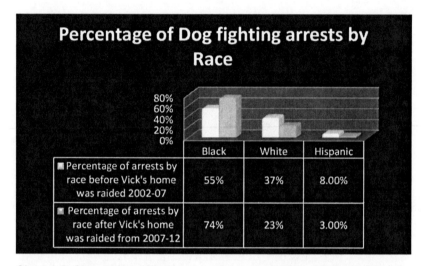

Percentage of Dog fighting arrests by Race			
	Black	White	Hispanic
■ Percentage of arrests by race before Vick's home was raided 2002-07	55%	37%	8.00%
■ Percentage of arrests by race after Vick's home was raided from 2007-12	74%	23%	3.00%

Chart 1-2: Shows the differences in the percentages of arrests for dog-fighting by race over a 10-year period, by comparing the five years before and after Michael Vick's property was raided on April 25, 2007.

Greater evidence of African-Americans being disproportionately punished over dog fighting is observable in the percentage of convictions for black and white defendants over the five years preceding and following Vick's dog fighting being exposed. The convictions of African-Americans charged with dog fighting increased by nine percentage points. By contrast, over the same period the convictions of white defendants decreased by twelve percentage points. In the case of Hispanics, the data show they are far more likely to be involved in cockfighting, which is popular in South America and Mexico. Still, the impact of a greater preoccupation with punishing street fighters may help to explain how the arrest rates of Hispanics for dog fighting decreased by five percent over a ten-year period, but like African-Americans, their convictions increased, albeit marginally by three percent (see Chart 1.3).

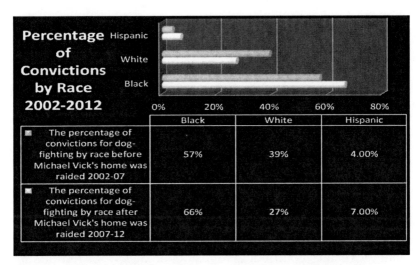

	Black	White	Hispanic
▣ The percentage of convictions for dog-fighting by race before Michael Vick's home was raided 2002-07	57%	39%	4.00%
▣ The percentage of convictions for dog-fighting by race after Michael Vick's home was raided 2007-12	66%	27%	7.00%

Chart 1.3: The data above shows the percentage of convictions for dog-fighting by race in the five years that precedes and follows Michael Vick's home being raided on April 25, 2007. Note: many of these cases are still open.

The Boudreauxs' 2008 acquittals are represented in this latter data, which, when taken as a whole, seems to reflect this dramatic shift where African-Americans were disproportionately represented among the increase in dog fighting arrests and convictions. Other questions of selective enforcement and equal protection of the law by race seem warranted, since the federal government never charged the Boudreauxs as they did Vick and his co-defendants. The question of race seems especially apropos, since the charges filed against Boudreaux and Vick were eerily similar, yet their respective outcomes were as different as black and white. The inaction on the part of the federal government is debatable, since the Boudreauxs did not go to trial until October 2008. Moreover, the amended AWA of 2007 was passed a year earlier.

Furthermore, the Department of Homeland Security aided the state of Louisiana's investigation by providing aerial surveillance of Boudreaux's property. Their investigation produced images and photos of what appeared to be a dog fighting operation that very much resembled Vick's. Additionally, U.S. Customs officials took an interest in the Boudreaux investigation, given his international sales of dogs from his world-renowned bloodline. Customers from as far as Mexico and Japan have purchased dogs from Boudreaux. Despite the evidence procured by the federal government and the amended federal law against dog fighting, no superseding federal indictments emerged against the Boudreauxs. The failure of the federal government to charge the Boudreauxs seemed to validate Surry County Attorney Poindexter's concerns that race may have been a factor in the federal investigation of Vick. Even more evidentiary was the relative silence of animal rights advocates like the Humane Society of the United States and PETA.

These organizations did not raise their voices in protest over the Boudreauxs' acquittals. Yet, in Vick's case, these animal rights advocates contributed to the public outcry for retribution. By contrast, when it came to Boudreaux, these rather powerful entities seemed to believe it was enough to get Michael Vick as the big catch who symbolized the sinfulness of dog fighting and was now the face of it. The effect merely perpetuated the idea that blacks are more criminogenic than whites. Other indices of differential treatment by race included the differential treatment accorded to the respective dogs in both criminal cases.

Selective Enforcement by Race

In Boudreaux's case, all of his dogs believed to be used for fighting were euthanized, per state law, following the raid. Furthermore, the Louisiana Society for the Prevention of Cruelty to Animals (SPCA) carried out the euthanasia without a rebuke from animal lovers. It is interesting to observe that in putting nearly sixty of Boudreaux's dogs to death, the government permitted the killing of more than seven times the number of dogs that Vick was charged with killing. On the contrary, rather than euthanize Vick's dogs, authorities acquiesced to outcries from so-called animal lovers and kept them alive. Consequently, Vick was made to pay over $1 million for their rehabilitative care. Such a hefty sum was among the economic costs that contributed to his bankruptcy. On the other hand, just months after Vick was released from federal prison in 2009, Boudreaux and his son, having been acquitted of all charges in 2008, filed a lawsuit seeking restitution from the Louisiana SPCA. The organization euthanized fifty-seven dogs from their infamous bloodline, which had an estimated value of $300,000. The suit was settled in 2011 without going to trial, with the terms undisclosed.[8] Thus the issue of race emerges as a relevant question in the differential enforcement of the law, particularly by the federal government, which prosecuted Vick, but never charged Boudreaux. Differential treatment is also observable in the compensatory damages paid out by Vick versus Boudreaux presumably being compensated for his losses. To ignore the question of race in light of these disparities is to deny the legacy of racism in America generally and in the criminal courts in particular. Yet the question of race notwithstanding that Vick's co-defendants agreed to testify against him in court meant there was little chance of him being acquitted on the charges for lack of evidence. Nor could he, like Boudreaux, rest his defense on being a licensed dog breeder or that the dogs were used for hunting.

Even worse for Vick, his co-defendants provided statements that he was not only principally involved in the dog fighting operation, but that he was the principal financier of the enterprise. Vick was also implicated as an accomplice in killing eight underperforming dogs. Then, one month after the federal indictment was handed down in July 2007, Congress proposed another stringent measure to the AWA, increasing the prison sentence for dog fighting from three years to five. With racketeering laws in hand, the federal government made plans to pursue a superseding indictment in August if Vick did not plead guilty to the escalat-

---

8 Richard Burgess (2011). *Dog deaths lawsuit settled.* Advocate Acadia Bureau. "SPCA euthanized 57 pit bulls; owners acquitted of any crime." Baton Rouge, LA.

ing charges. So in a span of three months, the Vick case invoked legal actions from the executive, judicial, and legislative branches of the federal government. With harsher penalties at their disposal, federal prosecutors induced Vick's co-defendants to take plea deals and testify against him. In the face of mounting public pressure, including threats against his life and the federal government's intentions of issuing a superseding indictment, Michael Vick decided to plead guilty to federal dog fighting charges.

In the end, Vick received a twenty-three month sentence. This was the longest of any of the co-defendants, despite Vick having no prior criminal record. On the other hand, Tony Taylor, the government's main informant, received a mere two month sentence, although the prosecutor sought probation for him. Both Peace and Phillips received twenty-one month sentences. Judge Henry Hudson, who presided over the high-profile case, would later say that Vick received the longest sentence because he initially lied about his role in killing the dogs. Surprisingly, Vick's attorneys failed to inform the judge that part of the reason the beleaguered quarterback lied about his role was that his life was being threatened by lynching. The gravity of the threats against Vick's life were real enough that upon his release from federal prison in 2009, corrections officials at the Leavenworth Prison did not divulge his departure time out of safety concerns. In the absence of receiving a broader perspective on why Vick lied, the judge sentenced him to prison despite evidence that the fallen star quarterback had undertaken several measures to demonstrate he was assuming responsibility for his actions, which could have lessened his sentence.

According to [9]ESPN.com: "Despite early surrender, a public apology, and participation in an animal sensitivity training course, Vick was denied an 'acceptance of responsibility' credit that would have reduced his sentence." Moreover, Vick received this more stringent sentence despite writing the judge an impassioned [10]handwritten letter. In the correspondence, Vick revealed

---

9 http://sports.espn.go.com/nfl/news/story/id.
10 Handwritten letter from Michael Vick to Judge Henry Hudson (n.d.).

how he grew up never understanding the severity of dog fighting. He observed that unlike other crimes, such as drug dealing and gun possession, dog fighting was not a serious crime in his neighborhood of Newport News. In the letter, Vick also intimated his love for his young children, who were agonizing over his ordeal. He also highlighted his charitable works through "Grateful to Give Back," which gave toys to underprivileged kids and families during the Christmas holidays and free turkeys at Thanksgiving. In a solemn attempt to show remorse and offer recompense to the public at large, Vick pledged to educate the community on the perils and pitfalls of dog fighting.

Furthermore, Vick received letters of support on his behalf that were addressed to Judge Hudson from notable luminaries, including former heavyweight boxing champion and entrepreneur [11]George Foreman; Hall of Fame Major League Baseball player [12]Hank Aaron; and the Honorable [13]Shirley Franklin, Mayor of Atlanta. All are renowned African-Americans. Additionally, Patrick J. Hughes, president and CEO of the Give Life Foundation, in Herndon, Virginia, wrote Judge Hudson with a stirring account of Vick's contributions to the victims of Hurricane Katrina in New Orleans in 2005. According to Hughes, Vick's contributions were timely and enabled the organization to deliver approximately $100,000 in relief supplies to the hurricane-ravaged area. This occurred while FEMA failed to reach many victims. In an interesting juxtaposition, Vick responded to human victims of this natural disaster faster than the Bush Administration. But it would be the federal government under the Bush Administration that would try him nonetheless for his mistreatment of dogs. Despite the revelations of Vick's generosity toward the needy, his support for the victims of Katrina, the appeals of prominent supporters, and his own pleas for leni-

---

11 Letter of support for Michael Vick from George Foreman to Judge Henry Hudson (n.d.).

12 Letter of support for Michael Vick from Hank Aaron to Judge Henry Hudson December 5, 2007.

13 Letter of support for Michael Vick from Mayor of Atlanta Shirley Franklin, December 5, 2007.

ency, Judge Hudson was unmoved. He sentenced Michael Vick, an All-Pro NFL quarterback, to federal prison for nearly two years for operating an illegal interstate dog fighting enterprise. (In November of 2008, Vick would also plead guilty to State dog fighting charges in Surry County, but his three-year prison sentence was suspended, in lieu of four years of good behavior.)

Although Vick was sentenced to nearly two years imprisonment for his crimes, the absence of a broader dialogue meant the public's view of animal cruelty was skewed to reflect the faces of Vick and other black males as street fighters of dogs. For example, in April 2009, just months after Vick had been released from prison, Rush Limbaugh recorded a public service announcement for the Humane Society in which he identified street fighters of dogs as "people like Michael Vick."[14] Such a reference did more to perpetuate the feeling that law enforcement's concern over animal cruelty should focus on black males. To further underscore this sense of subliminal race baiting that unfurled in the wake of the Vick case, animal advocacy groups such as the Humane Society and PETA, along with academicians, and the media perpetuated the idea that an estimated 100,000 street fighters of dogs, found mostly in urban cities, were the biggest problem with dog fighting, rather than breeders and dog men from the rural back roads like Boudreaux. But, in an ethnographic study, using participant observation, Evans, Gauthier, and Forsyth (1998), faculty from the University of Louisiana at Lafayette, found that of the thirty-one dog men interviewed for their study, ninety percent were white males. Despite such documented realities that have held across generations in rural white communities, more evidence of racial profiling followed. Rather than explore the different racial groups involved and the various geographic locales where dog fighting persists, the media, academicians, and animal advocacy groups blamed Vick's demise on hip-hop artists who are black, such as Jay-Z, DMX, and Missy Elliott.

---

14 Rush Limbaugh recorded a public service announcement for the Humane Society of the United States of America, April of 2009.

These popular recording artists were cited as factors that influenced Vick, given the dog fighting inferences in their music videos. But such attempts to distort the bigger picture of why Vick became involved in the blood sport were more questionable, than they were meaningful in providing answers. Still, a more immediate question that Vick himself seemed unable to adequately answer was why would a star quarterback, with the highest-paying contract in the history of the NFL, gamble away his career and livelihood by bankrolling an illegal dog fighting ring? Was it his attempt to maintain *street cred* as some have suggested? Was it because of hip-hop's gangsta rap culture, as others noted? Or was it simply a reflection of his depraved indifference to animals?

Why Did Vick Become Involved in Dog Fighting?

In the aftermath of Michael Vick's conviction and sentencing, the most outstanding question remained: Why did he do it? Dave Zirin, an attorney and critically acclaimed author, observed, "I don't know what led Michael Vick down the road to Bad Newz Kennels. I also don't pretend to know."[15] While Zirin was more tactful in avoiding shallow explanations that eviscerated Vick, other renowned journalists, such as Bryan Burwell (2007) of the *St. Louis Post-Dispatch* and Jason Whitlock (2007) of the *Kansas City Star*, did just the opposite. One of the fastest-moving bandwagon explanations that hitched a lot of riders was the rather feeble and fallacious theory that Vick's involvement in dog fighting was influenced by hip-hop's gangsta rap culture.

Was Vick Influenced by Gangsta Rap in Hip-Hop?

In a column titled "*Vick is the latest to take rap for the rap in our culture,*"[16] Burwell noted that somewhere between Jackie Robinson and Vick, black athletes somehow sought "Street Cred

---

15 Editorial from Dave Zirin edgeofsports@gmail.com. Subject: "Inching toward Insanity: Why Michael Vick is Not a Fascist." Ron Stewart, Ph.D., forwarded to Kenneth N. Robinson, August 24, 2007.
16 http://www.stltoday.com/stltoday/emaf.nsf/Popup?ReadForm&db=stltoday%5Csp orts%5C.

validation from hip-hop culture." Additionally, he stated there is a "misguided notion that the only way to appeal to the young demographic of the sneaker-buying public was to adopt the negative attitudes of the thug life popularized by black hip-hop/ gangster rappers." Ironically, while Burwell speculated about Vick's attempts to appeal to a *sneaker-buying public*, he failed to attribute the potential influence of Nike. The shoe and sporting goods manufacturer hired Vick to endorse their sneakers. On the other hand, Nike actually produced a commercial in 2003 that inferred a dog fighting match that was not dramatically different from the hip-hop music videos of artists like Jay-Z and DMX. Rather than chastise Nike for its hypocrisy, Burrell stayed with the hip-hop theme, adding that details in Vick's indictment were "readily identified as a part of the dark side of that culture." Rather than offer a counterview, Jason Whitlock, his cross-town colleague from the nation's *Heartland*, was even more heartless in driving home a similarly misappropriated theme.

In an article titled [17]"Vick can evolve from hip-hop prison culture," Whitlock expressed hope that Vick could develop to become "another wake-up call for black athletes to reject the hip-hop/ prison culture that glorifies much of the negative behavior and attitudes that has eroded the once-dignified and positive reputation of African-American athletes." He added, "As much as I love dogs... this case primarily repulses me because I believe Vick got involved with breeding vicious pit bulls because rap-music culture made it the thing to do." On the one hand, I applaud Burrell and Whitlock for attempting to address the question of why the star quarterback got involved in illegal dog fighting, as most journalists chose not to. Still the suggestion that the quarterback was attempting to maintain "Street cred" or that hip-hop was the influence is simply erroneous. For example, in the federal indictment a confidential informant described being chastised by Vick's comrades in crime for loudly stating the quarterback's name during a dog fighting contest.[18] This

17 http://www.kansascity.com/sports/columnists/jason_whitlock/story/195760.html.
18 United States of America v. Purnell A. Peace, Quanis L. Phillips, Tony Taylor, Michael Vick. July 2007, p.15.

account makes it apparent Vick was intent on being low-key in the dog fighting culture and was less concerned with street cred. Additionally, despite Vick's involvement being described on the plane of street fighters, he was actually a professional dog fighter, where secrecy is at a premium. How else could this easily recognizable NFL star exist in the underworld of dog fighting without the larger public knowing? Furthermore, the writers' overriding suggestion, like that of others, that hip-hop culture's gangsta rap influenced Vick to engage in dog fighting is even more implausible.

Rappers who subscribe to gangsta rap as a music genre are themselves largely influenced by a *parent culture* of violence, albeit far different from dog fighting. Instead of renowned dog fighters like Floyd Boudreaux, also known as the godfather or don of dog fighting, gangsta rap celebrates organized crime figures like Michael Corleone of *The Godfather*. Such characters are celebrated by hip-hop's gangsta rappers for their propensity to commit violence with guns, not dogs. Still, Burwell and Whitlock were not alone in misconstruing the view that hip-hop music's gangsta rap was somehow responsible for Vick's involvement. The Humane Society, sports reporters, and academicians also furthered this notion. However, it may be more plausible to suggest that the same parent culture that influenced Vick also influenced the rappers. Furthermore, the suggestion that hip-hop is somehow responsible seems even less likely since this music form did not exist prior to the 1970s. In addition, gangsta rap did not become popularized until the early 1990s. Given these timelines, the idea that Michael Vick's involvement in the blood sport was influenced by gangsta rap is not only unsubstantiated but untenable.

By contrast, there is evidence that the blood sport of dog fighting, as demonstrated by Vick, has a parent culture that is traceable to ancient Europe. The practice of using dogs to attack other animals increased in popularity as it evolved over centuries and spread throughout Europe before being transplanted to America in the nineteenth century. Throughout the twentieth century, many Americans, particularly in the South, embraced dog fighting as a sporting spectacle. As noted, the United Kennel Club (UKC) and the American Pit Bull Terrier Association, two dog fighting organizations, promulgated this parent culture of violence, making them ancestral parents of Michael Vick's Bad Newz Kennels. Once more, Vick himself indicated that his involvement in dog fighting was influenced by a "so-called culture." Vick's reference to this *so-called culture* was an apparent attempt to explain something beyond him and far more in depth than hip-hop culture's gangsta rap, which he could have easily identified. Therefore, rather than hip-hop's gangsta rap, Vick adopted dog fighting from a parent culture of violence which emanated from Europe. This culture was transplanted to America, where it would spread throughout the South, including Vick's hometown of Newport News, Virginia. There, in the Ridley projects, he inculcated the behavior through a process of social learning. In bolstering this view, Burke (2007) stated, "A pursuit once practiced chiefly in the rural South has moved to the mean streets of the 'hood.' Today dog fighting can be found in rural Southwest Virginia as well as in housing projects of Newport News" (p.2). The proceeding analysis will explore the history of this parent culture of dog fighting violence, which is pivotal to utilizing the subculture of violence theory as a reliable explanation for Vick's dog fighting misdeeds. Author Dave Zirin was quite poignant in observing of the Vick scandal: "Preemptive Strikes are abounding against looking at some broader social context."[19]

Subculture of Violence Theory

The subculture of violence theory was first postulated by [20]Marvin E. Wolfgang, along with Franco Ferracuti, who based this perspective in part, on the study of violence among blacks in Philadelphia in 1958. Ironically, it was also in the city of Philadelphia where Michael Vick resurrected his NFL career

---

19 Editorial by Dave Zirin, edgeofsports@gmail.com Sent to: Ron Stewart, Ph.D. on August 23, 2007, who forwarded commentary to Kenneth N. Robinson on August 24, 2007. p. 2.
20 http://www.criminology.fsu.edu/crimtheory/wolfgang.htm, p.1.

with the Philadelphia Eagles in 2009, some fifty years after Wolfgang's study. His findings showed that black males in the inner city often used toughness and violence as expressions of male virility. As this discussion will highlight, centuries ago in ancient Europe and even presently in America, men who engage in dog fighting have viewed the combating dogs as an extension of their own masculinity and toughness. Evans et al. reported that the dog men in their study not only used the dogs for fighting, but to also serve as symbolic expressions to validate their own masculinity (p.10). This is significant, whether discussing the parent culture or its subculture of dog fighting violence. Both have parallel conduct norms such as the aforementioned baiting, betting, fighting, and killing underperforming dogs. But because the term *culture* is the root word of *subculture,* and was used by Vick in discussing his involvement in dog fighting, it will be meaningful to gather a definition of it.

Culture: The Root of Subculture

As early as 1871, E.B. Taylor, who is described as one of the first to define *culture*, referred to it as "that complex whole which includes knowledge, belief, art, morals, law, custom, and any other capabilities and habits acquired by man as a member of society" (Wolfgang & Ferracutti, 1967, p. 95). On the other hand, a *subculture* has been defined as "a normative system of some group or groups smaller than the whole society" (Wolfgang & Ferracutti, p. 103). In examining the intra-racial violence amongst blacks, Wolfgang surmised that such violent behavior was, among other factors, the result of a *parent culture* that influenced this propensity. This *parent culture* of violence in America was often demonstrated by whites against blacks, initially during plantation slavery. Such wanton acts of terror and viciousness continued as a staple of the Jim Crow South. These conduct norms produced a subculture of violence that influenced blacks to commit violence against other blacks as an expression of power and toughness. Thus the violence exhibited by blacks toward one another was acquired through social learning, given the tradition of senseless violence committed by whites against them, particularly in the South. For example, whites who committed acts of violence against blacks did so often using the dreaded "N" word to convey their utter contempt for their victims. Similarly, blacks who commit senseless violence against other blacks also use the "N" word and are equally as scornful. These realities fill a void in explaining how a subculture of violence arises, yet, gives credence to Wolfgang's theory that the violence exhibited by blacks is only partly different from the parent culture of violence in this country. Although Wolfgang's perspective was developed observing levels of violence by human beings against one another, this discussion of Vick's dilemma will use this theory to discuss human beings committing violence using dogs.

The factors that will bridge and bond this historical connection between the parent culture and the succeeding subculture is what Wolfgang referred to as *conduct norms* (p.101).

Conduct Norms of Dog Fighting

The conduct norms associated with dog fighting as a parent culture, which are also apparent in the subculture of dog fighting violence exuded by Vick, include: dog fighting as a blood sport; dog fighting organizations; gambling, baiting, and the killing of underperforming dogs. Again, such conduct norms emanated from Europe and were transplanted to America in 1817, where they continued to shape the culture of dog fighting throughout the twentieth century (Gibson, 2005). Ultimately, such norms became central characteristics in the operations of Michael Vick's Bad Newz Kennels. It is also a historical norm, like Vick's own experience, that dog fighting attracted the rich and poor alike.

For centuries, animal combat involving dogs was featured throughout Europe, including at the Roman Coliseum, to entertain all social classes (Villavicencio, 2007). That both the prosperous and the paupers attended dog fighting matches gives greater clarity to Vick's involvement in animal combat as a poor youth growing up in public housing projects and during his lucrative NFL career. Centuries ago, dogs were used in combat against bulls, bears, and even human beings. In addition, dogs were baited and bets were placed on these contests, just as Vick had done. Baiting was the practice of using another animal, whether big or small, to entice dogs to attack it. In Italy, dogs would be restrained in large sacks where they could not escape. There they were beaten with sticks. The dog was then released, and a smaller animal would be placed in direct view to serve as bait. The dog would then attack and kill the smaller animal (Gibson, 2005, "The Scope of Dog fighting"). Interestingly enough, the American public grew angrier when it learned that Vick practiced baiting using smaller family animals to induce his dogs to attack. While both the media and animal advocacy groups like PETA vilified Vick for this heinous practice, neither explained to the public that baiting was a historical conduct norm of dog fighting that he acquired through social learning.

In fact, when it was reported that Vick had practiced baiting, PETA suggested he needed to have his brain examined before the NFL reinstated him. Surprisingly, such a request from PETA was not met with questions of racism, given the racist history of anatomical studies being used against blacks in America. But if PETA wanted to better understand Vick's use of smaller animals as bait for his dogs, there was no need to examine his brain; rather, an examination of dog fighting's history would have sufficed. Such a study of animal combat as an artifact of European culture would readily show that baiting was passed on to blacks like Michael Vick as a subcultural phenomenon. Another decadent and descendant conduct norm that Vick practiced, which was also passed down from a parent culture of violence in Europe, was the act of killing dogs that did not perform well.

In Vick's operation, dogs that underperformed in test match-ups or that lost in an actual contest were put to death. The same norms prevailed centuries ago, where fighting dogs who failed were seen as shaming their owners and were similarly put to death. Therefore the failure of the media, academia, and animal advocacy organizations to properly include such historical facts during the Vick saga created the impression that this practice was exclusive to his Bad Newz Kennels. Instead, the practice was but another indicator that Vick's conduct was acquired from a parent culture. Yet another translucent conduct norm that has stood the test of time is gambling on animal fights.

In Europe, spectators would place wagers on dogs fighting against animals such as bulls and bears. During the fight, a dog would be declared the winner if it could grab the bull or bear by the nose or lip and pin them down. The larger animal was declared the winner if it could prevent such a fate. Gambling on dog fighting matches became a greater part of the lure and lore of the blood sport that drew countless spectators who placed bets on the outcomes. Therefore, Vick's involvement in gambling on dog fights was hardly a novel idea. In fact, during chattel slavery, blacks would train dogs, chickens, and cocks to fight for the benefit of their white slave masters who would gamble on the outcomes. The latter was demonstrated in Alex Haley's epic story *Roots*, which became a made-for-television mini-series, first broadcast on ABC in 1977.[21] The series featured the story of Chicken George, who earned his nickname given his ability to train chickens to fight and kill for the benefit of his master, who gambled on such events. George's skills ultimately won him his freedom. This illustration from *Roots* was a reflection of how black slaves participated in animal combat as "plantation games."

Other notable indices of a dog fighting culture among black slaves occurred in Louisiana (Burke, p.4). It was in the Congo Square of New Orleans where black slaves would enjoin a number of cultural experiences from Creole dancing and singing to dog fighting (Doster, n.d.). One Louisianan dog breeder observed that blacks and Cajuns had been fighting dogs for over 200 years. Additionally, it was in the state of Louisiana that the Cajun rules of dog fighting were created and where the infamous dog man Floyd Boudreaux built his legend. These rules not only

---

21 *Roots*, 1977 ABC Mini Series, based on Alex Haley's best seller *Roots: The Saga of an American Family*.

illustrate the ongoing influence of an evolving parent culture, but also show the evolution of conduct norms that now govern dog fighting matches around the world. Moreover, Taylor's description of how culture is "acquired by man as a member of society" remains especially meaningful when one considers that the adaptation of blacks from slavery to freedom involved the acquisition of these conduct norms that reflected the folkways of this identifiable parent culture. This broader perspective on dog fighting was never given to the American public because the media chose instead to excoriate Michael Vick in the process of labeling him the face of animal cruelty.

Given the relative continuity of these historical developments, including the preceding parent culture of dog fighting violence, Wolfgang's subculture of violence theory provides a great canvas for redrawing the discussion of Michael Vick's involvement in dog fighting. This next section will highlight how dog fighting as a form of animal combat has evolved over time from a relic of European culture, to a plantation game during slavery, to sporting spectacle, to a criminogenic vice. In order to solidify this extraordinary connection between centuries-old practices of dog fighting as a parent culture of violence to a subculture of violence involving Michael Vick's Bad Newz Kennels, it will be useful to highlight in brief the evolution of dog fighting.

The Evolution of Dog Fighting

[22]Edmund Russell (2007) of the University of Virginia noted in his editorial on the Vick dog fighting issue, "The persistence of dog fighting reminds us that it is hard to change something unless we understand it, and gaining that understanding sometimes means paying a visit to the past" (A Tale of Two Smithfields, para. 15). Although dog fighting as a vicious blood sport was thrust upon America's conscience with Vick's scandal in 2007, we now know dog fighting is centuries old. Kalof and Taylor (2007) found that the history of dog fighting as a blood

---

22 http://www.virginia.edu/topnews/facultyopinions/2007/russell.html.

sport goes back to the fifth century BC. Dogs were also used for hunting as well as to protect the property of owners, just as they are commonly used today. But more importantly, even during ancient times, the dog was supposed to reflect the power and prestige of its owner. Such idealism still exists today where dog men view the fighting dog as an extension of themselves.

[23]Monica Villavicencio (2007) of National Public Radio reported that the evolution of dog fighting was also influenced by clashes between the Romans and Britons as far back as 43 AD. Both used fighting dogs in the battlefield, with the invading Romans often prevailing. However, the British dogs were observed to be the more fierce fighters. As a result, the Romans began importing fighting dogs from Britain, not merely for war, but to stage dog fighting matches as sporting spectacles. These events involved using dogs to attack other animals for exhibition in the famous Roman Coliseum. Villavicencio and others found that by the twelfth century, dog fighting as a spectacle mainly involved the practice of baiting. These spectacles that involved dogs attacking smaller and larger animals were carried out with great fanfare. During the sixteenth and seventeenth centuries, dog fighting as a blood sport became even more popular in Europe, particularly among the rich and royalty of England.

[24]Russell observed,

> The public outcry over the Michael Vick dog fighting case would have shocked Queen Elizabeth I. Elizabeth, who ruled England from 1558-1603, loved animal combat, hosted contests for visiting dignitaries, and would have been astonished to see such contests suppressed (para. 1).

Yet at the height of the Vick dog fighting scandal, none of this history was rehashed by the mainstream media. In addition, the church in England would often host dog fights as fundrais-

---

23 A History of Dog Fighting, Monica Villavicencio National Public Radio, July 19, 2007.
24 http://www.virginia.edu/topnews/facultyopinions/2007/russell.html.

ers (Kalof and Taylor, p.322). The historical participation of the queen and the church, the two ruling authorities in England, who also hosted dog fights, underscores the normalcy of the blood sport in European culture. Because such high-ranking social elites were involved in dog fighting means that Vick's involvement as a star NFL quarterback, was not at all incongruent with this tradition. Interestingly enough, animal combat using dogs to attack larger animals had significant impact on England's market economy.

The English use of dogs for baiting bulls was seen as necessary for tenderizing the animal's meat for human consumption. Bull-baiting through animal combat had become so functional that English law required that no bull would be butchered before first being baited. Incidentally, Russell found that the largest cattle market in London where bulls were baited for dog attacks and then slaughtered was named, ironically enough, "Smithfield" (para. 2).

From Smithfield of London, to Smithfield, Virginia[25]

That animal combat using dogs was an essential element of the Smithfield Market in London amounts to a cruel but interesting irony. Vick's property where his dog fighting enterprise functioned was in Smithfield, Virginia. Thus, the name Smithfield accounts for dogs attacking other animals for revenue-generating purposes in London and America, albeit centuries apart. Russell rather aptly noted, "There is a direct line from (fighting dogs in) bull baiting at the Smithfield market in London in the early 19th century to dog fighting (involving Michael Vick's Bad Newz Kennels) in Smithfield, Virginia, in the early 21st (century)" (para.14). It is notable that the term "line" is the root word of lineage, which adds greater authority to the view that Vick's conduct was influenced by an ancestral parent culture of animal combat. Perhaps the most direct line between the ancestral traditions of dog fighting in Europe to Vick's dog

---

25 http://www.virginia.edu/topnews/facultyopinions/2007/russell.html.

fighting in America is the evolution of the fighting dog itself. While Europe gave us the bulldog, Americans would adopt its direct descendant, the American Pit Bull Terrier.

The Bull Dog

As the practice of animal combat evolved, the need arose to breed bigger and stronger dogs to take down bulls. Cross breeding created the bulldog, whose large head and strong jaws made it ideal for taking down bulls during animal combat. The English were so impressed with the strength and tenacious fighting abilities of the bulldog that the animal became their national symbol (Russell, 2007, para. 4). Did the decision of the English to adopt the bulldog as their national symbol have any influence in America? Indeed, the influence of this transplanted symbolism is observable in the widespread use of the fighting bulldog as the official mascot of upwards of 300 high schools, colleges, and universities in America.

Even Georgetown University, a Catholic institution, uses the bulldog as its mascot. That a Catholic university would select the fighting bulldog as a symbol of its identity is not as odd since historically the church in England hosted dog fights as fundraisers. Yet none of these realities evoked discussion from these academic institutions or the mainstream media. Questions about the hypocrisy of vilifying Vick, while interscholastic and intercollegiate institutions glorify the tradition of dog fighting through nicknames was never posed. Additionally, the media, which blitzed Vick from all sides, has also perpetuated this culture of animal violence and cruelty. For example, the early morning edition of the daily newspaper is referred to, oddly enough, as the bulldog edition. Historically, newspapers in America would publish the results of dog fighting matches in their sports sections. Therefore, it is safe to conclude that the nexus between popular culture, sports, the media and dog fighting as a blood sport in America, was in place long before Michael Vick's scandal. But rather than discuss these historical connections, with the symbolism of the bulldog as Exhibit

A, critics carelessly blamed Michael Vick and hip-hop culture. Conversely, as this broader analysis shows, dog fighting evolved with the evolution of the fighting dog. This fighting bulldog was later cross bred with the smaller, quicker, terrier dog, creating the Staffordshire terrier, which ultimately became the American Pit Bull terrier. Of course it was this latter breed that was used in dog fighting by Michael Vick's Bad Newz Kennels.

Dog Fighting in the Jim Crow South

The idea of fighting pit bulls is unique to America. Official records from Alabama's archives show the American Pit Bull Terrier Association was staging dog fights in America as late as the 1930s. Herein lies but another example of parental conduct norms, which ultimately influenced Vick. Throughout the nineteenth and twentieth centuries, these norms evolved to include dog fighting organizations like the American Pit Bull Terrier Association and the United Kennel Club (UKC).

Such organizations were not only predecessors but also progenitors of Vick's Bad Newz Kennels. Ortiz (2010) found that in 1898 the UKC upheld the American Pit Bull Terrier as the "standard breed" for dog fighting and the American Dog Breeders Association did the same a decade later (Ortiz, p.7). While the UKC staged dog fighting matches complete with referees, by the twentieth century, the American Pit Bull Terrier Association was fighting the breed on an interstate basis. The existence of these dog fighting organizations for over two centuries reflected a shift in the culture of dog fighting in America. Vick indicated that his participation in dog fighting was influenced by a so-called culture. This culture included a widespread popularity that was especially endemic in the American South. Yet, as this section will attest, part of what allowed this culture to fulminate were various branches of the law enforcement community, which turned a blind eye to dog fighting, as Vick noted. The discussion that follows will rehash the cruel but interesting irony of Vick being sent to prison for dog fighting, which had been tolerated and even promulgated by prominent members of the legal community. Part of this review will necessarily include historical indices of such acceptance and its impact on the spread of the blood sport, particularly in southern states. In the final analysis, Vick was made to carry the weight for centuries of sins over dog fighting that was often condoned and in some cases perpetuated by law enforcement officials.

Dog Fighting and the Law

One of the most under-probed facets of the Vick narrative was his remarkable revelation that he did not believe dog fighting was terribly bad because the police in his neighborhood ignored it. In his letter to Judge Henry Hudson, who presided over his case, Vick intimated that police in his neighborhood did not make arrests for dog fighting as they did for more serious acts of criminal deviance. Yet, despite the uproar that his case created, neither the public at large, including the media, animal rights organizations, federal prosecutors, nor the presiding judge, were moved. But Vick's account of the police overlooking dog fighting should have received more consideration, perhaps as a mitigating factor, especially since the inaction of the police to dog fighting is congruent with the historical evolution of the blood sport. A review of these historical indices of law enforcement's culpability in the progression of dog fighting is meaningful in understanding how and why Vick victimized the dogs. Included in this review is an interesting exchange from the 1930s among the American Humane Society, the Tuscaloosa Sheriff's Department, the Alabama governor's office, his legal adviser, and the solicitor general. All were party to a trail of communications where concern was expressed over an impending dog fighting convention being hosted in the state by the American Pit Bull Terrier Association. Indeed, these sources demonstrate that the culture of dog fighting was alive and thriving in the Jim Crow South. An analysis of these correspondences will show how organizations like the American Pit Bull Terrier Association towed the fine line between dog fighting, which was not always illegal, and animal cruelty, which was. The latter question is especially apropos given Vick's account of how police in his community looked the other way when they observed him and others participating in a dog fight.

The American Pit Bull Terrier Association in the South

Official Alabama archives reveal a letter written by the field secretary of the American Humane Society of Albany, New York, dated January 20, 1934, which addressed concerns over dog fighting in the state. [26] The correspondence was sent to the Honorable B.M. Miller, Governor of Alabama, alerting him of an impending dog fighting match to be hosted in Tuscaloosa by the American Pit Bull Terrier Association. The letter, which implored the governor to prevent the matches from occurring, also warned that other members of the American Pit Bull Terrier Association from other states were planning to bring their dogs to stage fights. The existence of this organization and its interstate dog fighting contests provide more evidence that Vick's own interstate dog fighting matches were a subcultural phenomenon. A second letter from the American Humane Society, dated January 22, 1934, indicated that the proposed dog fights were to be hosted "at the American Pit Bull-Terrier Association Convention, January 27-28, 1934."[27] That a convention was held shows how well organized and attended these matches were.

In response to concerns raised by the American Humane Society, the solicitor general of Alabama and the sheriff of Tuscaloosa offered reassurance that the law would be upheld and the dog fighting match would be prevented. In a letter to the governor, dated January 24, 1934, R.L. Shamblin, Sheriff of Tuscaloosa County, advised, "I will see to it that this crime is not committed in this County if they do they will be arrested and brought to justice." [28]

---

26 State of Alabama archives, letter from American Humane Society, Field Secretary to Hon. B.M. Miller Gov. of Alabama, January 20, 1934.

27 State of Alabama archives, letter from American Humane Society, General Manager, to Hon. B.M. Miller Gov. of Alabama, January 22, 1934.

28 State of Alabama records, letter from Sheriff Shamblin to Governor Miller, January 24, 1934.

In a letter of similar import sent to the governor by the office of solicitor general, Edward De Graffenried, of the 6th Judicial Circuit of Alabama, committed to, "stopping the present intention of staging this fight…" But, curiously enough, he added, "…should they attempt to change their minds and stage the fight anyway it will be nipped in the bud if it is possible for us to do so."[29] (Notice the qualifying contingency of nipping it in the bud, *if it is possible*.) Then on January 26, just one day before the convention was to begin, [30]John H. Peach, legal advisor to the governor, wrote a letter to the American Humane Society, which stated in part: "The Governor has instructed (the) Sheriff of Tuscaloosa County to enforce Alabama law against cruelty to animals." Yet, in the last sentence, the governor's legal advisor reminded, "The State does not have a law prohibiting dog fights." So it is clear from the series of correspondences between the American Humane Society, the governor of Alabama, the sheriff of Tuscaloosa, the solicitor general, and the governor's legal advisor, that the law enforcement tone relaxed considerably as the American Pit Bull Terrier Convention drew closer. Undoubtedly, the conventioneers were fervently opposing plans to prevent their dog fights. In addition, the organization no doubt reminded the governor of Alabama and the state's legal community of the distinction between laws that punish animal cruelty versus no laws against dog fighting.

The preceding analysis indicates that Vick's Bad Newz Kennels was anything but a novelty. Nevertheless, an organization like the American Pit Bull Terrier Association is an example of how dog fighting organizations had historically staged dog fighting matches on an interstate basis. Vick of course was indicted, convicted, and sent to prison on federal charges for staging the same sort of dog fights across state lines. This account from the state of Alabama illustrates how lenient the law enforcement community was toward dog fighting throughout the South, which is another point Vick made. Perhaps in no other part of

---

29 State records letter from Solicitor General to Governor Miller, January 25, 1934.
30 State records from Governor's legal advisor to Richard Cravan, Field Secretary, The American Humane Society, January 26, 1934.

the American South was the dog fighting culture more firmly entrenched and law enforcement more laidback in allowing the blood sport to flourish than in the state of Louisiana.

"Cajuns and Blacks Have Been Fighting Dogs for Over 200 Years"

By the 1950s, dog fighting as a so-called sport became even more popular in the South, with law enforcement still walking the fine line between upholding laws against animal cruelty and no laws against dog fighting. Still, such a lackadaisical stance from the police as Vick witnessed as a youth is undoubtedly related to the historical participation and influence of law enforcement officials in the development of dog fighting as a sport. It was the mid-twentieth century when Lafayette, Louisiana Police Chief G.A. "Gaboon" Trahan developed what is known as the "Cajun rules" of dog fighting, which are still upheld worldwide. According to a report by Bill Burke of the *Virginia Pilot*, in 1950 the Lafayette police chief "hosted dog fights that drew attendees from all over the South long before animal activists demonized the activities and legislatures criminalized it."[31] This report of the Lafayette police chief hosting dog fighting matches throughout the South provides additional proof that Vick's own interstate operation was indeed influenced by a "so-called culture" of dog fighting, but in this case, perpetrated by a police chief. That the interstate dog fighting culture, as demonstrated by the United Kennel Club, the American Pit Bull Terrier Association, and Police Chief Trahan, ultimately influenced Vick's conduct is deducible from facts in his criminal case. The federal indictment showed that Vick's Bad Newz Kennels participated in dog fighting contests across such southern states as Virginia, Maryland, Alabama, North Carolina, and South Carolina, like the aforementioned had done. When taken as a whole, there is significant support for the notion that Vick was swayed by these traditions of dog fighting matches carried

---

31 Retrieved from http://www.hamptonroads.com/node/283641.

out across interstate lines. The role of the Lafayette police chief in creating rules for dog fighting matches underscores how widely accepted the blood sport had become, and how authorities of the law viewed it as a less serious social problem. It was also in this laidback law enforcement environment of Lafayette's dog fighting culture that Floyd Boudreaux, who traded fighting dogs with his comrade in canine combat, Chief Trahan, earned his reputation as the don of dog fighting. Additionally, in the 1990s Evans et al. of the University of Louisiana at Lafayette discovered a very fertile dog fighting culture in the American South. When combined, these factors help to explain why the Boudreauxs, whose case was tried in the same Lafayette Parish where Trahan once presided as police chief, were acquitted on all forty-eight charges of dog fighting in 2008.

Parent Culture vs. Subculture: And the Winner Is?

While there have been stark differences between the parent culture and subculture of dog fighting historically, those differences are still observable today. To further underscore how endemic and powerful dog fighting is in the state of Louisiana, the prosecution in the Boudreauxs' case was not allowed to present Kathy Strouse, the superintendent of the Chesapeake Animal Control Unit in Virginia, as an expert witness. Incidentally, Strouse aided the prosecution in getting a conviction against Vick. Incredulously, Boudreaux's attorney successfully argued in court that Strouse could not be considered an expert since she had not published anything in writing on the subject and it was her first time testifying in a legal matter that she had not investigated. It seems, on the latter point, the defense attorney and judge agreed that Louisiana's tolerance of dog fighting was perhaps different from Virginia's. For what did it matter that she had not personally investigated the Boudreauxs? Even more appalling, the federal government never became involved in the investigation of the Boudreauxs, despite having the amended Animal Welfare Act at their disposal. Such disparate outcomes in these respective dog fighting cases reveal the differences in how the courts treated whites like Boudreaux and his son, versus blacks like Vick and his co-defendants. The differences also illustrate the disparities between Boudreaux being more closely aligned with the parent culture of dog fighting in the South versus Vick being a reflection of the subculture.

Given the weight of the preceding analysis and the documented support, it is logical to surmise that this parent culture of dog fighting violence and its aforementioned conduct norms have evolved over centuries. Additionally, it has produced a subculture of violence that is now widespread throughout America, particularly in the South. Not so ironically, these influences were identifiable in the drama involving Michael Vick's Bad Newz Kennels, and as such gives credible authority to the subculture of violence theory as a reliable explanation for his involvement in dog fighting.

Conclusion

One of the greatest travesties associated with the Michael Vick dog fighting dilemma was the failure of the media, animal rights groups, the larger contingency of academia, and the politics of the state to more thoroughly examine and explain the depths of this historical social problem. While there were a few exceptions, in large measure the failure to include a relevant historical review negated the opportunity to infuse a theoretical perspective on the Vick dog fighting scandal. This chapter has provided historical and theoretical analyses of dog fighting's evolution over centuries in Europe, beginning as early as 5 BC and 43 AD, before being transplanted to America in the nineteenth century. Greater evidence of this identifiable parent culture involved the exploits of dog fighting organizations like the United Kennel Club of 1817 and the American Pit Bull Terrier Association of the 1930s, which served as progenitors of Vick's Bad Newz Kennels. This analysis rehashed Vick's concession that his actions were influenced by a "so-called culture." Qualitative research in this work shows the irony of this so-called culture being traceable to the Smithfield market in London of the nineteenth century and ultimately to Michael Vick's property in Smithfield, Virginia, in this the twenty-first century.

This historical review is reliable in identifying a parent culture of dog fighting violence, which provided a foundation for utilizing Wolfgang's subculture of violence theory. This theory helps explain how Michael Vick's adaptation to dog fighting occurred through a process of social learning. It should be noted, that this chapter did not offer a concise definition of the subculture of violence theory, but neither did Wolfgang. Instead, he employed terms like *culture* and *subculture,* as part of an *integrated conceptualization* that explains rather than defines such phenomena (Wolfgang & Ferracuti, p.163). Hence, Wolfgang's perspective is useful in explaining, among other factors, that the violence exhibited by blacks, like Michael Vick in this case, is only partly different from a parent culture of violence.

Other Social Implications

In retrospect, the failure of the media and the academic community to present a broader perspective on Vick's involvement in dog fighting resulted in a host of unfortunate consequences. Although Vick's participation in dog fighting constituted criminal conduct, it was lost on the American public that the behavior was learned from a parent culture much bigger than him. Thus, a significant opportunity was lost to better educate the public and the likes of Michael Vick, which could stem the tide of dog fighting as a social problem. Secondly, without a forum to discuss historical and theoretical analyses of Vick's conduct, his defense had no chance of offering such explanations as mitigating factors had he gone to trial. Consequently, Vick pleaded guilty and was sentenced to federal prison for nearly two years. Even worse, data uncovered in this chapter, shows that following Vick's criminal probe and conviction, African-Americans were arrested and convicted of dog-fighting, in greater proportion than other racial and ethnic groups. Another caveat that emerged in the wake of Vick's dog fighting case is that other forms of animal cruelty such as hoarding, abuse, neglect, and bestiality, which is also centuries-old, and more often perpetuated by deviant whites, is rampant throughout America, but is not punished like dog fighting.

Subsequent to the Vick scandal, Congress amended the AWA (P.L. 110-246, June 18, 2008), which increased the maximum prison sentence from three to five years. But there are no federal laws against other forms of animal cruelty like bestiality. Additionally, all fifty states made it a felony to fight dogs, yet in only twenty-nine states is it illegal to have carnal relations with dogs or other animals (and in only fifteen of those states is it a felony). This chapter sought to provide historical and theoretical perspectives of Vick's involvement in dog fighting with the hopes that such a perspective might prevent the proliferation of dog fighting in America and the world. Lastly, the manner in which Michael Vick was made to bear the burden of centuries of sins involving dog fighting was, in large part, owing to the powers of influential authorities. The role of the NFL, the media, corporate sponsors, and the politics of the state helped to quicken Vick's demise. These groups exercised their ability to label others as deviant as they saw fit, and to also label behaviors as well. Hence, Michael Vick was indicted, convicted, and sentenced to prison.

CHAPTER II

From Superman to Super-Masculine Menial

How the NFL and Its Dominant Alliance Sacked Michael Vick

"We place dogs above human beings...and there's something wrong with that picture."

—Juanita Abernathy[32]

In 2007, the idea of Michael Vick as *Superman* in the NFL was surely tested by his dog fighting dilemma off the field. If Vick, who has a tattoo of Superman's insignia on the back of his right hand, was akin to Superman on the field, then the dog fighting scandal proved to be his kryptonite. Rather than any mild-mannered Clark Kent away from professional football, the egregious charges in the criminal complaint against Vick cast him as the villainous ringleader of an illegal dog fighting operation. No matter how fast, exciting, elusive, or heroic he may have been on the gridiron, Vick's renown as the high-flying Superman was abruptly brought to a grinding halt. But the dog fighting dilemma was not the sole source of Vick's downfall. In the absence of any influential super-friends of his own, the

---

32 Juanita Abernathy is a Civil Rights heroine and the widow of Reverend Ralph Abernathy. She was quoted in an interview by Wright Thompson of ESPN. Thompson, W. (2007). *A History of Mistrust.*

NFL and its dominant alliance of superstructures, made up of the media, corporate sponsors, and the politics of the state, converged upon Vick like a Legion of Doom. These powerful institutions, which were also instrumental in developing NFL football into America's number one spectator sport, gang-tackled Vick for his role in the dog fighting ring.

This chapter will discuss Michael Vick's downfall in the context of the league and its dominant alliance of superstructures (public and private), which quickened his demise. Such a review is pivotal to show how these institutions reduced Vick from proverbial superman to super-masculine menial, with race as an interceding variable. Historically, the perception of blacks as super-masculine menials was used to justify their mistreatment during slavery and later during the era of the Jim Crow South (Sabo and Runfola, 1980). The term *superstructures* (Gramsci, 1971), which will be used interchangeably with the term dominant allies and powerful partners, refers to authoritative entities, public and private alike, that exploit others who lack significant social capital in a capitalist society.

Because blacks have lacked major social power historically, the NFL and their alliance of superstructures have perpetuated racism against them. Each of the aforementioned entities discriminated against them using racist stereotypes such as sambos, i.e., ignorant plantation darkies, and jungle savages, making them akin to primitive beasts (Oriard, 2001). As this discussion will show, such unfortunate notions influenced the NFL to discriminate against blacks with its gentlemen's agreement, which barred them from playing beginning in 1934. Following reintegration thirteen years later, discrimination became the norm as blacks could not play thinking positions like quarterback. These disparaging references that shaped the larger societal view of blacks were used in various forms of media, including movies, radio, television, books, newspapers, advertisements, and newsreels. Such negative notions have plagued blacks perpetually. These ideas influenced lawmakers and the courts to treat blacks with less consideration than whites in American society. When combined, the ideas of sambo and savage make up the composite of the super-masculine menial.

47

This awful tradition of racial discrimination against blacks has permeated every segment of American society, which has resulted in differential treatment by race in nearly every significant institution. The vestiges of such racial discrimination were apparent in the disownment that the league and its alliance of superstructures showed toward Vick when compared to prominent whites in the NFL who committed acts of deviance.

To wit, men like Bill Belichick, head coach of the New England Patriots, and Ben Roethlisberger, quarterback of the Pittsburgh Steelers, were blameworthy in transgressions that may have been criminal. Yet the reaction of the NFL and its dominant partners was relatively calm when compared to Vick's dilemma. The effect reinforced the traditional view in America that blacks are more criminogenic than whites and should be punished more severely as a result. Other indicators of blatant racism toward Vick that went largely unpublicized was the incessant use of the dreaded "N" word by angry partisans, who also called for him to be lynched. Exploring the racial angle in the Vick debacle is important to show that the vitriolic reaction of the public and the punitive sanctions imposed by the NFL and its dominant allies appeared to be outside the concern over dogs. But why would the NFL, mainstream media, corporate entities, and the politics of the state react so strongly to the Vick scandal?

Why Did Race Matter?

Beyond the differential treatment by race, there was great concern on the part of the league and their dominant allies that Vick's legal transgressions posed a threat to their multi-billion dollar partnerships. Historically, the NFL had always been wary of the perceived negative impact black players might have on their game's popularity and revenue. In 1934, the NFL believed that the presence of black players was a factor in their inability to attract fans, so they established a gentlemen's agreement that barred them for thirteen years. Subsequent to reintegration in 1946, which the league reluctantly acquiesced to, the NFL continued to discriminate against blacks. In light of the widely accepted view that blacks were ignorant sambos, so-called thinking positions like quarterback, the marquee position, was off limits for blacks. The historical intolerance to using *black quarterbacks* in the NFL may help to explain why the league and its powerful partners were so quick to excommunicate Vick. But before addressing the issue of race and how the NFL and its alliance of superstructures reduced Vick from superman to super-masculine menial, it will be meaningful to discuss how these same superstructures first shaped the NFL into a multi-billion dollar sports institution.

The NFL's Alliance of Superstructures

The league's dominant alliance of superstructures maintains a vested interest in the growth, popularity, and prosperity of NFL football. These interests helped develop the NFL into a multi-billion dollar behemoth of a sports business giant. Television networks advanced the NFL from an also-ran among spectator sports in the early twentieth century to king of the hill by century's end. Today CBS, NBC, Fox, ESPN, and DirecTV pay upwards of $9 billion in licensing fees to broadcast league games to millions of loyal fans, a significant number of whom were very angry at Michael Vick for his dog fighting crimes.

Historically, it was the nexus between television and corporate sponsors like the Falstaff Brewing Company (Powers, 1984), and Admiral, a manufacturer of television sets (Petersen, 1997), that brought NFL football into the living rooms of American families and mainstream culture in the 1940s. The relationship between the NFL and television spearheaded unprecedented growth in the game's popularity and prosperity. The increasingly higher ratings of NFL games on television have generated increasingly higher revenues and have had the added effect of attracting a virtual who's who among major corporate sponsors in America.

Corporate Sponsors Contribute Billions to the League

Many of the league's major sponsors have included such multinational companies as Pepsi, Visa, Coors, IBM, Verizon,

Reebok, Nike, and others who collectively contribute billions more in revenues to be official sponsors of the NFL. Corporate sponsors market themselves in the NFL through advertising during games and in league stadiums. Other corporate partnerships are established with league teams through the purchasing of luxury suites, which continues to drive the league's competition for revenue-generating super stadiums (Harris, 1986). But the most indispensable ally of pro football has been the politics of the state, consisting of local, state, and federal branches of government that have contributed mightily to the NFL's meteoric rise. Moreover, the politics of the state, in particular the federal government, have passed legislation and established court rulings that have enabled the NFL to accumulate considerable wealth, primarily through television.

The Politics of the State Shaped the NFL

Among the first significant developments that propelled the NFL forward in the era of television was a federal court ruling in 1953 that allowed the NFL to impose a blackout rule (Rader, 1984). This provision gave the league the latitude to blackout local telecasts of football games for the home team, whether the game was sold out or not. This induced local fans to buy tickets or they risked having very little entertainment on a Sunday afternoon. Realizing the rule was not at all fair to fans, in 1973 Congress passed a measure that required the NFL to lift the blackout if tickets sold out seventy-two hours in advance. Although this ruling was significant, it came more than ten years after Congress passed the revolutionary Sports Broadcasting Act of 1961. This law gave the NFL its most sweeping victory, as it allowed professional sports leagues to negotiate television contracts as a single entity. Prior to this landmark legislation, television contracts in professional sports were negotiated on a per-franchise basis, which enabled Major League Baseball to remain the nation's pastime while professional football remained an afterthought. But it was television that catapulted NFL football past professional baseball in the

1960s and into the mainstream of American culture (Rader, p. 121). While the Sports Broadcasting Act of '61 constituted a significant development for the league, it also increased the competition between the NFL and the rival American Football League, which was founded in 1959.

For upward of six years, the NFL and AFL warred over players. While the AFL signed a greater number of black players than the NFL, both adhered to the inflexible belief that blacks should not play quarterback. While the NFL was more of a "three yards and a cloud of dust" sport, the AFL was considered more entertaining. It featured greater scoring and a wide-open passing game that showcased the throwing quarterback. Congress would end the war when it granted a limited exemption from anti-trust laws, permitting the merger between the NFL and AFL in 1966. Although the merger enjoined the rivals into one league, the one constant that remained was the intolerance to playing *black quarterbacks*, which still exists today. Donovan McNabb, a former All-Pro NFL quarterback, who is black, stated that he and others like him were treated differently because of their race.[33]

Differential treatment of *black quarterbacks* in the NFL is rooted in racist notions promulgated in the media. These derogatory descriptors cast blacks as ignorant, lazy, and uncivilized; and whose athletic prowess was honed in the jungles of Africa. In the case of Michael Vick, the residual effects of such stereotypes formed the composite of the super-masculine menial, which is what he was reduced to as a result of the dog fighting scandal. As for the NFL and its alliance of superstructures, each has contributed to the league's growth and each has practiced racism against blacks. To better explain the role of racism in how Michael Vick was treated by the NFL and its allies, a brief review of how each has demonstrated racial intolerance against blacks in America will follow.

---

33 Retrieved from http://sports.espn.go.com/nfl/news/story?id=3035308. *McNabb says black QB's under more pressure*, 2007.

Kenneth N. Robinson, MS

The Not Fair League: Racism Against Blacks From the NFL and Its Allies

The Media

In the twentieth century, blacks in America attempted to participate in spectator sports like football amidst racist depictions of them in the media as indolent, primitive, and dangerous. From its inception, football as sport was created for Anglo-Saxon white males who were student athletes on the campuses of America's most prestigious universities, such as Harvard, Princeton, and Yale (Oriard, 2001). Although black stars like Fritz Pollard, who attended both Brown and Dartmouth, and Paul Robeson of Rutgers, starred in college football and the NFL, they did so despite prevailing stereotypes of them as sambos and savages promulgated in the media. These negative ideas created a caste system, known as *stacking*, that kept blacks from so-called thinking positions. It lasted for decades, and is still observable today. Although a greater number of black males have started at quarterback in the NFL in recent years, they are still a mere two of every ten starters in the game, despite their greater propensity for success. There appears to be a general reluctance by NFL owners to use them, except for their undeniable ability to mete out success. In addition to the media, corporate sponsors also discriminated against blacks historically by using some of the same disparaging images of blacks in marketing their products.

Corporate America

Corporations routinely used disparaging images of blacks as happy sambos, such as the images that still appear on the cover of *Cream of Wheat* cereal, *Uncle Ben's* rice, and *Aunt Jemima* pancake mix. Other corporations marketed products like soap and detergent using caricatures of blacks who were portrayed as dirty savages. During the Vick narrative, a corporation began selling the *Vick Dog Chew Toy*, which was marketed to dog owners.[34] While the doll was supposed to look like a toy for a dog, it was actually reminiscent of racist images and demeaning caricatures like *Little Black Sambo*.[35] To further underscore how desensitized the public had become, no one cared that dog owners placing the *Vick Dog Chew Toy* in the jaws of their dogs evoked the history of dogs biting blacks during the civil rights movement. Although most companies are less overt with their discrimination against blacks in marketing their products, still the climate of racism in corporate America is no less pronounced.

In the last twenty years, a number of racial discrimination lawsuits filed by blacks were settled by corporate giants like Texaco ($176 million) and Coca-Cola ($192 million). Incidentally, Nike settled a class-action lawsuit for $7.6 million with its black employees at its Niketown store in Chicago, Illinois (Sadchev, 2007). Nike, of course, had signed Vick to an endorsement deal and then dropped him after he was charged with dog fighting in 2007. The so-called shoe giant re-signed Vick to endorse their shoes after his redemptive 2010 season, in which he was named the NFL Comeback Player of the Year. But because most private corporations have leadership hierarchies, much like the NFL, where white males comprise better than 90 percent of the CEOs, racial discrimination is fairly common and predictable. Yet historically, it has been the politics of the state that has been the greatest purveyor of racism against blacks in America. Whether at the state or federal level, governmental entities have exercised their power to make discrimination against blacks the law of the land.

Politics of the State

In 1857, the Supreme Court ruled in the Dred Scott case that blacks had no rights that whites were bound to respect. Questions of Vick's rights to due process were raised by African-Americans

---

34 Michael Vick Dog Chew Toy sold on eBay during the dog fighting scandal. See photo at VickDogChewToy.com.
35 Illustration of Little Black Sambo, from the Helen Bannerman book: *The Story of Little Black Sambo* (1900).

given the incendiary media coverage of his case, which seemed to disable his right to a fair trial. In 1896, the nation's highest court ruled in *Plessy vs. Ferguson* that separate but equal was the law of the land. It was this ruling that allowed institutions and states to legally discriminate against blacks in America. Such racial discrimination was particularly embedded in the South, where Jim Crow segregation prevailed. The *Plessy* ruling would stand until 1954, when the Supreme Court upheld arguments developed by Charles Hamilton-Houston (who died in 1950) and Thurgood Marshall, lawyers of the NAACP, who asserted that separate but equal was unconstitutional. Although the ruling struck down legalized segregation in public schools, it did not strike down racism. Instead, racism has remained a part of every significant cultural institution in America, including the NFL and its partners. As this discussion on Michael Vick's case will show, the NFL and its alliance of superstructures—public and private alike—have reacted more punitively to the transgressions of blacks than whites.

The League and Its Superstructures Converge on Vick

In response to the Michael Vick dog fighting scandal, each of the league's alliance of superstructures acquiesced to angry fans with punitive sanctions against the quarterback. Fearing that Vick's presence in the NFL could affect the popularity and prosperity of the game, including television ratings and ultimately the feelings of fans, the league and its dominant allies moved to oust him. Given the historical role of state and federal governments in developing the NFL, the focus on the retributive reaction against Vick begins in the political sphere. Interspersed in this commentary will be references to race in the differential treatment accorded to Vick by the NFL and their dominant allies.

Politics of the State: Reaction to Vick

Racism emerges as an important issue in the Vick scandal for several reasons. The system of justice in the United States has been plagued by racial inequalities that have adversely affected blacks historically, particularly in the South. In Vick's case, Gerald Poindexter, the Surry County Commonwealth's Attorney, questioned whether the federal government's probe of Vick was based on the player's celebrity and race.[36] Conversely, high-profile acts of what seemed to be criminal deviance involving whites in the NFL, such as Bill Belichick's Spygate scandal and two separate rape allegations involving Ben Roethlisberger, did not result in any criminal charges.

Vick vs. Spygate

While the media, corporate sponsors, and the politics of the state all punished Vick, who is black, very little public disdain and certainly no legal sanctions followed the misdeeds of the New England Patriots' head coach Bill Belichick. It is worth noting that the respective scandals of Vick and Belichick came to light in the same year. Yet in a very insidious manner, the media used the Vick scandal to push Belichick's Spygate scandal off the public's radar. Even more revealing is that Belichick's scandal came to light after Vick's downfall. Secondly, as egregious as Vick's deeds were, his deviant conduct did not involve his NFL job with the Atlanta Falcons. Vick noted that he would fly to Virginia on his days off to engage in dog fighting. Conversely, Belichick carried out his misconduct in the course of his NFL job. By surreptitiously videotaping his opponents to gain a competitive advantage, Belichick may have committed wire fraud and unfair trading practices in violation of anti-trust laws in the course of interstate commerce. Were Belichick's actions in the Spygate scandal serious enough to warrant a Congressional investigation and federal charges? Indeed, his deviant actions were that serious, and Congress's failure to act is questionable given the extraordinary attention and punitive sanctions it accorded in Vick's case.

---

36 http://usatoday.printthis.clickability.com/pt/cpt?action=Local .2007. *Local dog fighting probe continues as Vick cancels camp.*

Congress had an obligation to act in response to Belichick's Spygate scandal since federal lawmakers gave the league a limited exemption from anti-trust laws with the 1967 merger between the NFL and AFL. Congress's rationale for the merger was that NFL football constituted interstate commerce. Belichick's conduct seemed to rise to the level of violating anti-trust laws as these illegal videotaping procedures conspired to undermine competition and fair trade in furtherance of interstate commerce. The depths of conspiracy not only included cheating, but training the team's video assistants to lie to authorities as well. The anti-trust law identifies a conspiracy as the involvement of two or more persons who unreasonably restrain trade for the purposes of limiting competition. In addition, the Spygate scandal should have been probed by Congress as a question of wire fraud. Federal Law 18 USC 1343 "makes it a Federal crime or offense for anyone to use interstate wire communications facilities in carrying out a scheme to defraud." However, in order to establish guilt beyond a reasonable doubt, two other conditions have to be met. It must be proven that the suspect knowingly and willingly devised a scheme to defraud. This first condition is met in Belichick's Spygate scandal, given that league rules prohibit teams from videotaping the opposing team during games. Additionally, he, along with thirty-one other head coaches, received a letter from the NFL's front office before the season opener of 2007 reminding them of videotaping restrictions. Yet Belichick did it anyway. The second condition requires that the suspect knowingly transmits or causes to transmit by wire, in the course of interstate commerce, "some sound" with the intentions of executing a scheme to defraud. Belichick's conduct, which he later apologized for, involved stealing his opponents' signals through wire transmissions using videotaping procedures in NFL stadiums or facilities in furtherance of interstate commerce. Furthermore, there was also speculation that Belichick had some of his players wearing microphones to steal signals as well. Despite these flagrant incidents of breaking NFL rules and perhaps federal laws, Belichick was not charged with a crime. The gravity of these serious transgressions notwithstanding, Congressional leaders on Capitol Hill remained relatively coy on the Spygate scandal. By contrast, congressmen such as Representative Tom Lantos (D-CA)[37] and the late Senator Robert C. Byrd (D-WV)[38] were vociferous in condemning Vick's deeds.

Aside from calls for an investigation and queries to NFL Commissioner Roger Goodell from U.S. Senator Arlen Specter (R-PA), Belichick's corrupt behavior was ignored on Capitol Hill. The question of racism and selective enforcement becomes especially relevant when you consider that Vick was charged by the federal government for conspiracy to engage in an illegal dog fighting enterprise in furtherance of interstate commerce. On the other hand, there was no federal investigation of Belichick or his Patriots staff for conspiring to gain an unfair advantage as well as committing wire fraud, despite their collusion in utilizing illegal videotaping tactics across state lines for nearly ten years. Additionally, the NFL was just as culpable of perpetuating selective enforcement on the question of race. For example, the league sent its security investigators, unsolicited, to assist state and federal authorities in the investigation of Vick in 2007. On the other hand, the league ensured there would be no federal investigation of Belichick when it destroyed the videotaped evidence, developed over nearly a decade by the Patriots staff, before an investigation could begin.

Senator Specter asked the league to explain why it destroyed the tapes, which he likened to the CIA's destruction of interrogation tapes.[39] The commissioner's response was that the tapes were destroyed to ensure that no other team would benefit from them. Senator Specter dismissed Goodell's explanation as something you would tell a kindergartner. But the league should have been questioned and punitively sanctioned by Congress for the

---

37 http://usatoday.printthis.clickability.com/pt/cpt?action=Congressman+seeks U.S. Rep Tom Lantos (D-CA.).
38 http://sports.espn.go.com/espn/print?id=2942677 Sen. Robert C. Byrd, (D-WV).
39 http://sports.espn.go.com/nfl/news/story?id=3225539 .(2008). Senator wants to know why NFL destroyed spy tapes.

potential legal harm of destroying evidence that may have been material in a criminal probe of Belichick and his staff. The decision by the commissioner to order the destruction of the tapes should have been reviewed by Congress as such actions could have amounted to obstruction of justice. Congress seemed altogether unconcerned about the larger implication of this unfortunate precedent in which an organization such as the NFL, which Congress regulates, destroyed potential evidence in what may have been a criminal matter. Even more evidentiary of selective enforcement by race, Senator Specter could not engender any of his colleagues on Capitol Hill to schedule so much as a hearing on the Patriots Spygate scandal.

By contrast, during discussions of the Vick scandal, members of Congress responded angrily and demanded the NFL act. But independent of any NFL punishment, Congress itself ensured Vick would be punished when it amended the Animal Welfare Act in 2007. Additionally, in August of 2007, Congress proposed added penalties that increased the prison sentence from three years to five years. Yet no states or the federal government took action against Belichick or the league for such deviant conduct, despite that fans as taxpayers have underwritten billions in the financing of league stadiums in NFL cities. However, former NFL player Willie Gary and several fans did file a suit in New Orleans that accused the Patriots of committing fraud, unfair trading practices, and racketeering over Spygate.[40] These lawsuits over Belichick's actions were not taken seriously enough by the courts it seems, and were ultimately dismissed. The latter outcome is undoubtedly attributable to the lack of continuing media coverage on the Spygate scandal. It was quickly swept under the rug. Yet these legal maneuvers underscored how harmful Belichick's illegal videotaping was to public confidence in the game. This was all the more reason that Congress should have reacted punitively to Spygate. There was a need to restore public trust and to send a message to major sports corporations like the NFL that they will be held to

---

40 http://www.usatoday.com/sports/football/nfl/2008-02-20-spygate-update (2008). *Goodell hopes deal close with Walsh on Spygate talk.*

the highest standards of the law. Even more revealing, the differential treatment accorded to these respective scandals by the
politics of the state ultimately led to differential labeling. Vick
became a criminal deviant and the face of animal cruelty, while
Belichick was restored whole as the best coach in the game.

These accounts highlight how race was seemingly a factor
in how differently Vick was treated by Congress and the NFL,
when compared to Belichick. While Congress erred by doing
nothing about Spygate, the NFL fined Belichick $500,000 and
the Patriots team another $250,000. In addition, the organiza-
tion lost a first-round pick. Unlike a plethora of black players
in the NFL who have been suspended for off-the-field conduct,
Belichick was never suspended for his surreptitious videotaping scandal.[41] On the other hand, Vick was suspended for
the 2007 season and served another four-game suspension in
2009. To further underscore the differential treatment between
the two subjects, Belichick was fined a mere pittance for his
scandalous ways, when compared to Vick, who lost a $130
million contract, and another $50 million to $60 million in
endorsement deals (Bell, 2007). The outcomes following the
respective scandals of Vick and Belichick were never more
apparent than at season's end in 2007. Vick was sentenced
to nearly two years in prison, and both his life and NFL
career were threatened. Conversely, despite Belichick's deviant
behavior, which may have actually been criminal, he was voted
the Associated Press NFL Coach of the Year. In the eyes of the
media, Vick has not been able to live down his dog fighting
misdeeds; but the press forgave Belichick almost as soon as
his scandal occurred. By 2011 Vick was still plagued by an
ongoing bankruptcy, despite signing another contract worth
$100 million. Conversely, Belichick is still highly regarded
by the media and is the highest-paid head coach in the NFL.
Yet the league's contention that Belichick's illegal videotaping
procedures did not help his team is a fallacy.

If Belichick is such a genius as the media has described
him, why would he engage in such rule-violating behavior for

---

41 (http://sports.espn.go.com/nfl/news/story/?id=3179438).

nearly ten years if it was not helping him? It is interesting to observe that before Spygate came to light, the Patriots under Belichick were 3-0 in Super Bowls. After Spygate was exposed in 2007, they lost the Super Bowl that year and again in 2011. It is also worth noting that since Spygate was revealed, in each of their last five playoff appearances (in 2007, and from 2009 through 2012), the three teams that beat them—the Giants (twice), the Jets, and the Ravens (twice)—all faced them during the regular season. Prior to Spygate being uncovered, the Patriots would have been able to illegally videotape these opponents to gain a competitive advantage in their next matchup. But after being caught cheating and being stripped of the illegal videotaping procedures, they lost to these teams in the playoffs. This is more than a strange coincidence and makes the inaction on the part of Congress even more alarming, given what appears to be Belichick's unfair advantage gained through the illegal videotaping of opponents. The non-response from Congress and relatively weak sanctions imposed by the NFL against Belichick provide more evidence of differential treatment by race that was also observable in the sports media. The league and the media have a penchant for treating blacks in the NFL as more seriously deviant than whites, and these respective scandals bear this out.

When troubled Hall of Fame linebacker Lawrence Taylor, who is black, was charged with rape in 2010, a reporter asked NFL Commissioner Roger Goodell if a player's off-the-field conduct should influence whether they are in the Hall of Fame. Goodell answered yes. But when Belichick's scandal was revealed, no reporter asked Goodell if a head coach's improper conduct, which included cheating on the field, should affect their Hall of Fame prospects. Despite the serious breach of public trust over the Spygate scandal, the NFL did not create any new policies or systems of control over such illegal videotaping. What were the consequences of the league's failure to implement better internal controls or dole out stricter sanctions for coaches who violate videotaping rules? Unfortunately for the NFL and its fans, there was Spygate II.

Spygate II

In 2010, Josh McDaniels, a Bill Belichick protégé and head coach of the Denver Broncos, was publicly chided for failing to inform his team owner and the league that one of his assistants illegally videotaped an opponent (Williamson, 2010). McDaniels and the Broncos organization were fined a combined $100,000. McDaniels had worked for Belichick in New England when Spygate was exposed. So he knew all too well the seriousness of such a transgression, yet he failed to disclose the illegal taping procedure, which occurred before a game against the San Francisco 49ers in London. McDaniels later fired the assistant, who had also worked for Belichick in New England when Spygate occurred. McDaniels too was later fired by the Broncos. Once again the league was embarrassed, but this time on an international stage. Despite the revelations of deviant conduct in 2007 and another episode of illegal videotaping in 2010, no member of Congress raised a question about this apparent connection, nor was there any discussion of a hearing to consider how widespread such breaches of public trust might be in the NFL. If the feeling on the part of Congress is that there are enough laws on the books to address unfair trading practices in industries regulated by federal lawmakers, then the question becomes why are they not being enforced when it comes to the NFL? The absence of any reliable explanation for why Congress would act unilaterally to punish Vick for his dog fighting scandal, but fail to punish the likes of Belichick, the Broncos, and the NFL, given a repeat episode of illegal videotaping, raises serious questions of selective enforcement by race. More evidence of differential treatment by race concerns the investigations of rape allegations against Pittsburgh Steelers quarterback Ben Roethlisberger.

Big Ben-eficiary of Race

Roethlisberger faced two separate allegations of rape, by two different women, in two separate states, Nevada in 2009 and Georgia in 2010. Yet he faced no criminal prosecution. No member of Congress spoke out publicly in either case, even though the purported Las Vegas victim filed a lawsuit claiming that he raped her in 2008. Even worse, no member of Congress uttered a word in the Georgia case, where Roethlisberger not only endangered the welfare of minors by serving alcohol to underage girls, but reportedly had sex with a college student in the bathroom of a bar. Even more disconcerting, the Georgia state legislature failed to pass any new laws against serving alcohol to minors. By contrast, at the height of public angst over Vick's mistreatment of dogs, every state in America made dog fighting a felony. Furthermore, members of Congress sent letters to Commissioner Goodell imploring him to punish the star athlete, and like all fifty states throughout America, the federal government made dog fighting a felony.

On the other hand, Congress's failure to show leadership in response to the investigations of sexual deviance involving Roethlisberger seemed to backfire. In 2010-2011, there were three sex-oriented scandals involving three male members of Congress. Congressman Eric Massa (D-NY) resigned in disgrace after it was revealed he made sexual advances toward his young male staffers. Congressman Chris Lee (R-NY) resigned after he sent pictures of himself, including one shirtless, to a woman on Craigslist. In 2011, Congressman Anthony Weiner (D-NY) revealed that he too had sent sexually inappropriate pictures of himself to a college student. While Weiner initially lied and said his Twitter account had been hacked, he later admitted that the picture was his and he indeed sent the inappropriate photos. In addition, it was also revealed that Weiner had inappropriate communications with at least six women, including a 17-year-old from Delaware. It was Weiner's cyber-trysts that really brought to light the hazard of Congress not acting in response to Roethlisberger's alleged sexual misdeeds, especially since Weiner seemed to harbor a preference for underage girls, including college students. Had Congress responded more stringently to Roethlisberger's deviant conduct toward women, maybe some of their members would have never attempted to sexually exploit young women and men. These disparate reactions by Congress to Vick's conduct versus no reaction to Roethlisberger's once more raises questions of selective enforcement by race on Capitol Hill. Why did Congress move to punish Vick for his deeds against dogs, but were less concerned about Roethlisberger's conduct toward young college girls? Left open for interpretation, the inaction of members of Congress toward Roethlisberger's misdeeds suggests there is apparently less regard for the treatment of women than there is for dogs. Still, the differential treatment by race in the Vick and Roethlisberger scandals was widespread throughout the executive, legislative, and judicial branches of government.

Even the courts took a different tact with Roethlisberger by scheduling his civil trial during the NFL's off-season in 2010, while Vick's court sessions in 2007 were scheduled during the league's regular season. It is also interesting to observe that Judge Henry Hudson, who presided over Vick's case, seemed to not only have knowledge of the court's schedule but the Falcons schedule as well. He scheduled Vick to appear in his court on July 26, which was the first day of the Falcons training camp. Additionally, he sentenced Vick on December 10, when the Falcons team faced the New Orleans Saints on *Monday Night Football*. Although Vick was suspended, these court dates guaranteed that Vick's appearance in Judge Hudson's court would gain national media coverage during significant times of the NFL season. On the other hand, in 2010, Roethlisberger did not have to worry about court dates during the regular season as his December 2010 scheduled appearance during the playoff race was moved to March of 2011. Thus Roethlisberger was effective enough to lead the Steelers to the Super Bowl in 2010, where they eventually lost. While the league did suspend him for the first four games, the NFL never became involved in the criminal investigation against him as they did with Vick.

The question of disparate treatment by race on the part of the league is especially apropos since the NFL sent its own security team, unsolicited, to assist state and federal investigators in the Vick probe. But, much like in the case of Belichick, the league did not send its security team to assist any law enforcement agency investigating either of Roethlisberger's alleged incidents of rape. The fundamental difference is that by sending their security team to assist an external law enforcement agency's investigation of Vick, the commissioner conveyed the message that the NFL had abandoned him. Conversely, rather than send their security team to help investigators in the Roethlisberger probes, the league sent them on a simple fact-finding mission for their interest only. Much different from the Vick case, the league's restraint in the investigation of Roethlisberger conveyed the message they had not abandoned him. In the end, despite eyewitness statements and the presence of physical evidence implicating Roethlisberger, the prosecutor decided not to pursue any charges against him in the Georgia incident. These inconsistencies raise additional questions of differential treatment by race on the part of the NFL and may help to explain the different outcomes in the legal dilemmas facing Vick and Roethlisberger. Did the league act in the case of Vick because African-Americans have been historically suspected of criminality? Did the league seek to protect Roethlisberger because it prefers white quarterbacks? It could be argued that Roethlisberger, as a member of the dominant racial group of whites in America, was treated with far more consideration by the NFL and other powerful entities. While there are a host of other disparities in the way Vick was treated versus Roethlisberger, a broader discussion to include *labeling theory* as an explanation will be covered in Chapter V. Whereas the preceding discussion addressed the differential social reaction to Vick versus Roethlisberger, in the mistreatments of dogs when compared to women, the following section discusses different forms of animal cruelty that are punished less severely. Particular attention is accorded to the crime of bestiality.

Animal Cruelty Laws in America: Street Fighters vs. Bestial Acts

As noted in Chapter I, while Vick was labeled the face of animal cruelty by the league's alliance of superstructures, other crimes associated with brutality against animals, such as neglect, hoarding, abuse, and bestiality (human beings having carnal relations with animals) are punished far less. These disparities in the enforcement of laws against animal cruelty warrant reflection given the apparent racial disparities in arrest incidents. Arrest data show that while blacks are more likely to be arrested for dog fighting, whites are more likely to be arrested for other crimes of animal cruelty like the aforementioned, most notably bestiality (www.pet-abuse.com). While the American public received no shortage of news on dog fighting as a social problem following the Vick scandal, hardly any mainstream media coverage is accorded to the crime of bestiality. This particular form of animal cruelty is especially notable. In 2007, while the Vick scandal was still a big-ticket news story, Troy Whitson, who is white, of Cinebar, Washington, was arrested for having sex with his two dogs (*Mercury News*, 2009).

Whitson's deviant actions did not result in an uproar of sensational mainstream press coverage as Vick's did. Neither the lay public nor animal rights advocates responded with the outrage accorded to Vick, despite such outrageous behavior by Whitson. In court, Whitson was allowed to enter a plea that was short of admitting guilt, but was a concession that he would be found guilty had he contested the charges. Still, he was sentenced to a mere thirty-day prison sentence for sexually abusing his dogs. In but another indicator of differential treatment by the law, the judge ruled that Whitson could not own a dog for two years. By contrast, Vick was sentenced to two years in prison, despite his confession of guilt, and was told he could not own a dog for three years while on parole. But it was the under-reaction from the media and the law enforcement community to Whitson's abuse that necessitated greater attention to the deviant subculture of bestiality. Such juxtaposition is noteworthy since arrest data show deviant blacks are more often involved in dog fighting as street fighters, while deviant whites are more often involved in other acts of animal cruelty, including bestiality. By no means is the crime of bestiality unique to one racial group. In 2009, Rodell Vereen, an African-American man from South

Carolina, was arrested and sentenced to prison for three years for repeatedly having sex with a woman's horse. But by and large, arrest data show that most of the individuals arrested for these crimes are deviant whites.

The argument from Capitol Hill when it increased the sentencing for dog fighting was that such people engage in other collateral crimes, i.e., robberies, assaults, gang violence, domestic violence, etc. Conversely, the federal government has no laws that prohibit bestiality, despite its seriousness and the propensity for collateral crimes committed by offenders. In fact, the sexually polymorphous theory observes that individuals who engage in bestiality are more likely to commit other acts of interpersonal violence toward human beings, i.e., rape, serial homicidal rape, child rape, etc. (*Humane Society, Bestiality Fact Sheet*, n.d.). Such acts of aggression toward animals and humans "become mutually inclusive" (Henderson, Hensley, & Tallichet, 2011; Hensley, Tallichet, & Dutkiewicz, 2010; Hensley, Tallichet, & Singer, 2006). Is race somehow a factor in the way state legislatures and the federal government uniformly punish dog fighting as felonious, while crimes like bestiality are not? The question is especially apropos when you consider that in the wake of Michael Vick's downfall, a significant number of arrests involving black males as dog fighters followed. On the other hand, since the Vick scandal, there has been a steady stream of deviant whites being arrested for engaging in bestiality. While the discussion over dog fighting evoked a strong social response that resulted in upwards of forty new laws to punish offenders, there has been very little public outcry over the widespread incidents of bestiality in America. This differential concern expressed by the media, and unequal distribution of animal cruelty laws in America, raises the question of whether the public's vitriolic reaction to Vick was more about race than the abuse of dogs. That state and federal laws punish dog fighting more severely than they do bestiality poses additional questions of selective enforcement by race. Before probing the question of selective enforcement over animal cruelty laws, this discussion will highlight the spate of bestiality arrests that have occurred in the last six years. This review will underscore the extent to which bestiality as a social problem is growing, while broadening the view that the unequal distribution of the law over animal cruelty reeks of unequal protection of the law by race.

Bestiality as a Growing Social Problem in America

In 2005, authorities were shocked to learn that a farm in Enumclaw, Washington, was a place where bestiality involving men having carnal relations with horses was commonplace. Evidence of this deviant sexual conduct came to the attention of authorities in the worst way. One of the culprits engaged in this deviant sexual behavior died of acute peritonitis—a perforated colon—after he allowed a horse to penetrate him (Sullivan, 2005). It was after this embarrassing episode that the Washington state legislature passed legislation making bestiality a felonious crime. Also in 2005, a blind man in Tallahassee, Florida, was found to be having sexual relations with his guide dog. Although he was initially charged with a felony count of animal cruelty, eventually these charges were reduced to "breaching the peace." In 2006, Walton County officials arrested a man who had sex with four goats, resulting in the death of one of them. Despite engaging in forced sexual intercourse with the animals, which constituted animal cruelty, the culprit was only charged with stealing the goats. In the state of Arizona, the legislature outlawed bestiality after a deputy fire chief was charged with having sex with his neighbor's lamb. In Gresham, Oregon, Brandon Vangthrongthrip admitted to police that he assaulted his pit bull "Rocky" as many as 400 times over five years, including 200 incidents of sexually assaulting the animal. To further underscore the differential treatment by the media and law enforcement of blacks and whites over concerns about animal cruelty, in July 2009, when Vick was attempting to gain reinstatement in the NFL, Laszio Arsenio Hovarth, who is white, admitted to seriously injuring his dog after having sex with the animal.

According to a published report, Hovarth duct taped the dogs legs closed and pressed a cloth against its lower half, in what may have been a futile attempt to treat the suffering animal (Hijek, 2009). Despite the dog's serious injuries, Hovarth refused to pay for the care of the animal, which was eventually euthanized. By contrast, Vick admitted to harming his dogs through fighting, and the court mandated that he pay $1 million in restitution for their care. Conversely, despite Hovarth's very bizarre behavior, the judge acquiesced to his request to be released from home confinement so he could enroll in culinary arts school. But Vick could not simply reenter society. Despite a contrite public apology and animal sensitivity training and his agreement to become an advocate for animal rights organizations, he was sentenced to prison. In 2010, a former insurance executive was served an arrest warrant when a veterinarian's office informed police that he admitted to having sex with his dog, a Great Dane named "Christie Brinkley." The veterinarian who examined the dog concluded that because she had been spayed, no other dog could have penetrated the animal, which showed evidence of forced sexual activity (Hijek, 2010). In yet another incident in the state of Florida, in 2011 a man's grandson found him in bed, nude, on top of the family's three-year-old female bulldog. The man's family contacted police, who promptly arrested him. He freely admitted to the police that he attempted to have sex with the dog, but would not do it again.[42] These shocking case studies are important to relate for several reasons. These incidents reflect deviant acts of aggravated animal abuse. Furthermore, such serious acts of animal cruelty should lead to changes in state and federal laws to punish this behavior uniformly as felonious, as with dog fighting. Even more alarming, many of the individuals who engage in this behavior believe that the animals can give consent for such sexual intercourse. By contrast, researchers have found that bestiality is best understood as "interspecies sexual assault." It is akin to the victimization of humans. Moreover, since animals cannot consent to sexual intercourse with humans, such conduct is not only unnatural and coercive but also potentially fatal (Hensely,

---

42 Retrieved from http://www.huffingtonpost.com/2011/06/28/eugene-hickman-florida-gr_n_885901.html.

Singer, & Tallichet, 2006). Thus, the failure of all fifty states and the federal government to pass laws making bestiality a felony means lawmakers are giving tacit consent for such behavior by default. To further underscore the need for change in laws against such aberrant behavior, researchers have found that for individuals who engage in bestiality it becomes mutually inclusive with aggressive behavior. Consequently, individuals who engage in bestiality are more likely to engage in interpersonal violence that is often sexual in nature. Despite the far-reaching incidents of bestiality and other crimes of animal abuse, animal rights organizations such as the Humane Society of the United States of America and PETA have been comparatively quiet. When considering the differential attention by the media and disparate treatment by the law enforcement community, the race of the respective defendants who are engaged in these deviant behaviors seems to be a factor.

The lack of uniformity in the laws against animal cruelty contributes to such racial disparities and warrants greater attention. Only twenty-nine states have laws that prohibit bestiality, and in only fifteen of those states is it a felony. Even more disconcerting, while there are no federal laws to prohibit bestiality, the one provision that prohibited such conduct by military personnel was repealed by the U.S. Senate in 2011.[43] All of which is stunning when you consider that individuals who engage in bestiality are more apt to commit other collateral crimes, including sexual assault on women and children. As noted, such multiple instances of sexually deviant behavior and other acts of interpersonal violence are explicable by the sexually polymorphous theory (Henderson, Hensley, & Tallichet, 2011; Hensley, Tallichet, & Dutkiewicz, 2010; Hensley, Tallichet, & Singer, 2006). This perspective addresses how one form of sexually deviant behavior, i.e., having forcible sex with animals, morphs into other acts of criminally sexual deviance such as assaults, serial

---

43 On November 15, 2011, the Senate Armed Services Committee voted unanimously to approve S.1867, the National Defense Authorization Act, which included a measure to repeal Article 125. This provision had forbidden military personnel from engaging in sodomy, whether homosexual or heterosexual, as well as bestiality. The full Senate voted 93-7 to approve the bill.

rape, and murder (*Humane Society, Bestiality Fact Sheet*, n.d.). Because the problem of bestiality in America is so widespread and is linked to sex crimes against women and children, more attention on this subject will follow in Chapter IV.

Other considerations that made race a factor in the differential treatment accorded to Vick were the responses of corporate sponsors who dropped him following the dog fighting scandal, but who showed unusual restraint by not dropping whites in the NFL who were embroiled in scandals.

Corporate Sponsors Drop Vick

The raucous reaction to revelations in the media of Vick's indictment over dog fighting caused sponsors such as Nike, Reebok, Rawlings, and Air Tran, among others, to cancel the all-star quarterback as an endorser of their products. Reebok, which had previously contracted with the league to design team uniforms, opted to stop selling Vick jerseys in the wake of the federal charges. Nike also dropped Vick after initially taking a wait-and-see approach.[44] Conversely, Nike did not drop Roethlisberger despite two serious allegations of rape by two different women in two different states. Incidentally, despite these alleged incidents, Reebok never stopped selling Roethlisberger's jersey as they did with Vick. In the case of Bill Belichick and his Spygate scandal, major corporate sponsors of his Patriots team such as Visa, Pepsi, and even the CBS network kept their deals with the organization. Despite that, Belichick's cheating besmirched his reputation, that of his team, and the NFL. Although Belichick and the Patriots team were fined up to $750,000 and lost a first-round pick, what followed was business as usual for him, the team, the media, the corporate sponsors, and the NFL. Had Belichick been black, would the aforementioned parties have been so lenient and forgiving?

On the other hand, not all calls for Vick's endorsers to drop him were predicated on race. African-Americans such as social activist Reverend Al Sharpton and hip-hop mogul Russell Sim-

---

44 http://msn.foxsports.com/nfl/story/7038442, Mark Kriegel, p.1.

mons joined PETA in calling for corporate sponsors to cancel Vick (Watkins, 2007). But race seemed to be an indirect factor in their outcry. Sharpton and Simmons were under significant media pressure to call for Vick's sponsors to cancel him, since they had done the same for controversial radio personality Don Imus. The difference, of course, is that while Imus lost his radio show on CBS for his remarks in 2009 that were widely perceived as racially offensive against the Rutgers women's basketball team, he landed on his feet with his show being broadcast on Fox. On the other hand, Vick's loss of sponsorships cost him between $50 million and $60 million in endorsement revenue, an insurmountable financial blow that eventually drove him to bankruptcy.

In filing for bankruptcy, Vick listed [45]$16 million in wealth and assets in the face of $20.4 million in liabilities. Had the quarterback been able to sustain roughly ten percent of his endorsement income, or $5 million to $6 million in endorsements, he would have probably averted bankruptcy. Even worse, the Atlanta Falcons organization, prodded by the NFL's front office, filed a grievance against Vick seeking to recoup over $22 million in bonuses paid to the quarterback.[46] But because the income was earned from roster bonuses, U.S. District Judge David Doty eventually ruled against the Falcons.[47] On the other hand, as a part of his bankruptcy, Vick agreed to pay the Falcons back salary lost during his prison stint in 2007 and 2008 (Clayton, 2009). Vick's decision to plead guilty reflected how weakened he had become not just socially but financially. Although powerful entities played roles in undermining Vick, no other dominant ally of the NFL had a more deleterious effect on his fate than the mainstream media.

While the Vick scandal was expected to garner some media attention, what the public saw was an example of how dangerous a force the media can be in this country, particularly toward

---

45 http://sports.espn.go/nfl/news/story/?id=3813868.
46 http://usatoday.printhis.clickability.com/pt/cpt/?action, p1.
47 http://usatoday.com/sports.football/nfl/falcons/2008/-02-04-vick-bonuses_N.htm, p.1.

blacks. Beyond the story of harm and mistreatment of the dogs, the media's coverage made Vick, in the eyes of most Americans, the most despicable and despised person in the nation. The mass media, including NFL.com, created a frenzied public furor that seemed to pique the interest of the federal government, which in turn superseded the state of Virginia's probe with its own investigation, indictment, conviction, and sentencing of Vick to federal prison. Additionally, as noted in Chapter I, blacks were particularly concerned that the media had instigated a rush to judgment that jeopardized the quarterback's right to due process. Given the firestorm of news coverage accorded by the press, there was a feeling that since Vick was found guilty in the court of public opinion, he had no chance for fairness in the court of law. Concomitantly, the mainstream media's myopic coverage of the Vick scandal resulted in a revival of racism in American sports, which had heretofore lain largely dormant. While some would rather believe that race had nothing to do with the overall reaction to Vick's dog fighting misdeeds, the underreported threats of lynching suggest otherwise.

Racism in the Media Coverage of Vick

In discussing the one-sided media onslaught, author Dave Zirin (2007) rather aptly queried, "Does this (media) discourse (on the Michael Vick case) make us smarter, or just more enraged?" This section will show that the anger and utter disdain that the public expressed toward Vick was spearheaded by the media and appeared to be beyond the dogs. Another important sequence in the Vick chronicle that went unattended to was the manner in which the NFL and media infringed upon the First Amendment rights of blacks, especially professional athletes who offered support for the quarterback.

As the Michael Vick scandal took hold of the public's attention, the quarterback faced some of the most malicious media coverage ever witnessed in America. While the majority of the American public was clearly against Vick for his mistreatment of dogs, the feeling that race was also a factor was widespread, especially among blacks. The Vick dog fighting scandal seemed to be the perfect storm for the NFL and the sports-reporting media to rail against the notion postulated by Rush Limbaugh in 2003, that they were desirous to see a black quarterback succeed out of social concern. Consequently, it appears that the mainstream media sought to use the Vick dog fighting scandal as an example of how very little social concern was harbored for blacks as quarterbacks in the NFL, and the league obliged for good measure. Limbaugh, perhaps still simmering over losing his coveted seat on ESPN's premier pregame show, *NFL Sunday Countdown,* over his remarks in 2003, could not resist taking a shot at Vick in 2009, when he recorded a spot for the Humane Society.

In the public service announcement recorded one month before Vick was released from prison, Rush Limbaugh referred to street fighters who participate in dog fighting as "people like Michael Vick" (Humane Society audio, 2009). Limbaugh's comments had the added effect of perpetuating the idea that black males like Michael Vick were the faces of animal cruelty. Furthermore, the inflammatory media stories that portrayed Vick as an animal abuser made him the most hated man in sports; an infamous distinction he carried in 2008, 2009 (Rogers, 2010), and 2010. Yet there was a strong feeling, particularly among African-Americans, that the media coverage of Vick was excessive, incendiary, overbearing, zealous, dangerous, and reeked of classical race-baiting.

When the Vick scandal broke, R.L. White, president of the Atlanta chapter of the NAACP, observed, "Michael Vick has received more negative press than if he had killed a human being."[48] Rather than being innocent until proven guilty, the mainstream media ensured Vick was guilty until proven innocent. The unilateral undoing of Vick with negatively worded press stories made it essentially impossible to find a potential jury anywhere in America where the quarterback could receive a fair trial, had he fought the charges. How could Vick have

---

48 http://www.usa.today.com/sports/football/nfl/falcons/2007-08-22-vick-wednesday_N. htm.

found a jury of his peers who had not been exposed to the dog fighting scandal in which the media seemed to convict him in the court of public opinion? Realizing the quarterback was intent on pleading guilty, apparently to cut his losses, media types such as Michael Ventre (2007) of MSNBC called for him to be permanently banished from the game.[49] The NFL, which initially took a wait-and-see approach, eventually barred Vick indefinitely from attending any team activities, including training camp in July 2007.

By the time the Atlanta Falcons training camp began, the public's venomous vengeance against the quarterback was in high volume and especially observable at the team's practice site in Flowery Branch, Georgia. One person flew a prop plane over the Falcons practice with a sign that suggested the team change its name to "Dog Killers."[50] Another fan, who, interestingly enough, admitted she was not a dog advocate, was creative enough to use the letters of the quarterback's last name, V-I-C-K, as an acronym for "Vicious! Inhumane! Cruel! Kills animals!"[51] But were the responses from such fans a strong reaction to the animal abuse or an overreaction? After all, there have been other professional athletes in the NFL and NBA who have been involved in dog fighting, yet there was not such a strong public reaction. It could also be argued that the media and fans overreacted to Vick's dog fighting misdeeds when compared to other NFL players who committed serious criminal offenses. As noted in Chapter I, other league players have been arrested for possession of drugs, illegal possession of firearms, sexual assault, domestic violence, driving while intoxicated, and even vehicular manslaughter. Yet the media scrutiny of such events was far less intense.

Then again, it could be argued that as a star quarterback in the NFL, Vick's high profile status necessitated such outstanding media coverage. But if his status as a high profile quarterback was a factor, why is it that the media reacted as strongly to the Vick scandal with wall-to-wall coverage that provoked a continuum of

---

49 www.thenation.com/doc/20070730/southpaw.
50 www.usatoday.com/sports/football/nfl/falcons/2007-07-26-camp-scene_N.htm.
51 www.usatoday.com/sports/football/nfl/falcons/2007-07-26-camp-scene_N.htm.

public protests, while Ben Roethlisberger's second rape allegation in a year in 2010 was here today, gone tomorrow? Incidentally, in 2007, before any rape allegations against Roethlisberger ever surfaced, [52]Rick Morrissey, a columnist of the *Chicago Tribune*, was intuitive enough to write in reference to the Vick scandal, "Abuse your dog, and people howl. Smack around your girlfriend or face charges of sexually assaulting a woman and people shake their heads and roll their eyes." Although Roethlisberger was suspended for four games by the NFL commissioner in 2010, there were no ongoing protests outside the team's practice facilities and none of the extraordinary media scrutiny that Vick was subjected to. In January 2011, ESPN provided more evidence of racial disparities in the media's coverage of the respective scandals involving Vick and Roethlisberger.

The network broadcast a special town hall meeting honoring the national holiday commemorating the birthday of Reverend Dr. Martin Luther King, Jr. This event, which was hosted in the New Ebenezer Baptist Church of Atlanta, Georgia, where Dr. King was once pastor, discussed inequities that remain in sports, including media coverage.[53] (It was previously known as Ebenezer Baptist Church when Reverend Martin Luther King, Jr. was pastor.) During the show, ESPN reported on data that showed the media was "least kind" in covering Michael Vick's scandal. Conversely, Ben Roethlisberger was treated "most kind" by the media while enmeshed in scandal. These findings are compelling when you consider that Roethlisberger played the entire 2010 and 2011 seasons in the face of a civil lawsuit in the Nevada case over rape allegations. To further underscore how differently the media covered both scandals, in 2007, ESPN first broke the story of an informant who said Vick was a "heavyweight" in dog fighting. The story seemed to ignite greater interest by federal investigators, who joined the probe after the feature was broadcast on *Outside the Lines*. Yet in 2009, when the first allegations of an alleged

---

52 Editorial from Dave Zirin. Received by Kenneth N. Robinson from stewarr@ buffalostate.edu, August 24, 2007, who subscribes to author Dave Zirin's edgeofsports@gmail.com.
53 ESPN Broadcast of a Town Hall Meeting, at New Ebenezer Baptist Church, Atlanta, GA. January 15, 2011.

rape involving Roethlisberger in Las Vegas surfaced, ESPN initially refused to report the story, citing its policy against reporting on allegations of rape that may have been untrue (Sandomir, 2007). For Vick, no matter how he attempted to recede from the public's eye, he was under constant watch as the story of his dog fighting deeds never let up. The public's anger was so great that Vick not only found his professional football career in jeopardy, but his life as well. The threats against his life, which included calls for him to be lynched, made it clear the strong public reaction had less to do with the dogs and more to do with his race.

"Hang (Him) From a Tree"

Perhaps the most confounding facet of the Vick story was the racist and contradictory way in which some advocates for dog safety were also advocating for violence against Vick, including death by lynching. Why would Vick's involvement in harming dogs be a cause for such a racist reaction from whites? Perhaps the popularity of the dog as "man's best friend" and more specifically, the white man's best friend helps to explain it (Colston, 2007). [54] Historically, the dog was seen as a symbol of a white man's ability to exhibit mastery and dominance over others, including blacks. During slavery, bloodhound dogs were used to hunt down black slaves who escaped the plantation and were wanted as fugitives. Adolph Hitler, who advocated for a pure Aryan white race, kept a trusted German shepherd named "Blondie" by his side. Dogs had also been used by European colonialists to suppress and intimidate blacks throughout Africa in general and South Africa in particular during Apartheid. In America, dogs had been used to attack blacks, particularly in the South during the civil rights movement, as an extension of the brutal racism wrought by Jim Crow segregation. Of course, such vicious tactics of using dogs to attack blacks in America was certainly not lost on the sons and daughters of the South who are black, including Vick. Is it illogical then that Vick and other blacks who ventured into dog fighting

---

54 http://www.usatoday.com/sports/football/nfl/falcons/2007-07-06-camp-scene_N.htm, Chris Colston.

may have reasoned that having dogs attack one another cannot be so bad since dogs had been used by the police to attack blacks? Still, Vick's actions toward the dogs seemed to evoke the kind of anger from whites that was akin to false allegations of black men harming white women, the mere suggestion of which could result in black males being lynched.

Zirin (2007) reported that America Online's Fanhouse message board was reveling with racist fans ranting for Vick to "hang from a tree" (p.2).[55] That the mainstream media's negative coverage of Vick contributed to this dangerous climate was one factor. Yet it is quite another to observe that calls for him to be lynched were ignored by the same mainstream media that fueled the animus. Somehow, while covering Vick, the media chose to ignore what history has taught about the role of the press in inciting violence against blacks throughout the twentieth century. In the past, the slightest provocation by a news story was enough to invoke whites to commit tumultuous bloodshed against blacks. The Vick dog abuse issue was more than enough for such a potentiality. The anger expressed by whites could have made blacks in general and Vick in particular an easy target for violence and murder. As late as 2010, Tucker Carlson of Fox News stated on air that for Vick's mistreatment of the dogs in 2007, he should have been executed (Chase, 2011). Despite the lessons of history, the connection between incendiary media hyperbole and the potential for widespread violence against blacks was never brought up during discussions of the Vick scandal, except for the likes of author Dave Zirin (2007) and ESPN's Wright Thompson (2007), both of whom are, incidentally, white, and who had the courage to discuss racism and lynching in their discussions of Vick.

Vick-tim of Racism

In discussing the Vick dog fighting case and subsequent media coverage, [56]Zirin made note of a "mob-mentality run-

---

55 www.thenation.com/doc/20070730/southpaw, p.2, Zirin, Dave.
56 Editorial by Dave Zirin sent to R. Stewart, Ph.D., who forwarded it to Kenneth N. Robinson on August 24, 2007. p. 2. Via edgeofsports@gmail.com on August 23, 2007.

amok" in addition to what he referred to as the "liberal" use of the "N" word, which accompanied calls for the quarterback to be lynched (p.1). On the other hand, in a feature titled [57]"History of Mistrust," Thompson (2007) discussed the Vick case within the larger context of racial strife in Atlanta historically, including accounts of white mob violence against blacks. The feature included discussions with civil rights heroine Juanita Abernathy, widow of civil rights icon Reverend Ralph Abernathy, and her son Kwame Abernathy. In addition, the story featured a living legend of the civil rights movement, the Reverend Joseph Lowery, who also discussed his concerns about the Michael Vick case. Thompson's story on the mistrust of the Atlanta community over Vick's legal quandary linked past incidents of blacks being lynched by whites in Atlanta, including an incident spurred by media reporting.

To make his point, Thompson cited an early twentieth century event in which a bourgeoning black middle class community was attacked mercilessly following newspaper reports of white women being assaulted by black men. While such reports were often unsubstantiated and even false, the mere suggestion was enough to precipitate white mobs forming, followed by violence against blacks that often led to death. The media in America seemed to not care that their provocative one-dimensional coverage of the Vick scandal created a greater divide between blacks and whites. To gather a better sense of the media's role in expanding the gulf between what white people were seeing in the Vick case versus blacks, a review of two events on July 26, 2007 is warranted. In one community, July 26 marked the first day of training camp for the Atlanta Falcons, where whites were calling for Vick's demise in full force. On the other hand, July 26 was for a number of African-Americans in Atlanta a day to remember the unsolved lynching of blacks at the hands of whites (Thompson, 2007, p.6).

---

57 http://sports.espn.go.com/espn/eticket/story?page=vicksatlanta&lpos=spotlight&l
id=tab2pos1, Wright Thompson.

July 26: The First Day of Training Camp, in Black and White

On July 26, the Atlanta Falcons held their first day of training camp in Flowery Branch, Georgia, which Michael Vick was barred from attending. Despite Vick's conspicuous absence, the camp was littered with the media, angry fans, and protesters, most of whom were white and who were calling for the quarterback's ouster and even death. On the other hand, for African-Americans and sympathetic whites, July 26 was a day to pay special homage to the innocent victims of an unprovoked, unsolved lynching that occurred sixty years prior (Thompson, 2007, p. 6). The commemoration of this tragedy included a complete reenactment of what occurred in the town of Monroe, Georgia, in 1946. These horrific crimes of lynching included the barbaric details of a pregnant black woman having her unborn child cut from her stomach. Such accounts represent examples of how inhumane human beings can be toward other human beings, much less dogs. Some may feel such a vicious account is irrelevant since it occurred sixty-one years prior to Vick's scandal. But for blacks, the injustice still breathes, since many of the perpetrators in the Monroe murders are believed to be still alive and have never been brought to justice. These sorts of accounts are rampant throughout American history and help explain why so many blacks in general and athletes in particular were downplaying the Vick case as a matter of *just dogs*.

Such sentiments seemed especially noteworthy given the horrendous history of blacks being murdered by whites without cause or conviction of the culprits. To this day, no person has been convicted in the awful death of Emmet Till, the fourteen-year-old boy from Chicago, Illinois, who was murdered in Money, Mississippi, in 1955. Yet many of these perpetrators are still alive, and others have given deathbed confessions of their involvement in the treacherous murder. If the scales of justice were balanced, whites who were involved in the unsolved murder of Till would not be allowed to confess on their death-beds; instead, they would be confessing in a court of law. If the federal government can build a case that made Michael Vick confess in court to killing dogs, why can they not do the same with whites who killed Till? That the perpetrators who have murdered and lynched blacks throughout history, including the killings in Monroe, Georgia, have never been brought to justice is an aggravating reminder of racism's legacy in America's criminal justice system. Additionally, the greater social harm in the failure to exact justice in the aforementioned cases means that others might be influenced to act similarly, believing, as whites often have throughout history, that black life is devalued in American society generally, and particularly in the courts. The murder of seventeen-year-old Trayvon Martin in February 2012, by George Zimmerman in Sanford, Florida, is certainly an example of that concern. The initial response by the police was to not arrest Zimmerman. But nearly a month after the Martin killing, a groundswell of public outcry prompted the state attorney general to appoint a special prosecutor who brought second-degree murder charges against the suspect. To further underscore the concern over black life being devalued in the criminal justice system, Zimmerman was acquitted of second degree murder in July of 2013. At the height of public outrage over the Martin shooting, in April 2012, two white males in Tulsa, Oklahoma, were arrested for shooting five black victims, three of whom died. Although an arrest does not equate to a conviction, it seems fairly obvious that the heightened public reaction to these respective incidents led to the arrest of these suspects. On the other hand, Vick being convicted and sentenced to prison for fighting and killing dogs in the face of many whites never being brought to justice for killing blacks sends an unfortunate social message that the lives of dogs apparently have more value in our society than the lives of blacks.

Additionally, such stark realities help to explain why civil rights leaders like Juanita Abernathy, Reverend Joseph Lowery, and organizations like the NAACP were concerned about the way Vick was being treated by the media and the law. Historically, sensational media coverage of criminal cases involving blacks contributed to their being treated unfairly by the courts.

Furthermore, the discussion about the unsolved murders of blacks who were lynched is particularly germane in this discussion of Vick given that his life was threatened with lynching.

The threats against Michael Vick's life were real enough that upon his release from prison in 2009, federal corrections officials withheld details of his departure from the public. While extraordinary details of the Vick case did not result in any reported random acts of violence against him or other blacks, the media seemed to kill any sentiments of support expressed for the quarterback, particularly by black athletes. Although the press is supposed to be a bastion of First Amendment rights in this country, the mainstream media seemed to curtail the freedom of speech of blacks who voiced support for Vick in 2007, particularly those who attempted to offer a more sobering perspective in contrast to the media-induced stupor.

No First Amendment Rights for the Second Class Citizen

The same media that vilified Vick also criticized any view contrary to "get Vick." For example, professional athletes such as Clinton Portis and Chris Samuels, then of the Washington Redskins, and Joey Porter, then of the Miami Dolphins, were widely criticized in the media for minimizing the Vick matter as simply involving dogs. The same happened to then-New York Knicks guard Stephon Marbury, who sought to downplay Vick's involvement in dog fighting (Fermino, 2007). Marbury made reference to dog fighting being a sport and was chastised by the media, which reacted incredulously. Oddly enough, Matt Buehrle of the Chicago White Sox, who is white, stated in 2010 that his father and grandfather hunted animals for game. But he mistakenly noted that dog fighting had never been a sport. Buehrle, who claimed that he and his wife were animal lovers, freely admitted that they wanted Vick to get hurt during his redemptive 2010 season (Borelli, 2011).[58]

---

58 Borelli, Stephen. (2011). 'Something Bad Needs to Happen' to Michael Vick.' USA Today, Sports, February 10, 2011.

While Marbury was right about dog fighting being considered a sport, Buehrle could not have been more wrong.

To further validate the widely accepted normalcy of dog fighting as a sports spectacle in America, local newspapers would often publish the results of dog fighting matches. While Buehrle was apparently unaware of this, both PETA and the Humane Society of the United States of America were, yet neither sought to clarify the truth. That the Humane Society would not properly inform the public that dog fighting was once thought of as a sport was especially galling since they agreed to work with Vick to educate the public. For his part, Portis made a pivotal point in 2007 about the prevalence of dog fighting as a blood sport throughout the South. He stated that he was from Laurel, Mississippi, where you can see a good dog fight in any backyard. Yet he too was ripped by the media, including NFL Commissioner Roger Goodell. As a result, Portis retreated from his support of Vick. Even comedian turned talk show host Whoopi Goldberg indicated that Vick's involvement with dog fighting was a part of southern culture and she too was criticized (Kalof and Taylor, 2007, p. 320).

In each case, as these various African-Americans attempted to broaden the discussion, they were shouted down by the mainstream media, most of whom were white and who seemed to suppress people's right to free speech. All of which raises questions of racial indifference in the way the media treated blacks and whites during the Vick discourse, especially athletes. For example, when then-Philadelphia Eagles quarterback Donovan McNabb made innocuous comments wishing Vick well in 2007, he came under fire by the press that demanded an explanation. McNabb sought to allay the strong media queries by simply noting that he had hosted Vick on a recruitment trip while at Syracuse University and wished him well. Conversely, not one media journalist asked Peyton Manning, a star quarterback of the Indianapolis Colts, who is white, to explain his expressions of support for Vick on NBC during a nationally televised NFL broadcast the same year. Incidentally, McNabb's well wishes were quite sincere, as he helped Vick land on his feet upon his release from prison when he persuaded his Philadelphia Eagles team to sign the embattled quarterback in 2009. On the other hand, it was remarkable to observe the inability of many NFL players who are black to offer sensible rebuttals to the media questioning them about their comments in support of Vick.

Portis could have countered the reaction from the media and NFL Commissioner Roger Goodell, who said he was "embarrassed" for the running back because of his remarks. He should have questioned whether the NFL commissioner was in any way *embarrassed* for the Washington Redskins team, whose nickname is the most racially offensive term in the lexicon of Native Americans. "Redskins" speaks to the heinous practice of Native Americans being skinned alive and their skins in turn sold at eighty cents for men, sixty cents for women, and twenty cents for children (Shropshire, 1996). While this matter should certainly be a workplace diversity issue in the NFL, the media has not asked the league to explain this blatant form of racism. Despite that, the NFL and the Redskins franchise that represents the nation's capital have been fighting the Native American community in court to keep the racist nickname.[59] Curiously, the NFL, the media, corporate sponsors, and Congress ripped Vick for his harm to dogs. But they all celebrate a league team whose nickname makes a mockery of the genocide of Native Americans. All of which bespeaks the level of hypocrisy in this country and the NFL. Whether the general public agreed or disagreed with comments from the likes of Portis, Samuels, Marbury, Porter, and Goldberg, these individuals had the First Amendment right to comment on the Vick case. While the media of course has the same First Amendment protections, an expression of those rights should never equate to suppressing the free speech of others. That said, the players' comments that Vick's conduct involved *just dogs* does not mitigate the wrong done or the seriousness of laws being broken over dog fighting.

But without a doubt, the most flagrant example of freedom of speech rights being abridged in an attempt to curtail support

---

59 http://www.usatoday.com/sports/football/nfl/redskins/2006-08-11-redskins-indians_x.htm.

for Michael Vick involved the NFL itself and one its employees, former All-Pro turned analyst Deion Sanders.

Not This Time, Primetime

Deion Sanders, who was inducted into the football Hall of Fame in 2011, is largely regarded as one of the greatest NFL players in the history of the game. He was known for his world-class speed, high-stepping antics and end zone dances, in addition to being the premier shut-down cornerback during his career. Upon retiring, Sanders entered broadcasting, first with CBS. Then, after returning for a partial season with the Baltimore Ravens, he re-retired from football and eventually shuffled to the *NFL Network,* which is owned by the NFL. During the Vick narrative in 2007, Sanders, who prides himself as a mentor to many young NFL players, wrote an impassioned column about the Vick case for the *News-Press*, his hometown newspaper in Fort Meyers, Florida. Like a small number of journalists, Sanders sought to broaden the perspective of why Vick was involved in dog fighting. He wrote, "You can still choose to condemn him, but I'm trying to take you inside his mind so you can understand where he is coming from" (Neus, 2007, p. 1).[60] By contrast, John Kincade of ESPN Radio condemned Sanders' column on Vick in a manner consistent with the largely white male-dominated media, which quelled any expressions of support for Vick, especially from blacks. According to Elizabeth Neus of *USA Today*, Kincade's critical comments of Sanders's article instigated "a wave of criticism from across the country, as well as from Sanders's hometown of Fort Meyers" (p.1). When Sanders sought to submit a rebuttal to the strong public response, the NFL stepped in and stopped the column from being published. Thomas George, the NFL Network's managing editor, wrote to Ed Reed, sports editor of the Fort Meyers *News-Press*, with the following: "This column and subsequent variations of it (are) not approved by the NFL Network. It cannot be

---

60 http://usatoday.printthis.clickability.com/cpt?action=cpt&title=NFL+Network+in
tercept.

run…" (p.1). It could be argued that Sanders's First Amendment rights were clearly violated by the NFL, except that he signed a contract giving the league control over his name and image when it came to league matters. Conversely, an argument could be made that the NFL's actions were not only wrong but in fact infringed upon Sanders's First Amendment rights.

Sanders's article actually discussed Vick's dog fighting deeds, which was a legal matter rather than a league matter. After all, Vick's dog fighting actions were never carried out on any NFL property. In fact, he freely admitted that he would fly to Virginia on his days off to engage in dog fighting. Therefore, the league cannot accurately assert that Vick conducted these affairs on NFL time. So why did the league and its NFL Network prevent Sanders's subsequent article in the *News-Press* from being printed? It seems rather apparent that the NFL's intent was to not only control the message associated with Vick, but it preferred to placate an angry public that was against him. Had Sanders written an article that was critical of Vick as the larger white-male dominated mainstream media had done, would he have been criticized by John Kincade of ESPN? Would the NFL had interceded and stopped Sanders's second column from being printed had he followed the trend of vilifying Vick? While not a gambling man, I would bet a dollar to a doughnut that Kincade and the NFL/NFL Network would have offered no such opposition had Sanders chided Vick. In fact, not only was the NFL unopposed to any negative views of Vick, but the league contributed to the rising tide of opposition against him.

In but another example of the NFL's unique ability to be both shameful and shameless simultaneously, during the time Sanders was being told not to write any columns about Vick, NFL.com and NFL Network, the two major media arms of the league, published a picture online of a woman holding a sign that read "Kick Vick." [61] The caption, which was viewable for several days, was published on July 23, 2007, less than one week after the quarterback was indicted. So while the NFL Network prevented Deion Sanders from writing in support of Vick on

---

61 http://www.nfl.com/nflnetwork/story/1026650.

July 30, one week earlier it exhorted millions of their fans on NFL.com to "Kick..." the fallen quarterback. For the league and its conduct-policy-cop-of-a-commissioner, Roger Goodell, to enjoin the public to carry out violence against the beleaguered Vick was reckless, irresponsible, and reprehensible. How is it that the NFL and its commissioner can attempt to hold its players to such a high standard of conduct, yet the league would use its media muscle to incite the public to commit violence against Vick? Moreover, that the NFL threw fuel on the fire that further infuriated a raging public that was threatening to lynch Vick is even more maddening.

Historically for blacks, being kicked and beaten were mere precursors to being lynched. Still, the inherent contradiction of the NFL telling Sanders he could not write in support of Vick while the league and its media arms directed an already angry public to attack him is but another example of the NFL as the "Not Fair League." Yet reporters like [62]Jemele Hill of ESPN, herself an African-American, said she found it difficult to defend what was occurring to Vick by the "white media" because there was no "moral high ground" for something so low as what he did to the dogs (Zirin, 2007, p.2). Perhaps Ms. Hill could have better inoculated herself from the toxic hate being fostered by the "white media" she identified had she sought a more cerebral and sensible perspective, like Dave Zirin or that of her colleague at ESPN, Wright Thompson, both of whom, incidentally, are white.

It was Thompson's historical connection that tied the discussion of Vick to a *History of Mistrust* in Atlanta in relation to the civil rights movement that invoked historical figures such as Reverend Dr. Martin Luther King, Jr. and Rosa Parks among others (2007, p. 2). Thompson's feature also engaged a host of living civil rights luminaries such as the aforementioned Juanita Abernathy and Reverend Lowery, juxtaposing

---

62 Editorial from Dave Zirin, edgeofsports@gmail.com Sent to: Ron Stewart, Ph.D. on August 23, 2007, who forwarded it to Kenneth N. Robinson on August 24, 2007. p.2.

these freedom fighters, alive and deceased, against a discussion of Vick's dog fighting dilemma and the unsolved lynching of blacks. Thompson, as noted, cited the horrific acts of devastating debauchery against blacks, including the killing of the pregnant black woman who had her fetus cut from her womb (p. 6). The concerns Thompson raised were substantial given that Vick was ultimately convicted, yet many of the killers that had lynched blacks with impunity are still alive and have never been brought to justice. Such references to blacks being lynched was especially apropos in light of Vick's life being threatened with lynching. Zirin (2007, p.1), who addressed the threats of lynching against Vick, also noted the awful irony of dogs being used against blacks during the civil rights movement, which Vick himself, being a son of the South, is no doubt keenly aware of. Again, if Vick has had to accept a history where the police used dogs to attack members of his own community, might he have also believed that using dogs to attack other dogs was not so bad? Yet the NFL, the media, corporate sponsors, and the politics of the state apparently cared less about such a meaningful connection. Instead, these superstructures made Vick the face of animal cruelty while aiding and abetting his indictment, prosecution, and imprisonment. In so doing, the NFL and its alliance of superstructures reduced Michael Vick from superman to super-masculine menial.

Conclusion

The preceding chapter discussed how the NFL's dominant alliance of superstructures, such as the mainstream media, corporate sponsors, and the politics of the state, all contributed to the NFL becoming the most popular and prosperous sports institution in America. Because of their influence on the development of the NFL, these powerful groups maintain a vested interest in the economic expansion and stability of the game. Consequently, in the wake of the Michael Vick scandal which created unease in the NFL, these superstructures contributed much to the strong public reaction that made him more susceptible to criminal prosecution. In addition to the commonalities these dominant entities share in developing the NFL, each has a documented history of practicing structural racism against blacks. While the NFL and its alliance of superstructures were certainly concerned about the effect Michael Vick's scandal might have on their multibillion dollar partnerships, their collective reaction helped to convict him and also raised questions of racial indifference toward him.

Conversely, these same powerful entities were more restrained in addressing scandals involving whites like Bill Belichick and Ben Roethlisberger. As a result, there was less public rage and the law enforcement community seemed to assume there was not as much concern. Thus their investigations were either halted or never pursued. Although the alleged rape incident involving Roethlisberger in Las Vegas became the subject of a lawsuit, which he settled in 2012, there were no criminal charges. In addition to the media, the NFL was just as harmful in its display of racial indifference toward Vick's precarious legal situation when compared to scandals involving Roethlisberger and Belichick.

In the case of Vick, the league sent its security team to help investigators who were combing through the quarterback's property in Virginia. Conversely, the league did not use its security to assist any law enforcement investigations of Roethlisberger's rape charges or Belichick's Spygate scandal. Consequently, the outcomes for these employees of the NFL could not have been more different. Vick of course was indicted and sent to prison, while Belichick and Roethlisberger were immunized from criminal sanctions. As a result, Belichick was not investigated by Congress nor charged by the federal government for committing wire fraud or conspiracy to violate anti-trust laws in the course of interstate commerce. Nor was the league punished, censored, or sanctioned in any way for destroying the Spygate tapes, actions that could have amounted to obstruction of justice. The league's other ally that contributed to the "get Vick" climate that quickened his precipitous fall were corporate sponsors.

Historically, corporate sponsors have been just as inclined as others to practice racism against blacks. Business corporations have marketed their products using disparaging images of blacks as ignorant sambos and jungle savages. These images constitute the composite of the super-masculine menial, which Vick was reduced to in the wake of the scandal. Such realities provide a perspective of how Vick went from tolerable to intolerable by corporate America.

Today, over ninety percent of all CEOs of private companies are white males. Such a skewed hierarchy at the leadership helm, which is also reflected in NFL organizations, means racism is not only relatively common, but fairly predictable. As for celebrated African-American athletes like Vick, corporations will use them to simply sell their products. Although several multinational companies, including Nike and Rawlings, paid Vick to endorse their products, they also contributed to his ruin over dog fighting. As these corporate sponsors dropped Vick, reports of him losing upwards of $60 million in endorsements weakened his resolve considerably, and he later filed for bankruptcy. Hurting financially, Vick did not fight the conspiracy charges over dog fighting and instead pleaded guilty. Incidentally, in 2011, Nike announced that it was re-signing Vick to an endorsement deal. It seems Nike is simply intent to exploit him once again after his brilliant comeback season in 2010. After all, when Nike dropped him in 2007, the company never conceded its own role in popularizing dog fighting with a 2003 commercial that inferred a dog fighting match. Beyond corporate sponsors, the superstructure that has practiced the most harmful racism historically is also the entity that claimed Vick's fate in the wake of the dog fighting scandal: the politics of the state.

Of course, the politics of the state, which in this discussion includes state and federal governments, have historically treated blacks with indifference. Supreme Court rulings like the Dred Scott case in 1857 and the 1896 Supreme Court ruling in *Plessy vs. Ferguson* established legal precedents that made racial discrimination the norm. Even today in America, there are real concerns over inequalities in the American criminal justice system, given the soaring rates of imprisonment for blacks and other underrepresented groups.

As much as the NFL unbraided Michael Vick for his harm to dogs, the league has been conspicuously silent on the senseless canine killings committed by China. These points will be addressed in the following chapter, given the NFL's peculiar business relationship with the communist state which broadcasts league programming for a fee.

CHAPTER III

The Height of Hypocrisy:

The NFL and China

"The city officials initiated a 'dog cull' order wherein every single dog in Xangxian was to be executed, whether by being beaten to death, sliced open, or just shot."
- Weird Asia News, 2009

"The order demanded that dog owners kill their dogs within 48 hours or have them killed by the military police at a cost of 100 yuan, or $16 each."
- Humane Society, 2009

The critical media backlash Michael Vick underwent over the dog fighting disaster far exceeded overkill in the eyes of African-Americans. Many felt Vick got a raw deal from the press because he is black. Even sports journalists who are African-Americans felt helpless in the face of the sensational subterfuge perpetuated by the largely white male-dominated sports media. For example, Jemele Hill of ESPN, who is also an African-American, found it difficult to defend Michael Vick in the face of what the "white media" had done to him, because there was no "moral high ground" for something as low as what he did to the dogs (Zirin, 2007, p. 2).

However, in searching for moral high ground in response to the white media's reaction, Ms. Hill could have referenced other atrocious acts against dogs in the world. She would have realized that neither the media nor the NFL had any moral high ground to stand on in condemning Vick's misdeeds against dogs. Especially since the league maintains its rather peculiar business relationship with the People's Republic of China, despite its wretched record of animal abuse against man's best friend. Although television networks in America pay the NFL for broadcast rights, the league pays China to broadcast its programming on state-controlled CCTV, despite the communist state having no laws against animal cruelty. What makes their business relationship questionable is the sheer level of debauchery and mass killing of dogs ordered by Chinese governments. These atrocities have been covered by the international media, including major broadcasting agencies in America. Despite this, no reporter had the gall or the gumption to ask the NFL about this blatant contradiction. How is it that the NFL could condemn and suspend Vick for his despicable conduct toward dogs but never suspend its ties to China, given its systematic killing of canines?

In 2006, one year before Vick's dog fighting depravity came to light, the Chinese government ordered the slaughter of 50,000 dogs in Shanghai (MSNBC, 2006). The dogs were killed supposedly because three people died from rabies (MSNBC, p. 1). But there is no evidence that the slaughtered dogs were tested or quarantined. There was widespread belief that the government used the small number of rabies cases as propaganda to justify the massive massacre. Additionally, the indiscriminant culling included the killing of tens of thousands of uninfected dogs who had personal owners. These atrocious actions by the Chinese government were condemned by animal rights groups worldwide.

In a ghastly scene played out before the international community, the state police, operating as killing squads, forcibly took dogs from their owners. Then in an utter display of disregard, dogs were beaten to death in front of owners who were helpless in the face of this brutality. Owners were offered sixty-three cents to kill their own dogs; otherwise, the state police would kill them without compensation. Despite the dog massacres in China, the media never asked the NFL to explain this inconsistency on its part. How is it that the league could condemn Michael Vick for killing a few dogs without commenting on or condemning China's massacre of thousands? Ironically enough, the NFL was so unconcerned about the 2006 mass killing of dogs in China that they proceeded with plans to play the first of its kind, "China Bowl," there in 2007. Even more unsettling, the league shamelessly promoted this exhibition in the American press during the same time it was publicly condemning Vick for his harm to dogs.

[63]*The New York Times* (2007) published a story on the China Bowl, an exhibition game that was to feature the New England Patriots playing against the Seattle Seahawks. Given the league's penchant for pomp and circumstance, the *Times* story included a photo and a caption of a Chinese kicker participating in tryouts hosted by the NFL. The contestants were vying to make history as the first Chinese person to placekick in an NFL preseason game. Despite such media buildup, no journalist in America saw fit to question the league about the oddity, if not sheer hypocrisy, of the NFL publicly flogging Michael Vick for his acts of animal cruelty while simultaneously planning a game in China, given its notorious record of animal cruelty. Furthermore, China, which is already infamous for human rights abuses, has no laws to prohibit animal cruelty, thus dogs are brutally killed with impunity (Global Times, 2009). Ultimately, the NFL's exhibition game in China was canceled, not over human rights issues or concerns about animal abuse, but a general lack of interest on the part of the Chinese people. As much as the NFL would like for China's billion-plus populace to embrace its game as it has the NBA, the Chinese see football as too violent.

Perhaps the scenes of bodies clashing violently and being thrown to the ground with reckless abandon are too reminiscent of reactions by the state to resistance from its citizens. So while the NFL and its allies in the media, corporate sponsors, and the politics of the state were castigating Vick's mistreat-

---

63   http://www.nytimes.com/2007/03/02/sports/football/02kickers.ready.html?ex= 1187150400. *Pro Football Grooms 3 Legs, With a Billion Eyes.*

ment of dogs, they all ignored China's systematic slaughter. The collective silence in the face of dogs being killed in China was indeed striking when you consider several factors. In 2007, the NFL posted a photo with a caption on its website of a protester holding a sign enjoining people to "Kick Vick" for his abuse of dogs. Yet the NFL turned a blind eye to China's mass execution of dogs, acts that reflect the state's long-standing abhorrence for dogs as a symbol of Western culture. The gross disparity in the number of dogs Vick was held responsible for killing versus the disproportionately greater number killed by China is staggering.

While Vick was charged and convicted of killing eight dogs in 2007, the Shanghai Province of China slaughtered 50,000 dogs the year prior. For every one dog Vick was convicted of killing, the Chinese government massacred upwards of 6,250 dogs during this single culling. Notwithstanding the international outrage, there was more canine carnage to come. Yet no major media outlet, corporate sponsor, or member of Congress, all of whom lambasted Vick, enjoined the NFL to question or condemn the issue given its business relationship with the communist state.

For Every One Dog Vick Killed, China Killed 13,750 (2006-2009)

While the NFL ignored China's massacre of dogs, Commissioner Roger Goodell vilified Vick publicly in response to allegations of his involvement in dog fighting. He stated, "We totally condemn the conduct outlined in the charges (against Michael Vick)."[64] Why would the commissioner publicly attack Vick without similarly assailing China? The NFL's conspicuous silence was an apparent attempt to preserve their business interests with the state-controlled China Central Television (CCTV).[65] In addition to CCTV, the NFL pays Sina.com, the

---

64 Gary Mihoces, *USA Today Sports.* 10 Questions in Vick Case: Potentially stiffer penalties possible factor in plea. August 21, 2007.
65 Retrieved from NFL.com-NFL News (2003). *NFL & China Central TV reach partnership.*

popular Internet hub on the mainland of China, untold sums of money to broadcast its programming.[66] By contrast, American television networks collectively pay billions in licensing fees to broadcast NFL programming. While the dog culling in China was never addressed by the NFL in 2006, another opportunity presented itself just three years later.

Since China has no laws against animal cruelty, the communist state authored what became a chilling trilogy of canine culling. In a cruel and twisted irony, just months after Vick was released from prison in 2009, two Chinese provinces ordered the senseless slaughter of another 60,000 dogs in the cities of Hanzhog and Heihe (Humane Society, 2009; www.weirdasia news.com, 2009; letter from Fred O'Reagan of the IFAW, 2009). So in three separate spates, between 2006 and 2009, upwards of 110,000 dogs were killed by officials from Chinese governments. Again, neither the American media nor any animal rights organizations asked the league to explain such a barefaced double standard. How could the league express such strong disapproval of Michael Vick, including enjoining people to kick him, yet have nothing to say about Chinese officials killing more than 100,000 dogs?

What explains the NFL's suspension of Michael Vick for nearly two years and another four games in 2009, despite having never suspended their business ties to China? It seems rather apparent that the NFL was not as concerned about the mistreatment of dogs as it was about its business interests. Its strong reaction to Vick's crimes against dogs was influenced by outrage in the community, fueled by animal rights organizations that threatened the league's business operations. For example, the Humane Society reportedly sent over 160,000 messages of protest to Nike in response to Vick's dog fighting dilemma (Sandomir, 2007). Conversely, in the absence of animal rights organizations threatening the NFL over its economic relationship with China, the league has continued with business as usual. While Vick's dog fighting crimes included drowning, hanging, electrocutions, and dogs being shot dead, those grotesque

---

66 LexisNexis Academic: Document. *NFL taps Sina.com to popularize American football on the mainland.* June 23, 2008. South China Morning Post, Business, p.3.

acts pale in comparison to China's systematic annihilation of 110,000 dogs in Shanghai, Hanzhong, and Heihe.

Upon his release from prison in 2009, the NFL told Vick he needed to show remorse for his mistreatment of dogs. Yet, the same time the league took a see-no-evil, hear-no-evil approach to the government-ordered slaughter of dogs in China. According to several reports, both stray dogs and those with owners were beaten to death. Similar to the culling of 2006, dog owners were told by the Chinese government to kill their own dogs or the government would do it. But in 2009, pet owners were fined for failing to comply. In Hanzhong, the Humane Society International obtained a copy of the government edict and reported, "The order demanded that dog owners kill their dogs within 48 hours or have them killed by the military police at a cost of 100 yuan, or $16 each" (Humane Society, 2009, p. 1). In Heihe, like in Hanzhong, the government gave dog owners an ultimatum that bore consequences both emotionally and financially. Residents were told if they did not kill their own dogs, "they not only (would) have to stand to see the dog killed (by the state police), but also pay a fine of up to 200 yuan ($29)."[67] Another Chinese news agency reported, "The city officials initiated a 'dog cull' order wherein every single dog in Xangxian was to be executed, whether by being beaten to death, sliced open, or just shot." Other cruel methodologies used during China's dog culling included this description:

> One by one, the dogs are pulled out with a pair of long metal tongs and brutally beaten with a stick. And then, even though it appears that some of the dogs may be still alive, they're tossed into a pit to be burned.[68]

The report also found that it mattered not whether the canines were stray dogs or had masters; all were ordered to be

---

67   http://blogs.law.harvard.edu/guorui/2009/05/23/heihe-city-government-ordered-to-kill-dog/.

68 http://www.isiria.wordpress.com/2009/06/16/dog-massacre-in-china-30000-dead-and-counting.

slaughtered. Not only did the Chinese government of Heihe use the state police to kill the dogs, but like the Shanghai culling, they employed killing squads. None of these tragic accounts of dog killings have prompted the NFL to reevaluate its business association with China. The NFL cannot play Pontius Pilate when it comes to the massacre of dogs in China. Especially since the NFL pays the Chinese government, which pays the state police, who were ordered to kill the dogs. On the actions of the state police, one animal activist observed:

> My husband could not sleep for several nights. What he had in his mind were the blood trails on the ground, dying dogs taking a last look at this not-so-friendly world, and the wailing howls of the dogs pinned down by the police (Weird Asia News, 2010, p. 2).

The government's explanation that the cull was an attempt to control the spread of rabies seems hardly tenable. Even vaccinated dogs were part of the culling in Hanzhog during the indiscriminant killings. Moreover, the government's response that stray dogs were biting people and spreading rabies was described as a "cleverly planned attempt" by officials to turn the region into a "dogless" Chinese city.[69] When taken as a whole, the 2006 culling of 50,000 dogs in Shanghai and over 30,000 each in both of Hanzhog and Heihe in 2009 amounted to a staggering 110,000 canines killed. Consequently, China's actions have come under international fire from organizations like the IFAW (International Fund for Animal Welfare), HSI (Humane Society International), and Animals Asia. Even PETA, which relentlessly hounded Michael Vick in 2007, was among the dog advocacy groups from around the world who condemned the slaughter of dogs by the Chinese government. How is it that the NFL and PETA were on one accord when it came to Vick's mistreatment of dogs in 2007, but on no accord when it came to China's massacre of dogs in 2006 and again in 2009?

---

69 http://www.weirdasianews.com/2010/02/12/china-dog-massacres-2009/.

As bad as Vick's Bad Newz Kennels was, how could its behavior rival the sheer volume of viciousness of dog killings administered by the Chinese government? Reports that Vick's organization killed eight dogs fueled plenty of public outrage. But for every one dog Vick and his comrades killed, China's provinces ordered the slaughter of 13,750 dogs in separate culls between 2006 and 2009. Hence, NFL consumers, animal rights groups in America, the media, and Congress should be just as outraged about the league's business relationship with China as they were about Vick. Yet these entities have remained conspicuously silent on the matter. Beyond the NFL's economic interest in China, Americans should be concerned about why China harbors such a deep-seated aversion to dogs.

Dogs in China: A Bourgeois Affectation

Since the People's Republic of China came into existence in 1949, China has viewed dogs contemptuously as a "bourgeois affectation" (MSNBC.com, 2006).[70] In other words, China views dogs as a symbol of Western culture and the economic system of capitalism. The underlying suggestion is if you can afford to feed another mouth, and that mouth belongs to a dog, then the impression is that you are doing relatively well in a capitalist society. The view of dogs as a bourgeois affectation in the West is traceable historically.

As far back as the nineteenth century, the French saw dogs and cats as a status symbol of the middle class (Fleming, 2007). This idea was adopted in America as dogs were not only viewed in the familial context, but were among the indices of middle class life in bourgeoning suburban communities. There is nothing in the history of this nation that did more to perpetuate the bourgeois affectation of middle class culture than the development of American suburbia. In a not so ironic twist, the expansion of these communities coincided with the advent of

---

70 http://www.msnbc.com/id/14139027/. *Chinese country clubs to death 50,000 dogs.*

television and the rise of the NFL as a spectator sport. These communities offered residents a reprieve from the hustle and bustle of urban life and were supposed to represent the fulfillment of the American dream in a capitalist society. The image of the family house, family car, and the family dog completed the picture-perfect scenario for the model American family. The idea of building suburban homes with large backyards was in part an accommodation for dogs. A family's ability to afford this lifestyle and care for a dog is an indicator of prosperity in a capitalistic society.

On the contrary, many rural Chinese are often too poor to take care of themselves, much less a dog. This stunning contrast is what gives China greater cause to resent the dog as a bourgeois affectation. While the country is worried less about its rural farmers developing a desire for dogs as indicators of a bourgeois persuasion, the same cannot be said about the younger, trendier Chinese. It is this next generation in the country's developing areas that have come to love dogs as pets. Officials have been intent to curtail the growing influence of Western norms and mores. The wider use of dogs as pets in China is especially pronounced in emergent urban areas where a number of veterinarian hospitals have sprung up. In shopping plazas, newer industries have unfurled for dog lovers, such as grooming parlors, where the pets can have their hair dyed fashionably. While the Chinese government has tolerated some change in caring for dogs, it remains leery of a growing affinity for such artifacts of bourgeois capitalism.

This may help to explain why so many of the dog owners had their pets forcibly taken from them only to be crushed to death in front of their eyes. Again, neither the NFL nor any of its dominant allies who criticized Vick seemed to care about these events. Even though the media and members of Congress were vociferous in enjoining the NFL to punish Vick, they have never asked the league to reevaluate its business relationship with China in light of its destruction of dogs. It is incumbent upon Congress to do so, not merely because it regulates the NFL as interstate commerce, but because its business relationship with

China falls under foreign commerce. If Congress as a whole is less inclined to question the NFL about this double standard over harming dogs, the Congressional Black Caucus (CBC) needs to initiate an inquiry. The need for the CBC to react seems especially apropos since the NFL contributed to the view that Vick and other African-American men are the faces of animal cruelty.[71] By contrast, perhaps no other country has projected a more brutal face of animal cruelty toward dogs than China. Moreover, as much as the United States has prodded China on human rights abuse, democracy, and pollution, the absence of animal cruelty laws there has been largely ignored.

So while Vick's involvement in dog fighting is explainable as a vestige of European culture and plantation slavery in America, China's killing rampage is a vestige of its contempt for dogs as a symbol of Western culture and the economic system of capitalism in America. China has also come under international condemnation for the continuous slaughter of millions of dogs and cats annually.[72] The absence of animal cruelty laws in China has made dogs and cats fair game to be skinned alive and their furs used for fur coats (*Fur is Dead*, n.d.). Does not the fur coat represent a bourgeois affectation in the West, particularly in America? In both Europe and the United States, fur coats are a status symbol in a capitalistic society.

Several undercover investigations have uncovered underworld markets where furs from dogs and cats are sold under the guise of expensive animal furs. Even more alarmingly, half of all furs sold to unsuspecting Americans are made in China. Unbeknownst to many Americans, the fur coats purchased in this country are likely off the backs of dogs and cats skinned alive in China, with nary a remark or rebuke from the league. But NFL football is supposed to be America's game. If so, why does the NFL continue to do business with China given its pro-

---

71 An analysis of dog fighting arrests by race shows the number of African-Americans arrested have increased in the five years that followed Michael Vick's home being raided, while the number of whites arrested have decreased. Arrest data was retrieved from www.pet-abuse.com.

72 http:/www.furisdead.com/feat-dogcatfur.asp.

pensity to kill dogs so impetuously out of contempt for Western culture? Yet on account of his dog fighting, Michael Vick was branded a dog killer of the worst kind. All of which goes back to the question of race and the power of labeling. If the reaction of the American public to Vick's scandal was not about race, then where are all the dog lovers on the question of animal cruelty in China? Again, if there was outrage about the NFL's relationship with Vick over his abuse of dogs, where is the outrage over the league's relationship with China, given its unmatched record of cruelty to dogs?

Perhaps one explanation for the media's inaction on the question of China is that television networks that broadcast NFL games help protect the league's image and brand. They remain wary of embarrassing the league and of jeopardizing their future licenses for broadcast rights of NFL games.

When the NFL Says Jump, the Networks Say, "How High?"

Although the networks have far more wealth than the NFL, they seem to be easily intimidated by the league. Traditionally, when the NFL says jump (as in paying more for broadcast rights), the networks have said, "How high?" If networks refuse to pay what the NFL demands, the league will simply sell the rights to the next highest bidder. NFL Commissioner Pete Rozelle was notorious for his ability to gouge television networks for excessive increases in licensing fees. His understudy and successor, Commissioner Paul Tagliabue, was no less inclined to use the power of the NFL brand to intimidate a television network. For example, in 2003, Commissioner Tagliabue was interviewed by Bob Costas for HBO's *Inside the NFL*.[73] Costas asked the commissioner about ESPN's highly rated but controversial show *Playmakers*. At the time, ESPN, along with its sister station ABC, held coveted licenses to broadcast NFL programming such as the NFL draft and the *Sunday* and *Monday Night Foot-*

---

73 HBO's *Inside the NFL*, fall 2003. Bob Costas interviews NFL Commissioner Paul Tagliabue.

ball packages. While the *Playmakers* series did not name the NFL in any way, it depicted pro football players in unflattering ways. Realizing this underlying concern, Costas asked Commissioner Tagliabue point blank: if ESPN does not pull the show, will it affect their ability to negotiate with the league in the next round of television contracts? If the ESPN show was to have no bearing on the league's television negotiations, Tagliabue would have said so. Instead, he opined dryly enough, "No comment." It has been said, "A hint to the wise is sufficient." Apparently ESPN reasoned the same, as the network canceled the highly rated award-winning television series because it was clear the NFL was not happy about it. This latter example illustrates the significant power and sway the NFL maintains over the television networks, which should concern Congress.

It was Congress that passed the Sports Broadcasting Act of 1961 that gave the league significant power over the television networks, including the ability to negotiate with them simultaneously. It should be noted that since canceling *Playmakers* in 2004, ESPN has been awarded the license to broadcast NFL programming without fail. In 2011, it was reported that ESPN will pay upwards of $2 billion annually to broadcast NFL shows, including the annual league draft and *Monday Night Football.* Interestingly enough, the 24-hour sports network pays more than twice the amount for broadcasting rights than does Fox, CBS, and NBC. The reason being, ESPN consistently turns a profit with NFL football because it collects subscriber fees through cable and satellite television. Profitability helps to explain why Disney Co., which owns both ABC and ESPN, moved *Monday Night Football* to ESPN. Conversely, the other networks go into their contracts with the NFL knowing they may not profit off their agreement. The cost of a license to broadcast league programming is so exorbitant that networks cannot charge advertisers enough to garner a profit. But networks continue to bid for the license to broadcast league games for the prestige and outstanding ratings that NFL football consistently delivers.

In addition, the high ratings allow the networks to mitigate fixed-in losses in revenues by connecting with a target viewership of males ages eighteen to forty-four and their families. Another incentive for television networks is that NFL broadcast rights enable them to turn a profit for their local affiliates. These same networks that do business with the NFL never broached the incongruity of the NFL failing to even comment on China's systematic extermination of dogs. The failure to question this inconsistency is noteworthy when you consider that CBS, CNN, and MSNBC, among others, filed reports on the tens of thousands of dogs being killed by the Chinese government. While Michael Ventre of MSNBC (Zirin, 2007, p. 1)[74] wrote that Vick should be banned from the NFL for life, he said nothing about the league's hypocrisy in doing business with China. Meanwhile, MSNBC published a meaningful account of the dog massacre in Shanghai in 2006.

The example of ESPN caving in to league pressure should be a huge concern given the potential for significant harm to the public. In his book *Supertube*, Ron Powers (1984) observed that the significant power that the NFL wields over the television networks makes it a perfect model for socialism. Powers's suggestion makes it easier to understand why the NFL never uttered a syllable of dissent over China's dog killings. It appears that the NFL has more in common with China than not. Although China is identified as a communist state, some would argue that the government's control over private industries also reflects a socialist model. But since the NFL functions much like a self-contained entity, it also exists as a governing force unto itself. While the NFL is certainly answerable to Congress, the sheer pomp and popularity of the sport captivates the very lawmakers who are supposed to regulate it. Consequently, even members of Congress seem to get swept up in the NFL's unique ability to cultivate a sense of blissful unawareness.

In fact, Congress rarely imposes its will on the NFL except over matters like the Vick dog fighting scandal. Other NFL issues that have been serious enough to warrant attention from Congress include the use of human growth hormones by players and the league's blackout rule. By contrast, Congress did

---

74 http://www.thenation.com/doc/20070730.

not address scandals involving Bill Belichick and Ben Roethlisberger. More recently there was scant attention accorded to the Bountygate scandal involving the New Orleans Saints organization in 2012, which was left up to the commissioner. Congress has deferred to the NFL on issues of player safety despite the debilitating effects of CTE (chronic traumatic encephalopathy). While there was a raucous reaction on Capitol Hill in response to what Michael Vick did to his dogs, not even the suicides of three former NFL players, believed to be linked to CTE, have prompted a Congressional hearing. The relative inattention of Congress to these grim concerns confronting the NFL is indeed surprising. Many observers see the NFL's outgrowth as harmful given its hegemonic monopoly over professional football and its influential sway over the media. In a twisted irony, although the NFL is touted as America's game, in too many ways the league more closely resembles the totalitarian rule that exists in China.

The NFL Like China

Both the NFL and China are very protective of their images. Both operate with centralized authority and have models of vertical revenue procurement. Each operates with binding control over the media. In 2008, the NFL placed severe restrictions on the amount of league highlights that can be shown on television on game days and the next seven days that follow.[75] These restrictions are enforceable on "regularly scheduled news programs" (local or national news shows), "sports wrap-up shows," and "loop news services" (channels such as CNN and ESPN). This tight grip on its footage not only allows the NFL to increase the value of its game highlights, but it gives the league added muscle over television and broadcast networks. Of course, China television is state controlled, so the content is always filtered and designed to bolster the standing of the communist nation. In recent years China's control over media content came

---

75 Retrieved from: http:abcnewsone.tv/?q=node/2199, *NFL Highlight Restrictions*, ABC NewsOne.

under international criticism when the state began censoring its citizens' use of social media. In 2012, China instituted even tighter restrictions on Internet access amid concerns of potential political unrest. When President Barack Obama visited China in 2009, government officials, wary of his international populist fame, ensured that his town hall meeting with Chinese youth was not broadcast on state television.

Both the NFL and China function with sweeping and unfettered dictatorial powers that include imposing harsh sanctions on rule breakers under their authority. The NFL's dreaded personal conduct policy, which allows the league commissioner to discipline players whose conduct breaks league rules or societal laws, has been the subject of debate. More recently, this policy and its enforcer have come under considerable scrutiny over the aforementioned New Orleans Saints bounty scandal. The scandal involved a system where Saints players were allegedly paid thousands of dollars to injure opposing players. The NFL commissioner used his unbridled authority to suspend coaches, front office personnel, and players from the Saints organization. But, it was the suspensions of Saints players for several games, and in some cases the entire year, without pay, that became the most cantankerous issue.

NFL players and their union argued that the commissioner's unchecked authoritarian rule prevented due process. Similarly, China has an organizational dictatorship where "might is right" prevails over its citizens. But unlike Chinese citizens who have very few options when addressing their grievances, there is a legal recourse for NFL players seeking redress of their grievances. Given the existence of a collective bargaining agreement between the NFL and the NFLPA (NFL Players Association), the players first sought redress through arbitration. When an arbitrator upheld the commissioner's suspensions, their fight was taken to a court of law.

Eventually, a three-member judicial panel heard the arguments of both sides and overturned the commissioner's suspension. But the panel did not rule on the legality of whether the players had actually participated in a bounty system. Instead, the panel only evaluated the procedures the commissioner under-took in punishing the players. The NFLPA protested Goodell's plans to preside over the appeal of his own decision. The commissioner then appointed his former boss and predecessor as NFL commissioner, Paul Tagliabue, who vacated Goodell's suspensions of the players. While Tagliabue affirmed Commissioner Goodell's findings that a bounty system existed, he voided the suspensions over a lack of precedence in suspending other players for similar behavior.[76] In this instance, even Tagliabue disagreed with Goodell's exercise of power. Of particular note, Tagliabue questioned Goodell's decision to issue longer suspensions for players who failed to meet with him when he only fined quarterback Brett Favre for doing the same thing in 2010. Three of the four players who refused to meet with him were African-Americans. Still, the commissioner's authority has often been criticized and challenged by the NFLPA and scrutinized both in the media and in the courts. In the years to come, the NFL will be spending more time in court.

Increasingly, a growing number of former NFL players have joined a class action lawsuit against the league over the debilitating effects of concussions sustained over their careers. The litigious matter is but another indicator of how touchy relations have become between the NFL and the players, both past and present. From the labor lockout of 2011 to the bounty scandal in 2012 to a pending lawsuit involving as many as 2,000 former players, there are very serious structural problems with the autocratic rule that rests with the league's commissioner. While the NFL would argue against the suggestion that its organizational model is a reflection of socialism, the only factor that has debunked it historically has been the existence of the NFLPA, the infrequent interventions of Congress, and the remedies and rulings from the courts. Left alone, the use of such unbridled authority, particularly in the NFL's planned economy, is more akin to a nation like China than America.

---

76 Tagliabue, Paul. (2012). In the Matter of New Orleans Saints Pay-for-Play Performance/"Bounty": Final Decision on Appeal.

Labor Versus Labor Power

Like the citizens of China, NFL players have often felt exploited given the physical toll their jobs take on them. In China it is the exhausting labor and long hours worked, whether in the fields, the factories, or in white collar professions that can be so taxing. In the NFL, it is work hard and play hard, with all the power you can muster. The end result is often debilitating injuries later in life. Their high salaries are not guaranteed beyond the signing bonus. By contrast, the contracts of head coaches, who are part and parcel to management, are guaranteed. Likewise, China has exploited the labor of its citizens, which mass produces goods from a wide range of industries and multinational companies from America. Although China's citizens earn considerably less, the socialist economy has allowed the country to emerge as an economic superpower.

Workers Stadium Versus Taxpayers Stadium

The NFL too has become an economic superpower by reaping the benefits of the game popularized by the players. In addition, the NFL has also placed the burden on taxpayers to underwrite billions to finance the league's super stadium race over the last fifty years. Ironically enough, in China the stadium that was to host the first China Bowl involving two NFL teams in 2007 is called "Workers Stadium." The title of course indicates that it was built by Chinese workers. Given such a reality, virtually every NFL stadium in America might be called "Taxpayers Stadium," given the exorbitant amount of taxpayer financing that has gone into constructing nearly all of the mega-structures on a revenue procurement model. Rather than naming these stadiums in honor of local communities, team owners sell naming rights to corporations to generate more revenue. Once NFL stadiums have yielded enough wealth for the owners, they seek newer venues to charge higher fees and generate more wealth. For communities that have refused to pay for new NFL stadiums or redesigned venues to create more wealth, owners have heavy-handedly threatened to move their franchises, and have often done so. For those communities that have forked over billions in taxpayer financing for new stadiums, they can expect to lose billions over the lifetime of such tax-exempt funding. Often the exorbitant costs of building new stadiums have been more than what local governments can afford. Consequently, the NFL has taken two newer approaches to help finance the construction of their super stadiums.

On the one hand, owners have turned to their customers by charging season ticket holders a PSL (personal seat license) to offset the costs of new stadium construction. The PSL, which can cost thousands of dollars, does not include the costs of season tickets, but gives the customer the license to buy a season ticket. This certainly appears to be taxation without representation and is an exploitative way of telling fans the license gives them an ownership stake. On the other hand, since the cost of building newer stadiums now exceeds $1 billion, which is out of range for taxpayers, team owners created their own G-4 monetary financing system for new stadium construction and renovations. Among other considerations, the loan program requires owners in need to put up the first $25 million, after which G-4 funding will match them by the dollar. The loan program will fund newly constructed stadiums up to $200 million and renovated stadiums up to $250 million. However, in order to qualify for the loan program, there must be a public-private partnership. Furthermore, local communities are still expected to pay more because G-4 funding is only expected to meet twenty-five percent of construction costs. That the NFL has a G-4 entity that resembles the G8 summit of eight great nations of the world underscores the suggestion of the NFL functioning as a self-contained quasi-state. Moreover, that this G-4 program lends money to owners to help finance new or redesigned stadiums indicates that owners have had the financing for some time. The NFL owners have minimized their own risks of investing in stadiums while maximizing the potential for profits at the expense of their consumers. This is reminiscent of public criticisms against China.

Such charges have included suggestions that China manipulates the value of its currency, thus lowering the relative price of exported goods. The effect is that China produces cheap goods, which undercuts the ability of companies in other nations to compete. The ability to have goods produced in China at such low costs continues to drive businesses to the Far East to set up operations. This allows the communist state to reap large economic gains while most of its citizens remain poor and while America continues to hemorrhage jobs. Despite considerable gains, China has been cited for shoddy construction, including schools that have collapsed, causing preventable deaths. Similarly, the Dallas Cowboys have had to contend with accidental deaths and an estimated 170 incidents of personal injuries related to work conditions in the construction of new facilities. In 2011 another worker fell to his death while putting up a billboard at the stadium. His family has sued and named the Dallas Cowboys franchise as a defendant. Given this new round of construction in the NFL's ongoing super stadium race, more accidents and tragic deaths may occur.

Of similar import, China has been chided for allowing unsafe working conditions. Chinese miners have been killed due to questionable safety regulations and hazardous work sites. The NFL is now the subject of a class action lawsuit by a growing number of former players who allege the league was negligent in denying the long-term effect of concussions. The former players may have a strong case. There is some evidence of negligence on the part of the NFL after the league commissioned a study on the effects of concussions.

Not What the Doctor Ordered

In response to repeated questions and concerns about the perceived long-term effects of concussions on players' health, the league authorized a 1994 study by its Mild Traumatic Brain Injury (MTBI) Committee. That the NFL would use the term "mild" trauma is an indicator of a deliberate attempt to downplay the seriousness of head injuries brought on by the game. Ultimately, the committee concluded there was no conclusive evidence that players who suffered concussions were more susceptible to recurring brain trauma.[77] This determination was made by Elliott Pellman, M.D., whom the league selected to chair the committee and research endeavor. Pellman was known in the NFL after serving as team doctor of the New York Jets. Oddly enough, it was later determined that Pellman was unqualified to study neuroscience. Rather than a neurologist or a neuropsychologist, who are qualified to study the effects of concussions, Pellman is a rheumatologist, who specializes in joints and muscles. That the NFL would place a doctor who treats joints and muscles in charge of an important study on player safety and the impact of brain injury is inexcusably negligent. It was later reported that Pellman misrepresented the truth of where he received his medical degree. Rather than SUNY Stony Brook, he attended medical school in Mexico, reportedly because his grades were too low to get into an American medical school. Instead of commissioning an independent panel, the league, ever intent on controlling the message, hired Pellman, who earned a living in the NFL. His finding that a concussed player was not at significant risk of suffering a subsequent concussion if he returned to the game has long been refuted. Moreover, his committee's findings, which were published in a peer review medical journal, indicated that there was no evidence that players were at risk of long-term effects from concussions. These findings were inconsistent with conclusions from several other medical studies authorized by the likes of the NCAA, the Center for the Study of Retired Athletes at the University of North Carolina, and the International Conference on Concussions in Sport (in Vienna in 2001 and Prague in 2004).

Today, we know that CTE (chronic traumatic encephalopathy) is a medical condition that describes the long-term effects and consequences of concussions sustained by players in the NFL. Several high-profile former NFL players, such as Andre Waters, Dave Duerson, and more recently, Junior Seau, have committed suicide, and CTE has been identified as a con-

---

77 Retrieved from http://sports.espn.go.com/espn/magazine/archives/news/story?page=magazine-20061106-article37.

tributing factor. CTE's debilitating effects include insomnia, headaches, loss of memory, and the onset of Alzheimer's. Some families have donated the brains of deceased NFL players to be studied at Boston University's Center for the Study of Encephalopathy. Despite these developments, most networks that partner with the NFL have accorded only meager attention to this serious issue. The stakes are too high, with too much NFL revenue at stake. Once more, these developments and the lack of quality attention devoted to this issue by the mainstream media indicate how harmful the NFL's influence over the media has become. Not only does CTE require more medical attention, but it also needs more media attention. Instead, the networks have allowed the NFL to function like a totalitarian state, using propaganda to control the message on a controversy. Rather than feature stories and interviews with former NFL players and family members of players who have committed suicide, most networks and news agencies have only accorded scant attention to this severe issue. On the other hand, in 2012, with growing concern over the safety of full-contact football and widespread fears of CTE, many parents and some reporters questioned whether children should be playing the sport. Even President Barack Obama commented that he would be less inclined to have a son play football, given the growing apprehension associated with CTE.

Realizing that little league football is where NFL dreams begin, the league rolled out an advertisement campaign for concerned parents featuring NFL stars Tom Brady and Ray Lewis to highlight the importance of safety improvements in the game. In addition, the spot included a physician who noted that millions of dollars in research is being committed to making football safer. The commercial was an obvious attempt to offset fears that football as a full-contact sport is too dangerous and debilitating. Of course, it was also designed for propaganda, given the pending lawsuits the NFL is facing. All of this is designed to allow the NFL to control the message, much like China does with its interests.

This preceding chapter showed that although the NFL is regarded as America's game, there are troublesome signs that suggest the league functions as a model of socialism. For the NFL to condemn Michael Vick for his harm to dogs while never criticizing or condemning China for its greater harm to dogs sends the wrong message to the public. The unfortunate thought is that China is a growing economic superpower, so it does not matter if they harm dogs. Nor does it matter if they do so because dogs are a reflection of their contempt for America's economic system. That the NFL has not condemned China is not good; that neither the media nor corporate sponsors nor members of Congress, who implored the league to punish Vick, have said anything is an even more ominous message.

Conclusion

It should now be clear why the league condemned and suspended Michael Vick while continuing to do business with China without comment and why this has gone unquestioned by the media. It appears the television networks are easily intimidated by the NFL despite their First Amendment rights to question such matters. Moreover, Congress should be alarmed about the league's supremacy and sway over television networks. This overbearing power was manifested not just in the media maligning Vick, but in other matters involving NFL players, including the concern over player safety and their long-term health. While injuries have always been a predictable consequence of violent sports, the growing awareness of CTE as a debilitating medical condition afflicting former players is a new concern. The power and influence of the NFL to seemingly control the message and the media's coverage over such a serious matter contributes to the idea of the league as a model for socialism. After all, Congress not only gave the NFL the power to amass such control over the mass media through the 1961 Sports Broadcasting Act, but federal law also gave it an exemption from Sherman Anti-Trust Laws in 1967. This legislation created the NFL as it is known today.

The NFL shapes the television coverage of its network partners with an understanding that future broadcast rights are contingent upon the networks making the league look good. This is potentially harmful to the public. This is especially true for African-Americans who have been historically labeled in uncomplimentary ways by the media. Such a tendency occurred in the media-induced anger and animus that arose against Michael Vick.

The public disdain for Vick was so great that when Commissioner Goodell reinstated him with a host of stipulations and restrictions, some in the media, like Bucky Gleason, a sports writer for the *Buffalo News*, praised it. He likened the commissioner's strict supervision of Vick as akin to keeping a dog "chained to the porch" (Gleason, 2009). But the failure of the media to question the league about its harsh treatment of Vick, compared to its silence on China, begs the question, who is really behaving like a dog chained to the porch? Neither the American media nor the general public nor Congress have held the NFL or corporations like Nike or Reebok accountable for brandishing Vick as the face of animal cruelty while remaining silent on China's debauchery against dogs.

These companies stopped doing business with Vick but continue to pay China to manufacture their goods without any evidence of greater human and animal rights being upheld. Additionally, investigators have found that the skins of dogs and cats from Asian countries are also used to make many products sold in the United States, including sporting goods. While NFL footballs are supposedly made of cowhide, are there any other league products that might include skins from dogs or cats killed in Asia? What about sporting goods made by Nike and Reebok? Future discussions of animal cruelty in America and around the world should include questioning multinational companies whose goods are made in China, where animal cruelty is not prohibited. Their collective silence is deafening and altogether revealing about the question of race in a capitalistic society like America, where they can denounce Vick[78] but continue to do business with China. Even though the NFL reinstated Vick in

---

78 http://nytimes.com/2007/08/01/sports/football/01sandomir.html.

2009, and Nike re-signed him in 2011, these companies, which took a position against him, should condemn China's systemic slaughtering of dogs. Additionally, it is incumbent upon athletes, particularly blacks who play in the NFL and who endorse the products of Nike and Reebok, to implore these organizations to condemn what China does to innocent dogs. Furthermore, these athletes should enjoin American corporations to pressure the communist state to adopt laws against animal cruelty. The athletes and organizations should know that in the absence of their doing so, their silence equals complicity.

Although Vick's actions against the dogs were illegal and wrong, there was plenty of wrong to go around. The general reaction from the NFL and its dominant allies was effective in not only making Vick the face of animal cruelty, but he easily became the most hated sports figure in America. Moreover, the actions of the NFL against Vick reflected a history of racial discrimination against blacks. Additionally, the league used its significant influence over the media to quell any support for the quarterback. Once more, the media never questioned the NFL about doing business with a country whose rampant rate of animal cruelty is unrivaled throughout the world. Yet the NFL continues to pay China to broadcast its programming. All of this helps explain why the networks and other media sources have not questioned the NFL. But why hasn't Congress questioned such matters?

American taxpayers, who contribute mightily to the NFL's wealth, and Congress, which regulates the NFL's business with China as foreign commerce, should be concerned. Congress has not held the NFL to the Vick standard in its business relation-ship with China. Vick's animal cruelty prompted members of Congress to demand the NFL take swift action against the quar-terback. Yet nothing from Congress has been heard on the NFL's business relationship with China, whose debauchery against dogs is, perhaps, unparalleled the world over. In fact, the only dogs that are protected from acts of animal cruelty in China are state-owned dogs. Hence, not only have more than 100,000 dogs been killed in recent years, but millions more are slaughtered each year for the illicit fur trade. Perhaps the most alarming aspect of all is that China's contempt for dogs reportedly stems from its view of the animal as a bourgeois affectation of capitalism, a symbol of Western culture and the economic system that exists in America. The adverse reaction to Vick versus no reaction to China is owing to the latter's status as an economic superpower. By contrast, Vick is seen by the NFL and its alliance of superstructures as the super-masculine menial.

The next chapter will discuss the impact of conservative talk show host Rush Limbaugh's comments in 2003 that contributed to Michael Vick being relabeled as a black quarterback. Additionally, in 2009, Limbaugh recorded a public service announcement for the Humane Society of the United States which contributed mightily to Vick being seen as the face of animal cruelty.

CHAPTER IV

Limbaugh's Lunacy:

Relabeling "People like Michael Vick"

"Rush (Limbaugh) is a great communicator and a fan with an acute sense of what's on the minds of listeners, combined with his ability to entertain and serve as a lightning rod for lively discussion, makes him the perfect fit for this new role."
—ESPN Executive Vice President Mark Shapiro, 2003[79]

In 2003 ESPN hired the controversial and socially conservative radio talk show host Rush Limbaugh for their *Sunday NFL Countdown* pre-game show, believing he would "provide the voice of the fan and to spark debate on the show," according to ESPN.[80] But if ESPN really believed that Limbaugh would provide the voice of the fan, then their fans must be divisive, vitriolic, and also of the opinion that the media and the NFL wanted to see black quarterbacks succeed out of social concern, as Limbaugh would state. According to Mark Shapiro, Executive Vice President of ESPN, the network sought Limbaugh's commentary to serve as a *lightning rod for lively discussion* (www.profootballweekly.com, 2003). Not only did Limbaugh serve as a lightning rod, but his controversial remarks against blacks as quarterbacks in the NFL would ignite a firestorm of racial discord in the NFL and America. Why would ESPN seek

---

79 http://profootballweekly.com/PFW/Features/They+Said+It/2003/said45.htm.
80 http://www.sptimes.com/2003/07/15/Sports/Limbaugh_to_join_ESPN.shtml.

such a volatile personality in Limbaugh for its popular NFL show? On the one hand, it seems obvious the network believed Limbaugh would boost its ratings for ESPN's *Sunday NFL Countdown,* which did occur.[81] Although ESPN's decision to hire Limbaugh increased its ratings, quite predictably, it also increased their risks.

The network was fully aware of Limbaugh's propensity for contentious commentary, but apparently appreciated more that his radio show is broadcast in up to 650 markets (NFL.com, 2003). Limbaugh has a strong following, especially among millions of young white males, the primary target audience of the NFL and their corporate sponsors. Furthermore, there are a host of NFL owners and executives that revere and respect Limbaugh. For example, Alex Spanos, owner of the San Diego Chargers, had Limbaugh write the foreword to his book, *Sharing the Wealth* (Spanos, 2002). Bobby Beathard, a former general manager with the Chargers and Washington Redskins, was said to have kept a picture of Limbaugh on the wall in his office. As late as 2009, there was serious talk of Rush Limbaugh becoming part of an NFL ownership group with Dave Checketts that was interested in purchasing the St. Louis Rams. Limbaugh is a native of Missouri and a self-professed fan of the game. Ultimately, the plan for NFL ownership was discarded due to strong public opposition from current and former African-American players. Left alone, the NFL was apparently open to the idea of Limbaugh joining its ownership brass. According to the controversial talk show host, he anticipated a negative public reaction, but was reassured that the idea was cleared at the highest levels of the league. Undoubtedly, this was a veiled reference to NFL Commissioner Roger Goodell and team owners, a significant number of whom are conservative Republicans. Throughout its existence the NFL has been a very conservative league that has been resistant to social change, especially on racial diversity. At no other position has there been greater opposition to blacks in the NFL than at starting quarterback.

---

81 http://www.usatoday.com/sports/columnist/martzke/2003-10-01-martzke_x.htm.

Historically all facets of the media, including radio, were instrumental in creating and perpetuating racial stereotypes of African-Americans, including the label of *black quarterback*. Furthermore, as this discussion will highlight, rather than the label being used to help blacks succeed at quarterback, it actually undermined their potential for success. Additionally, this review will demonstrate that subsequent to Limbaugh's racially charged remarks, which led to his firing at ESPN, a noticeably negative shift in the sports media's coverage of black quarterbacks followed. This change was particularly observable in succeeding NFL drafts beginning in 2004, just months after his blundering rant. Subsequent NFL drafts would show that rather than the media exhibiting social concern for black quarterbacks, they appeared to follow Limbaugh's lead by diminishing the value of blacks as quarterback prospects in favor of white prospects. In an ironic twist, it was during the 2007 NFL draft when reports first began surfacing that Atlanta Falcons All-Pro quarterback Michael Vick, the first overall pick of the 2001 draft, was involved in illegal dog fighting.

The following chapter will explain that Vick's legal dilemma not only became a lightning rod for controversy; it also became the perfect storm for the NFL and sports media to rail against the notion perpetuated by Limbaugh that they wanted to see a black quarterback succeed out of social concern. Additionally, it will be shown that Limbaugh never forgot that his criticisms of black quarterbacks cost him his dream job as an analyst on ESPN covering NFL football. In 2009, when Michael Vick was released from prison, he would find Rush Limbaugh lurking in the shadows. In an apparent attempt to once more evince his utter contempt for black quarterbacks, who, perhaps in his mind, cost him his perch on ESPN, he exacted what seemed to be an act of revenge against Michael Vick.

In April 2009, Limbaugh recorded a public service announcement for the Humane Society of the United States (HSUS) in which he chided Vick. The timing of the announcement not only coincided with Vick's release, but oddly enough, it occurred after the Humane Society agreed to collaborate with the beleaguered quarterback on his road to redemption. Consistent with his attempts to label others as he sees fit, Limbaugh derided street fighters of dogs as "people like Michael Vick." However, it is white males who have always been principals in the blood sport of dog fighting and remain as such. This chapter will also show that subsequent to Limbaugh's public service announcement, which placed greater attention on "street toughs," the number of African-Americans arrested and convicted for dog fighting increased sharply. Conversely, the number of whites decreased.

While Chapter VII addresses various dog fighting types (i.e., professional, hobbyists, and street fighters), this chapter will touch on other forms of animal cruelty (i.e., neglect, hoarding, abuse, bestiality, etc.) that are often overlooked but no doubt harmful in our society. Before discussing the wider impact of Limbaugh's comments and other incendiary insinuations that interplay with this narrative on Michael Vick, I will review Limbaugh's comments about black quarterbacks. I intend to not only debunk Limbaugh's ridiculous and racist rhetoric, but will also present a framework for a larger perspective on the history of structural racism in the NFL. I'll include a retro-analysis of the harmful effects of being labeled a black quarterback in the NFL. I argue that the tradition of racial intolerance toward African-Americans as quarterbacks in the NFL contributed to the venomous and vitriolic reaction against Michael Vick, more so than just his involvement in dog fighting warranted. I'll show that revelations of Vick's involvement in the illegal blood sport played into the hands of the NFL and media. As a social reaction, the NFL and media made it clear there was no such social concern for black quarterbacks with Michael Vick as Exhibit A. Before delving into this broader discussion, the outstanding question remains: why did ESPN hire Rush Limbaugh in the first place?

Why Did ESPN Hire Limbaugh?

ESPN is renowned for its popular "Top 10" highlight reel, which shows the most exciting sports plays every day. By contrast, the network's decision to hire Rush Limbaugh was listed in the top ten (number eight overall) of *GQ Magazine's* twenty-eight worst decisions ever made in television.[82] While ESPN conceded that it hired Limbaugh to be a lightning rod for discussion, the network got more than it bargained for. Were there other underlying factors that seemed to influence the popular sports network to take such an ill-fated risk? We later learned that a multitude of white fans apparently shared Limbaugh's thoughts about black quarterbacks. In the aftermath of his remarks, many of them expressed support for his controversial comments.

Stunningly, Limbaugh had the unmitigated gall to imply that the media showed social concern for black quarterbacks while working for ESPN, the so-called "Worldwide Leader" in sports. The twisted irony is that the television network is also the worldwide leader in hiring former quarterbacks who are white to work as NFL analysts. In fact, at the time Limbaugh made his baseless remarks about then Philadelphia Eagles quarterback Donovan McNabb and black quarterbacks in general, ESPN had as many as five former NFL quarterbacks, all of whom were white, working for the network on NFL shows. Such a representation of former league quarterbacks working for ESPN hardly suggested any social concern for black quarterbacks. Just the opposite, it reinforced the perception that white quarterbacks understand the game better than blacks and therefore should be the preferred norm at this leadership position in the NFL.

It is also worth noting, ESPN hired Limbaugh after the NFL adopted its interviewing mandate, which was then called the minority hiring policy, also known as the Rooney Rule. It now requires NFL teams to interview minority candidates for head coaching and front office management positions. Many observers of NFL football, including the media and fans alike, did not appreciate this form of affirmative action. This no doubt had Limbaugh, among others, seething. While the media's attention to Limbaugh's racial remarks focused on McNabb, who was mentioned by name, lost in the shuffle was that he also targeted "minority coaches." Are there other factors that explain why

---

82 *GQ*, October 2012. *The XVIII Worst Decisions in Sports History.*

ESPN took such a calculated gamble in hiring the politically conservative radio host who had no particular background as a football analyst? It seems fairly obvious that someone at Disney, which owns both ABC and ESPN, harbored an affinity for Limbaugh. In 2000, he auditioned to join ABC's *Monday Night Football* before joining ESPN in 2003. How could ESPN have believed Rush Limbaugh might amount to a qualified studio analyst on ESPN's *Sunday NFL Countdown* given his penchant for partisan and problematic political perspectives?

Within the first month of his new job with ESPN, Limbaugh answered the question in the negative. First, he sought to diminish the import of the league's "minority hiring policy," although his comments did not yield much attention. Not to be discouraged, in the weeks that followed he upped the ante with racially inflammatory remarks, suggesting black males as quarterbacks and head coaches were beneficiaries of "social concern" from the NFL and a media that was "desirous" to see them succeed (Martze, 2003). While ESPN would eventually fire him for what many blacks and others perceived as rabble-rousing racism, the damage of his delusional and discordant denunciation could not be undone. Subsequent to Limbaugh's lunacy on ESPN, there was an observable shift in the media coverage of blacks as quarterbacks in the NFL. Limbaugh's comments spurred a spate of subversive sports reporting against such quarterbacks. In addition, Limbaugh's remarks relabeled such players as *black quarterbacks*, while using Philadelphia Eagles quarterback Donovan McNabb as a case in point. In the months and years that followed, blacks as quarterbacks in the NFL would suffer a range of insults and less favorable media attention than their white counterparts. This was never more apparent than during the Michael Vick dog fighting scandal, which completely disavowed the suggestion of social concern for a black quarterback. Furthermore, Limbaugh's virulent views about the NFL and the media being partial to blacks at quarterback were totally incongruent with reality, both historically and presently.

Blacks attempting to play quarterback in the NFL have experienced some of the harshest forms of structural racism from the league and the sports reporting media. Rather than the media harboring any unique consideration for them, as Limbaugh suggested, the social concern and desire to see quarterbacks succeed has seemingly been reserved for white quarterbacks. Before discussing the effects of Limbaugh's remarks against blacks at quarterback in the NFL, it is important to review in brief Limbaugh's statements on ESPN.

Wide Right II: No ESP at ESPN

Rush Limbaugh wasted no time at ESPN launching an attack on black quarterbacks. Limbaugh's decision stemmed from his awareness that this leadership position was traditionally exclusive to whites. That Limbaugh strayed off course with his rhetorical ramblings on race was but another indicator that his hiring by ESPN harbored neither rhyme nor reason in preparing football fans for NFL games. The job that Limbaugh had on the set of ESPN was odd enough. He was placed alone at a studio desk by himself, away from the entire cast of *Sunday NFL Countdown.* There he could issue a "challenge" that allowed him to interject during commentary from other analysts on the show. The challenge granted to him was a poorly conceived parody of the NFL's own challenge rule that grants head coaches the power to halt the game to contest a ruling on the field. That Limbaugh would be edified to a role akin to a head coach on a sports network show was another sign there was a lack of fit and reality to his role.

The 2003 cast for *NFL Countdown* included Emmy Award-winning host Chris Berman and former All-Pro NFL players turned studio analysts Tom Jackson, Steve Young, and Michael Irvin. Jackson, Young, and Irvin had stellar careers as All-Pro football players in the NFL with eight Super Bowl appearances between them. The three former All-Pros were expected to offer a reliable insider's perspective to complement Berman's expertise as a sports broadcaster. But what did Rush Limbaugh have to offer besides the potential for controversy? Limbaugh would not last past the first month of the NFL regular season before his propensity for polemical polarization came into play. During a week four discussion on ESPN's *Sunday NFL Countdown,* Limbaugh indicated live on air that Philadelphia Eagles starting quarterback Donovan McNabb, an All-Pro, who is black, was never as good as he had been touted, but had been given too much credit for the team's success by the media that was "desirous that a black quarterback do well," out of "social concern" (Martzke, 2003, p. 1). Limbaugh's comments were widely perceived as a personal attack rather than a professional assessment of McNabb, who had already established himself as one of the best quarterbacking talents in the game. Moreover, his contentious critique of McNabb seemed especially harsh and untimely given that the season was only in its first month. Furthermore, it is not uncommon for a veteran quarterback to struggle with a couple of bad games only to bounce back. McNabb should have been no exception.

When the Baltimore Ravens won the Super Bowl in 2000, its offense failed to score a single touchdown for the entire month of October. Trent Dilfer, who is white, became the starter on October 29 of the season. Although the Ravens went 7-1 with Dilfer as the starter, the defense was the catalyst. Yet no one sought to discredit him as a beneficiary of a great defense, nor did anyone suggest the NFL and the media were desirous to see a white quarterback succeed out of social concern. Because Dilfer did not have to answer such controversial questions on race as McNabb did, he simply rode the wave of the Baltimore Ravens defense, which led the team to a Super Bowl championship. To further underscore the latter point, the Ravens released Dilfer shortly after winning the Super Bowl. Incidentally, Dilfer currently works for ESPN as an analyst on NFL programming. His ability to become a Super Bowl champion quarterback on the strength of a dominant defense only to retire and become an analyst on ESPN's NFL programming is a revealing irony. It underscores how fallacious Limbaugh's remarks were, that the media was desirous to see a black quarterback succeed.

To further underline how imprudent Limbaugh's comments were, if there was so much social concern for black quarterbacks in the media, why didn't someone on the *Countdown* set criticize Limbaugh's remarks? McNabb himself questioned as much, noting that even the cameraman should have said something. Moreover, no other media source raised a question about the controversial remarks. In fact, Limbaugh's statements only became a national story when U.S. Senator John F. Kerry, an aspiring Democratic presidential candidate, made it an issue. To further accentuate how nonsensical Limbaugh's remarks were, beside ESPN, television networks that partner with the NFL, including CBS, Fox, Showtime, NBC, and previously ABC and HBO, share a historical tradition of hiring former quarterbacks as NFL analysts who have invariably been white. All of which has allowed them to sustain their occupational dominance at quarterback in the NFL. Hence, even in today's game, where blacks represent nearly two out of every three football players in the NFL, white males dominate at starting quarterback by a ratio of eight to two. Such occupational dominance by whites is consistent with their occupational dominance in broadcasting roles with television networks that partner with the NFL. Even more striking, Limbaugh's comments were particularly backward given the history of the pejorative term *black quarterback*. It disparaged African-Americans to no end and curtailed their chances of becoming successful quarterbacks in the NFL. Moreover, his use of the term created a hierarchy of naming, which actually favors white quarterbacks. Sabo and Messner describe this *hierarchy of naming* as "a linguistic vehicle for reinforcing status differences…between whites and blacks" (p. 151). Such derogatory labeling of African-Americans playing quarterback misplaced the focus on their race rather than their talents, which worked to their disadvantage in the NFL.

Labeling

Perhaps no other people in America have been more adversely affected by the harmful effects of labeling than African-Americans. Labeling theory speaks to the social process whereby individuals, groups, and organizations with social power negatively label others with less social power. Such labeling will impact the social interaction between those labeled and those doing the labeling. The larger consequence of such pejorative labeling is that it can influence the social reaction of the wider society against the groups so labeled. Hence, racial prejudice and discrimination against groups like African-Americans have remained commonplace in our society. Throughout their often calamitous journey in America, from slavery to freedom, racial stereotypes have plagued blacks in perpetuity. Even worse, blacks who attempt to demonstrate their worthiness are often saddled by such negative suggestions about them. This lackluster ideation, often perpetuated by the media, is rooted in falsehood rather than facts. Even stereotypes of blacks as lazy, shiftless, ignorant, and animalistic have prevailed with a degree of permanence, permeating every facet of their social lives. Perhaps in no other sphere of American cultural life have stereotypes been more visibly pronounced than the canvas of spectator sports. Ironically enough, the labeling theory, which is a branch of the social reaction perspectives, re-emerged in the 1960s, just as social scientists were paying closer attention to issues of race in sports institutions like the NFL. Sociologists were particularly drawn to the manner in which black players were steered away from coveted, so-called thinking positions like quarterback.

Centrality in the NFL

The idea of *centrality* held that whites would be assigned to positions of central importance like middle linebacker, offensive center, and quarterback, given the need for intelligence (Ashe, 1993; Loy & McElvogue, 1971). This unwritten rule in the NFL, which assigned blacks to skilled positions that relied more on athleticism like running back, wide receiver, and defensive back, became known as *stacking.* As much as we would like to believe that these practices have changed, the data on assigned positions on NFL teams suggest otherwise. Hoose (1989) found that the further an offensive player is away from the football, the more likely he is to be black. These trends have changed very little in recent years. According to the 2009 report on race and gender in the NFL, whites were still eight in ten starting quarterbacks; they are also the majority of offensive centers (seventy-four percent) and guards (fifty-three percent), while a slight majority of offensive tackles, which require more athleticism, are African-Americans (fifty-one percent).[83] In addition, running backs and wide receivers, which are skilled positions in the NFL, are filled by African-Americans at a rate of eighty-five and eighty-nine percent respectively. Still, the disdainful labeling that blacks have been subject to in football goes back to the nineteenth and twentieth centuries' when newspapers, newsreels, movies, radio, and television, all perpetuated racist ideas of black football players as sambos, savages, and later the mindless super-masculine menial. These stereotypes were used to appease white fans who preferred to not see blacks playing the game of football, a sport that from its origins was created for young white males (Oriard, 2001). The enduring legacy of such racist stereotypes is that they left an indelible mark on black players, forever shaping their participation in the gridiron game. At no position did such negative stereotypes have a more adverse impact than at quarterback. One of the most awful outcomes of Limbaugh's lunacy expressed on ESPN was that he reopened old wounds of racism when he relabeled African-Americans as *black quarterbacks*. The reference called attention to the players' race first, which had the effect of overshadowing their talents. It also created this hierarchy of naming, which reinforced status differences between quarterbacks who are black and white, which favored the latter. Quarterbacks who are white were simply referred to by their names, rather than their race, which created the impression they were amply qualified. By contrast, the idea of a black quarterback not only brought attention to their race but also to the weighty burden of discrimination in America. The next section will review the tumultuous history associated with the term *black quarterback*. I will show unequivocally that the idea

---

83 The Race and Gender Report Card: National Football League (2009). By Richard Lapchick with Chris Kamke and Derek McMechan.

of a black quarterback never bred any social concern from the media or the NFL. Rather than having any influence on such a quarterback's success, it actually quickened the demise of many. This history is important to review, not only in debunking the misguided notion that African-Americans were beneficiaries of preferential treatment, but to underscore the significant social harm associated with the undercutting effects of labeling. Had Michael Vick been better informed about the perils, pitfalls, and pathologies associated with African-Americans being typecast as black quarterbacks, perhaps he would have avoided the pathway that claimed his freedom for nearly two years.

The "Black Quarterback"

Rush Limbaugh's erroneous suggestion that the media and the NFL wanted to see black quarterbacks succeed has no fit with reality during any time in history. In the NFL, being identified as a black quarterback curtailed many careers and simply killed others.

Throughout the twentieth century, a multitude of outstanding quarterbacks were denied their rightful chance to compete for starting positions because of their race, even when they demonstrated their capabilities. Shortly after the NFL's gentlemen's agreement ended, which barred blacks from 1934-1946, black quarterbacks like George Taliaferro and Willie Thrower made inroads into the quarterback ranks of the NFL during the 1950s. Taliaferro, who alternated between halfback and quarterback, was an All-Pro on three different teams. Thrower had an outstanding career as a quarterback at Michigan State and longed for a career as a passer in the NFL. But one game in Thrower's career underscored the pangs associated with being labeled a black quarterback in the NFL.

In a 1953 contest between the Chicago Bears and the San Francisco 49ers, George Halas, head coach of the Bears, sent in Thrower to replace an ineffective George Blanda. Thrower went three for eight passing, moving the Bears into scoring position at the 49ers four yard line. Then Halas substituted Thrower out in favor of Blanda, and the Bears scored a touchdown. When the press asked Halas to explain why he substituted Thrower in that situation, he claimed the team was using plays Thrower wasn't familiar with. In truth it seems rather obvious why the change was made. Halas did not want to embarrass Blanda, who was white and who was being outshined by a quarterback who was black. Realizing he had no future playing quarterback in the NFL, Thrower ultimately left to play football in the Canadian Football League (CFL). Sadly enough, many African-Americans who wanted to play quarterback in the NFL had to realize their dreams north of the border.

From the Not Fair League to the Canadian Football League

Hoose (1989) reports that during a time in which NFL teams simply did not play black quarterbacks, between fifty and 100 had to play in the CFL. As early as 1951, when Bernie Curtis, an ex-Syracuse University star quarterback, played in Canada, black quarterbacks were accepted in the CFL. In but another contorted irony, history has recorded that thousands of black slaves escaped to Canada to find freedom unavailable in America in the nineteenth century. Yet in the twentieth century, remnants of such racism forced blacks who were not free to play quarterback in the NFL to go to Canada. Others to follow included Sandy Stephens, who excelled at the University at Minnesota, where he led his team to a win in the Rose Bowl. He arrived in the NFL in 1961, eight years after the departure of Thrower.

After being drafted by the Cleveland Browns in the second round, Stephens was traded to the Detroit Lions, who had no plans to use him at quarterback. Stephens reminded the coaches that he was first-team All-American and a Heisman candidate at quarterback, and therefore wanted a shot to compete for the position. He was told the team already had that position set, but at running back he would "throw the option pass every now and then" (Hoose, p. 56). Like others before him, Stephens eventually left the NFL for the CFL to play quarterback. Perplexed, his parents once asked him, "Why is it we have to go all the way to Canada to see you play (quarterback) before people who aren't even our own countrymen?" (Hoose, 1989: p.56). Other black quarterbacks, such as J.C. Watts, who starred at the University of Oklahoma (1977-1981), and Warren Moon, of the University of Washington, played in the CFL (1978-1983) because of structural racism in the NFL, which demanded that they change their position. Watts had success playing for several CFL teams from 1981 to 1986. The New York Jets drafted him in the eighth round with the intentions of making him a running back. Incidentally, Watts was the offensive MVP of the Grey Cup as a rookie in the 1981 title game against Moon's Edmonton Eskimos, which prevailed. Moon, who won six Grey Cup championships, including five in a row, was the game's MVP (p. 52). Despite leading his University of Washington team to a Rose Bowl championship in 1978 against Michigan, Moon was not drafted by any NFL team to play quarterback. Moon would later sign with the Houston Oilers in 1984 for what was at the time the richest deal in the history of the NFL. When Moon retired from the NFL after a very successful career and a number of playoff and Pro Bowl appearances, he had over 60,000 passing yards as a quarterback in both the CFL and NFL. In 2006 he was named to the Pro Football Hall of Fame on his first time on the ballot. Although he retired from the NFL having never won a Super Bowl, he left the game with a more significant victory: his dignity and the distinction of defeating structural racism in the NFL. After Watts's playing career in the CFL concluded, he returned to his home state of Oklahoma and eventually won a seat to the House of Representatives as a Republican member of the United States Congress. One cannot help but wonder what Watts thought of his fellow Republican, Rush Limbaugh, given his remarks about black quarterbacks benefitting from social concern in the NFL. While many of the aforementioned quarterbacks seemed to shake off the harmful effects of being called a black quarterback, others were not so fortunate.

The reluctance to play blacks at the marquee position in football was widespread throughout the league and articulated from the highest office of the NFL. In his 1975 book *Pioneers of Black Sport*, Ocania Chalk observed, "The positional discrimination at quarterback has an ally in the office of the (NFL) football commissioner" (p. 238). In commenting on the non-use of black quarterbacks as early as 1969, Commissioner Rozelle stated, "… many of your Negro football players (quarterbacks) have not had the early football training that the white boys had…" (p. 238). The commissioner's comments were a veiled reference to black quarterbacks from historically black colleges and universities, some of the only institutions that allowed blacks to excel at quarterback in college football. On the other hand, NFL teams had used predominantly white colleges as their pipeline for white quarterbacks, which is what Rozelle's comments were alluding to. Rozelle's comments reflected how insincere the league was on the question of racial discrimination at the quarterback position. For example, Willie Thrower had starred at Michigan State, where he completed over sixty percent of his passes in the 1950s, and Sandy Stephens excelled at the University of Minnesota as an All-American quarterback in the 1960s. But they were denied an opportunity to play quarterback in the NFL despite excelling at these national powerhouses. The observations by Rozelle make it abundantly clear that unlike what Limbaugh suggested on ESPN, there was never any desire to see black quarterbacks succeed in the NFL. While historically black colleges were considered inferior football programs that produced less capable quarterbacks, these notions too would be debunked.

In 1987 Doug Williams, an African-American quarterback from Grambling State University, a historically black college, led the Washington Redskins to a Super Bowl blowout, 42-10, against John Elway of predominantly white Stanford University and his Denver Broncos. Williams's play was so outstanding he was named the game's MVP. This stunning outcome not only trounced the Broncos but also Rozelle's theory that the "Negro boys" were unable to play quarterback in the NFL because they lacked the training of the white boys. But before

Williams could triumph, there would be many trials and tribulations for African-Americans attempting to play quarterback in the NFL. It is a history that the Michael Vick's of the world should be required to study—a history that ESPN should have studied before it hired the likes of Rush Limbaugh. For even when African-Americans were good enough to start and lead, the negative notion of being a black quarterback undermined their chances.

Eldridge Dickey: "The Lord's Prayer"

In his book *Michael Vick: Finally Free*, Vick (2012), who attended Virginia Tech, extolled the distinction of being the first African-American quarterback drafted first overall in the NFL. In 1968, Eldridge Dickey of Tennessee State, a historically black college, became the first black at quarterback to be drafted in the first round when he was selected by the Oakland Raiders. But structural barriers associated with being labeled a black quarterback would ultimately prevent Dickey from succeeding in the NFL. In an open competition for starting quarterback, Dickey, whose nickname was the "Lord's Prayer," beat out Ken Stabler, who was also drafted in 1968, but in the second round, out of the University of Alabama. Stabler, who was left-handed, was no match for Dickey, whose ambidextrous skill-set allowed him to throw the ball with both his right and left hands. Rather than accept that Dickey won the competition fair and square, Stabler quit and would not return until 1970. On the other hand, despite Dickey's talents, he was tarnished by the label of a black quarterback and had to switch his position to wide receiver to remain with the team. Sadly, Dickey's career never amounted to anything in the NFL, no matter that he was the rarest of talents at quarterback. The trials associated with being labeled a black quarterback and being denied an opportunity to play the position in the NFL seemed to influence his descent into drug addiction. The same year that Dickey became the first black quarterback to be drafted in the first round, Marlin "The Magician" Briscoe, a rookie for the

Denver Broncos, became the first black to start at quarterback in the modern era.

Marlin "The Magician" Briscoe

While Vick has the distinction of being the most gifted quarterback in the NFL, given his ability to throw and run, the first quarterback to showcase such rare gifts among African-Americans in the modern era was Marlin Briscoe. Nicknamed "The Magician," given his unique playmaking abilities, he starred at Omaha University because the University at Nebraska did not recruit him to play quarterback. At Omaha he set passing records as a collegian. Still, he was drafted by the Denver Broncos of the AFL to play defensive back. Since Briscoe had the option of going to Canada's CFL to play quarterback, he used the leverage to negotiate a three-day tryout at the position with the Broncos. He seized the opportunity and dominated the throwing drills, despite receiving far less repetitions than the white quarterbacks. During his rookie season, the Broncos' quarterbacking corps was depleted by injuries, which thrust Briscoe into action by default. He excelled by setting a rookie passing record for the Broncos in throwing fourteen touchdown passes against thirteen interceptions in just five starts. To further underscore Briscoe's output at quarterback, Hall of Famer John Elway threw the same number of touchdown passes as a rookie quarterback for the Denver Broncos, but in twice as many starts, in 1983. Briscoe's performance at quarterback in just five starts earned him runner-up for AFL Rookie of the Year in 1968. Despite his heroics, he proved to be too good for his own good. Because of structural racism associated with being a black quarterback in the NFL, Briscoe would never play the position again. He would later say of Broncos head coach Lou Saban, "I believed it was racial." Years later Saban would say it was his size, but Briscoe stated the head coach "simply would not have a black QB (quarterback)" (Briscoe, 2002, p.107). He was released by the Broncos and ultimately signed by the Buffalo Bills, who changed his position to wide receiver.

Briscoe starred at the position and made All-Pro his first year. Incidentally, in Briscoe's first year with the Buffalo Bills, the team drafted James Harris, a quarterback who is black, out of Grambling State University.

James Harris

Among the teams who reportedly showed interest in signing Michael Vick after he was released from prison in 2009 were the Buffalo Bills. The mere interest in Vick was striking because aside from the controversy surrounding his dog fighting crimes, forty years earlier the team refused to play a black quarterback. In 1969, the Buffalo Bills drafted James Harris out of Grambling State University in the eighth round. Despite having the physical tools to play the position in the NFL, Harris's career in Buffalo did not amount to much. In three seasons, he started just three games as quarterback. This was hardly an opportunity to show his mettle at the most coveted position in the NFL. Moreover, his three years in Buffalo were marred by racial intolerance. According to Harris, he received racially charged hate mail on a regular basis including death threats, which led him to conclude "it did not pay to be black in Buffalo" (Knox, 1988). Harris stated, "There was a lot of hate mail, a lot of name-calling during that time, a lot of postcards with negative pictures" (*Buffalo News*, Mark Gaughn, Sports 2/23/04). Harris never got the chance to prove his worth at quarterback in Buffalo and later signed with the Los Angeles Rams as a free agent in 1973, where he was named the starter in the sixth game of the 1974 season. Harris, who was genuinely surprised by the move, stated, "…Knox (the head coach) comes in one day and tells me I am the starter, and I think, does he know what he's doing? Remember, although I was the backup quarterback, I am black" (Knox, 1988, p. 150). Would race be a factor in how Harris was treated by Rams fans? Despite leading the Rams to consecutive NFC West division titles in 1974 and 1975, as well as two appearances in the NFC Championship games, and a Pro Bowl selection in 1975, Harris frequently received racist hate mail, including death threats, given his identity as a black quarterback. His head coach, Chuck Knox, attempted to hold the quarterback's hate mail so it would not reach him. Harris observed, "He (Knox) said he held my mail? He sure didn't hold all of it. I would get terrible letters on a regular basis. I remember one letter contained a drawing of Knox and me in a toilet, being flushed down together. I would get two or three letters like that a day" (Knox, p. 154). Eventually, pressure from fans and the team's owner resulted in Harris being benched in 1976, notwithstanding back-to-back appearances in the NFC Conference Championship. Despite losing the starting job in week six of the season, and that his replacement Pat Haden started seven games at quarterback, Harris still finished the season as the team's leader in passing yards. Harris later stated, "As a quarterback I had done all I could, more than most people could, and it still wasn't enough for the Los Angeles Rams to accept me just as a quarterback, not a black quarterback" (Knox, p. 158). Clearly, Harris's comments indicate the negative impact of being labeled a black quarterback, which contributed to this hierarchy of naming. He would later remark that in the NFL you get two chances to play quarterback, "a chance and a nigger chance" (Ashe, 1993, p. 45). While Harris's promising playing career was cut down by racism in the NFL, he has had success as a front office executive with the Baltimore Ravens (Super Bowl champs in 2000), the Jacksonville Jaguars, and currently with the Detroit Lions. But during the same years when Harris was looking for a fair chance to prove himself at quarterback, Joe Gilliam of Tennessee State was attempting to do the same with the Pittsburgh Steelers.

Jefferson St. Joe Gilliam

While Michael Vick is renowned for his quick, snap-like throwing motion, Jefferson St. Joe Gilliam had a quick release side-arm throw that could strike like a cobra. He was an extraordinary talent, but like Dickey, Briscoe, and Harris, he had to contend with being labeled a black quarterback in the NFL. He was drafted in 1972 out of Tennessee State by the Pittsburgh Steelers. Tennessee State is the same HBCU (Historically Black Colleges and Universities) that produced Elridge Dickey. So Gilliam was aware of the trials and tribulations associated with attempting to play quarterback in the NFL for people like him. Despite having the quick release and superior physical tools, Gilliam's race became a factor. After he was named the starting quarterback of the Pittsburgh Steelers in 1974, he led the team to a dominating victory over the Baltimore Colts in the season opener. While Gilliam's performance should have quelled the media's preoccupation with his race, the label was magnified when *Sports Illustrated* (1974) featured him on its cover with the title "Pittsburgh's Black Quarterback." The negative influence of the media against Gilliam increased when a Pittsburgh newspaper conducted a fan poll, asking who should be the team's starter at quarterback. Terry Bradshaw, who the Steelers drafted number one overall in 1970, but had been benched, placed second behind Terry Hanratty in the poll, while Gilliam finished third. Despite leading the team to a successful start at 4-1-1, his time as starting quarterback was mired by racial taunts and death threats. He was benched in 1974 after the sixth game of the season. Rather than the media showing any social concern for Gilliam as a black quarterback, just the opposite occurred. After being benched by the Steelers, his career was never the same and his life spiraled out of control given his addiction to drugs. The burden of structural racism through negative labeling was confounding to a young Gilliam, but toward the end of his life reality settled in. In 1999 he told a reporter for the *Tennessean* (Nashville), "I thought if you played well, you got to play. I guess I did not understand the significance of being a black quarterback (in the NFL) at the time" (Briscoe, p. 161). Unfortunately, Gilliam's story shows how the burden of being labeled a black quarterback in the NFL can have dire consequences. Sadly, his life ended tragically due to a drug overdose on Christmas Day, 2000.

Gilliam's ill-fated outcome stemmed, in no small measure from the strain of racial stratification at the quarterback position. In more than a strange coincidence, Briscoe found that he, Dickey, and Gilliam all had problems with drug addiction, which he attributed to the racism they experienced in the NFL, which included the negative identity associated with being labeled a black quarterback.

This historical review shows that contrary to what Limbaugh suggested, the term *black quarterback* was never used by the media or the NFL to benefit blacks or as a sign of concern. Instead, the suggestion created a hierarchy of naming that favored white quarterbacks over black quarterbacks. Limbaugh's decision to resurrect this racist relic was only part of the problem. The media covering the NFL, which Limbaugh chided, seemed to intentionally counteract his suggestion by interjecting the term "pedigree" in the league's lexicon. The use of the term shaped a new form of hierarchy in naming. This concept, which became an indirect reference to white quarterbacks, was introduced during the 2004 NFL draft and followed Limbaugh's remarks on ESPN.

The 2004 NFL Draft and the Advent of "Pedigree"

In 2004, just months after Limbaugh's racially charged remarks on ESPN, there were indicators of an undercurrent of media backlash against blacks playing quarterback in the NFL. First, there were no black quarterbacks drafted in the first round of the NFL draft in 2004. Between 1999 and 2003, several blacks were drafted as quarterbacks in the first round. They included Steve McNair, Donovan McNabb, Dante Culpepper, Byron Leftwich, and Michael Vick — all of whom had success in the league. But in the first NFL draft following Limbaugh's attempts to diminish the stature of black quarterbacks, all of the quarterbacks drafted in the first round were white. They included Eli Manning, Philip Rivers, Ben Roethlisberger, and J.P. Losman. While Roethlisberger and Rivers were highly regarded, the biggest media story of the draft's class became Eli Manning and this newly-minted notion of quarterbacking "pedigree." The term speaks to an individual being connected to an ancestry, family background, or history. Although, the media used the Mannings to project a family pedigree of NFL quarterbacks, history has shown that white quarterbacks were portrayed as a unique pedigree, all their own.

The traditional idea of quarterbacking pedigree in the NFL embodies the characteristics of leadership and intelligence, which blacks were supposed to be bereft of. Hence they were not allowed to play the position. Given the emergence of this notion, which came on the heels of Limbaugh's indictment of the media, sports reporters covering the NFL seemed deliberately intent on edifying white males at quarterback like never before. It is not clear if the Manning family wittingly or unwittingly emerged as the model to inculcate the notion of pedigree into the league's lexicon. But this newer concept, which fortified white males as the preferred norm at quarterback, used the Mannings as Exhibit A, with the NFL draft as the backdrop.

"Pedigree," the Manning Model

The Manning family made a huge media splash at the 2004 NFL draft when Eli, the projected first pick out of Ole Miss, where his father Archie once played, openly dissuaded the San Diego Chargers from drafting him. Eli had indicated that if the Chargers picked him, he would forgo his NFL career and attend law school. Even more peculiar than Eli's stance was the sight of his father, former All-Pro NFL quarterback Archie Manning, publicly telling another league team not to draft his son. Keep in mind this was not a football dad going mad at a Pop Warner event. This was the NFL draft, hosted by the most popular sport in America, held in New York City, the media capital of the world. Then there was the sight of Eli's older brother, All-Pro quarterback Peyton Manning, standing beside him, equally as intent to support his brother's defiance of the NFL's draft selection process. Interestingly enough, no one in the media criticized the Manning family for this deliberate affront to the draft. When Eli decided to enter the draft, he knew that any team could select him as long as he was available. Rather than disparage the actions of the Mannings, the press relished and reveled in this notion of pedigree. All of which seemed deliberately intent on offsetting Limbaugh's remarks months earlier that the press was desirous to see black quarterbacks succeed. The lack of critical commentary indicated a greater interest in seeing a white quarterback succeed with the help of his famous family, and in subverting draft proceedings, no less. Eventually the San Diego Chargers drafted Manning against his wishes, but honored his desire to play elsewhere by trading him to the New York Giants. What would have been the reaction if a black quarterback such as Michael Vick had sought to subvert the propriety of the NFL draft as Eli did? Would the media have been so reluctant to criticize it? It is worth noting that Eli and Peyton Manning have been two of the greatest quarterbacks of their era, with four Super Bowl appearances and three championships between them (two for Eli and one for Peyton). On the other hand, their family's actions at the 2004 draft were questionable but not unprecedented. Their collective defiance of the draft process far exceeded John Elway's demands that he not be drafted by the Baltimore Colts in 1983. Similarly, the Colts drafted Elway but traded his rights to the Denver Broncos, where he played his entire career. The notion of pedigree in referring to a brand of quarterback that was introduced at the 2004 draft had connotations beyond the Manning family.

It was also a way of beating back the prevailing notion that quarterbacks with stealth builds and athleticism, like the aforementioned blacks, were becoming the preferred model in the NFL. Especially after a plethora of legendary NFL quarterbacks from the 1990s, including Steve Young, Troy Aikman, Dan Marino, Joe Montana and Jim Kelly, all retired after concussions, injuries, or decreased mobility. A more recent example is the criticism of quarterbacking sensation Colin Kaepernick of the San Francisco 49ers in 2012. David Whitley of the *Sporting News* derided Kaepernick's tattooed anatomy. In doing so, he erroneously suggested that the quarterback's body art made him akin to a prisoner or a parolee. Because Kaepernick is an African-American, the comments were criticized for their racial undertones. But to further underscore the existence of a media-designed Manning model among quarterbacks, Whitley added, "When our kids said they wanted a tattoo, we could always point to the Manning brothers."[84] The latter comment, nearly ten years after Limbaugh's lapse, is an indicator of how 2003 marked a shift in how blacks as quarterbacks would be portrayed in the media.

The 2004 draft became a referendum on the desirability of blacks as quarterbacks in the NFL. In subsequent NFL drafts, African-American quarterback prospects would be overshadowed by favorable coverage of white quarterbacks. This was especially true in the media reporting leading up to the 2005 draft.

The 2005 NFL Draft: Smith or Rodgers

In the run-up to the 2005 draft, Alex Smith of the University of Utah and Aaron Rodgers of the University of California were the most publicized among the projected first-round picks at quarterback. On the other hand, there was Jason Campbell, an African-American quarterback from the University of Auburn, who was also projected to be a first-round pick. As a senior, Campbell led his team to a 13-0 record against some of the toughest competition in college football's Southeastern Conference (SEC). But he was largely ignored by the media during discussions of the top quarterbacks available in the first round. Despite Campbell's success, where he excelled as a pocket passer, the media pundits pondered who would be picked first: Smith or Rodgers, both of whom are white. In the end, Smith went first overall. Rodgers fell to the twenty-fourth pick, just one spot before Campbell, who went twenty-fifth overall. So the exclusion of Campbell from the discussion on which quarterbacks were the top prospects was totally unwarranted, except that it edified white males as the preferred model. Once more, the maltreatment of Campbell seemed to reflect the media's preoccupation with disavowing Limbaugh's comments about blacks being the beneficiaries of social concern. Furthermore, Campbell being thrust to the background of the draft proved to be a harbinger of things to come. Despite leading the Washington Redskins to a playoff berth within his first three years in the league,

---

84 Story was retrieved from http://aol.sportingnews.com/nfl/story/2012-11-28/colin-kaepernick-tattoos-49ers-qb-start-alex-smith-stats-contract-draft. David Whitley.

he was traded to the Oakland Raiders in 2010, only to lose his starting job in 2011 due to injury. Campbell's career numbers include a completion percentage of over sixty percent, with seventy-four touchdowns against fifty interceptions. By contrast, despite struggling for most of his NFL career, Smith remained a starter with the San Francisco 49ers, while Campbell signed with the Chicago Bears in 2012 as a backup. Of the three, Aaron Rodgers of the Green Bay Packers has been the most successful, including a Super Bowl championship in 2010 and league MVP in 2011. Of the three top quarterbacks from 2005, only Campbell's career has stalled.

The 2006 NFL draft would show more disparate media coverage involving blacks as quarterback prospects, but would include a new low, as Vince Young and the Wonderlic aptitude test saga presented a major setback to black quarterbacks. It allowed the media to resurrect age-old stereotypes that blacks lacked the requisite intelligence to play quarterback.

2006: Young Versus Leinart

The 2006 NFL draft sparked great interest and anticipation. Two of the most talented quarterbacks in the draft were USC star quarterback Matt Leinart, the Heisman Trophy winner, and the University of Texas star quarterback Vince Young, the reigning national champion. What added to the drama was that Leinart and Young had just battled to the finish in one of the most exciting NCAA Division I-A National Championship football games ever played. Young put on one of the most electrifying performances for a quarterback in the history of college sports. He amassed over 400 total yards, and was equally balanced, passing and running for over 200 yards each in leading his team to victory. Still, commentators predicted Leinart, who had won a national championship previously, would go first. Media reports even suggested the Titans would draft Leinart over Young because the team had hired Norm Chow as their offensive coordinator, a position he held at USC where he coached Leinart. Moreover, the media pundits stated that Young's side-arm delivery would encounter problems in the NFL. While the sports reporting media mashed and bashed Young excessively, the NFL contributed to the doubters. While the Texas quarterback had led the nation in passing efficiency in his last year of college, NFL scouts still labeled him a running quarterback, a disparaging notion for a quarterback who is black. But nothing was more indicative of the NFL's and the media's role in negatively label-ing Young than the infamous Wonderlic test score attributed to him during the annual NFL Scouting Combine.

In the midst of the "Combine," which is an invitation-only event for the nation's top pro-football prospects, the media quickly spread a story that Young scored poorly on the dreaded test. The aptitude test is administered to all players at the annual pre-draft scouting combine, supposedly to measure their ability to think under pressure. While the test results are supposed to be confidential, the disclosure seemed deliberately contrived to hurt Young's draft stock. The test is also seen as an important mea-sure of a player's intelligence, especially for quarterbacks, given their need to think quickly. Young ended up taking the exam a second time when he reportedly scored a thirteen, which is still considered too low for a quarterback. The media seemed to use Young's test score to drum up stereotypes of black quarterbacks as lacking the requisite intelligence to play the position in the NFL. To further underscore this point, during the same combine, the press ignored the fact that Bruce Eugene, a black quarterback from Grambling State, posted a forty-one (out of fifty) on the Wonderlic. Eugene's score was the highest for any quarterback at the 2006 NFL Scouting Combine, including USC's Matt Lein-art (thirty-five). In fact, the Grambling quarterback's score was higher than a number of current and former NFL quarterbacks such as Peyton Manning (twenty-eight), Tom Brady (thirty-three), Ben Roethlisberger (twenty-five), Eli Manning (thirty-nine), Steve Young (thirty-three), Troy Aikman (twenty-nine), Brett Favre (twenty-two), and John Elway (twenty-nine), among others. On the other hand, the inordinate amount of media atten-tion accorded to Young's score appeared to be racially motivated. The media could have mitigated race as an issue in Young's poor performance given Eugene's top score for a quarterback, which offset that perception. The racial angle seems especially plausible when you consider that the low score plagued Young before he took to the field. By contrast, it was initially reported that Tim Tebow posted a low Wonderlic test score at the combine in 2010. Yet no one held that against him, nor has it been mentioned, regardless of how poorly he throws the ball at times.

That race was seemingly a factor in the reaction to Young's score is also seen from the non-reaction to white quarterbacks who fared poorly on the exam, such as Dan Marino and Jim Kelly, both of whom reportedly scored a fifteen. But, much different from Young, both played their entire careers without media references to their poor test scores. Both Kelly and Marino went on to have great NFL careers that won them enshrinement in the Pro Football Hall of Fame, which further underscores how overrated the test scores can be. Mirabile (2005)[85] found that intelligence as measured by the Wonderlic Test has had no significant relationship to a quarterback's performance in college or in the NFL. On the other hand, Mirabile found that race was statistically significant for collegiate quarterback prospects. Although non-white collegiate quarterbacks drafted in the NFL have been relatively few, they had higher passing efficiency ratings (8.9 points more than their white counterparts) and greater offensive production (44.8 more yards per game) than white quarterbacks. It is worth noting that although Mirabile's study only covered the subjects through their rookie years, a high percentage of non-white quarterbacks have led their NFL teams to the playoffs within their first three years. Of relative importance is that Mirabile's study came two years after Limbaugh's disoriented digression. Despite his study and its findings, the culture of differential treatment of black and white quarterbacks continued during the draft unabated.

Russell or Quinn in 2007

In the 2007 NFL draft, the league and media again showed their unwavering bias for white quarterbacks. First, the media

---

85 McDonald, Mirable (n.d.) Intelligence and Football: Testing for Differentials in Collegiate Quarterback Passing Performance and NFL Compensation.

created the question about which quarterback would go first: JeMarcus Russell of LSU, who is black, or Brady Quinn of Notre Dame, who is white. Quinn was touted for his intelligence, with constant references to his devotion to schoolwork, while Russell's slow-talking southern drawl created the impression that he was just another physical talent imbued with more brawn than brains. That Russell could throw the football sixty-five yards in the air—on one knee—only contributed to the notion.

The Oakland Raiders, which held the number one pick in the 2007 draft, ultimately picked Russell first overall. Sadly, he went on to fulfill the low expectations many media pundits had panned him for. But as one former Raiders coach stated, he was doomed for failure, as the Raiders coaches never wanted to draft him. In 2010 the Raiders released Russell, which resulted in him being labeled the biggest draft bust ever. Shortly after being released, Russell was arrested for his involvement in a drug sting. What makes the 2007 draft so memorable is not what Russell failed to become, but what the media and the NFL did in illustrating social concern for a white quarterback, Brady Quinn. This desire to see him succeed occurred on draft day in front of a national television audience.

Social Concern for Quinn

Despite the pre-draft hype of who would go first in 2007, Brady Quinn nearly fell out of the first round. Team after team passed him over, including his hometown Cleveland Browns. The explanation that no team needed a quarterback does not fit the conventional wisdom associated with the NFL draft, which says you select the best guy available at the time of your pick. As Quinn continued to get passed over, ESPN, perhaps not so ironically, continued to film the Notre Dame quarterback, persistently asking him how he felt after every pick. But the questions were posed out of sympathy rather than cynicism. After each pick, Quinn became visibly more anxious. He began unbuttoning his shirt and loosening his tie as the embarrassment of being passed over was clearly affecting him. The awkward sequence prompted ESPN's Tony Kornheiser to quip that if Quinn continued to get passed over, he would soon be "naked."

What followed next is still stunning to recall and unprecedented in the chronicles of NFL draft day events. In response to this unfortunate spectacle surrounding Quinn, NFL Commissioner Roger Goodell took the unusual step of removing him from the floor to spare him more humiliation and placed him in the confines of his private suite. How many black quarterbacks were passed over entirely by the NFL but received no special treatment from the NFL commissioner or sorrowful attention from the media? At the 2013 NFL Draft, Geno Smith, an African-American quarterback out of West Virginia, who was projected to be a first round pick, was similarly embarrassed, over being passed over in front of a national television audience. But unlike Commissioner Goodell's unique consideration for Quinn, he did not offer Smith refuge in his private suite, to spare him more anguish. Smith was eventually drafted in the second round by the New York Jets. But more importantly, the preferential treatment Quinn received by the NFL commissioner and the media underscored the fallacy of Limbaugh's suggestions of social concern for black quarterbacks in the league. The draft day drama involving Quinn was but another sign that contrary to what Limbaugh suggested about black quarterbacks in the league, it is actually white quarterbacks that have benefitted most from social concern out of a desire to see them succeed.

Incidentally, the Cleveland Browns, which had used their own first pick to draft an offensive lineman, traded to get back in the first round and selected Quinn. While Russell's NFL career was a huge disappointment, Quinn's career never got off the ground in Cleveland, and he was traded to the Denver Broncos in 2010. There he descended to third string behind Kyle Orton and Tim Tebow in 2011. In 2012, he was signed by the Kansas City Chiefs, which reunited him with his former head coach Romeo Crennel, who initially drafted him. The preferential treatment Quinn received from the media and the NFL was but another example of a dramatic shift in how these sports entities accorded different treatment to black and white quarterbacks. Although the 2007 draft placed the media spotlight on JeMarcus Russell and Brady Quinn as rookie prospects, the focus of the sports world would soon shift to a veteran NFL quarterback and an ensuing scandal. It was on the eve of this same draft that stories of Michael Vick's involvement in dog fighting began swirling.

In a rather twisted irony, Vick participated in this NFL draft as an alumnus despite growing speculation of his involvement in dog fighting. Before being allowed to participate, Vick was asked by Commissioner Goodell if the reports were true, and Vick denied them. But the public was less convinced, which was evident from the cascade of boos from fans when he was introduced in Radio City Music Hall. When it finally came to light that Vick had lied to the commissioner, the wrath of the league's front office and the sports media would hit him like an anvil. Although there was an observable pattern of disparate press coverage accorded to black quarterbacks following Limbaugh's remarks, such indices were merely the calm before the storm. The Vick dog fighting scandal became the perfect storm for the NFL and media to disavow Limbaugh's suggestion that they wanted to see a black quarterback succeed out of social concern.

Perfect Storm

The media swarm that overwhelmed Vick in the aftermath of the dog fighting allegations was more dogged than any fierce pass rush he had ever faced. The elusive quarterback, whose career was catapulted to superstar status given his speedy ability to outrun his opponents, would be unsuccessful in the face of his greatest opposition yet. While the law was in hot pursuit, the NFL and media hounded Vick like bounty hunters, assisting in no small measure to his prosecution. In no uncertain terms, both the NFL and the sports reporting media disemboweled Michael Vick in front of the world.

Goodell also used the growing scandal to make an example out of Vick to tout his new law and order personal conduct policy. The media, in turn, revved up the public's anger meter with wall-to-wall coverage, which quickened Vick's precipitous tumble from the top of the NFL. Their overindulging coverage raised very serious questions of whether Vick could have gotten a fair trial had he fought the charges. The media's portrayal of Vick as a malicious dog fighter also brought out the animal rights advocates, which riled up the public even more with protests. What followed was a slew of punitive sanctions against Vick, both formal and informal.

Formal and Informal Sanctions

While African-Americans worried that the media's inflammatory coverage infringed upon Vick's rights to due process, the majority of white Americans wanted retribution. A host of informal and formal sanctions against the quarterback mounted. Informal sanctions increased after considerable outcry from animal rights groups such as PETA and the Humane Society. This led an increasingly angry public to act whether they cared about dogs or not. The groundswell of public acrimony increased when ESPN's *Outside the Lines* broadcast a feature on the blood sport, which further implicated Vick.

Even though the qualifications of the commentators on the show were questionable, the network gave them a platform nonetheless. ESPN interviewed an individual who was identified as a "confidential informant" who had been a dog fighter and who had competed against Vick in the blood sport. He described Vick as a heavyweight in dog fighting. But the network never stated what established this individual as a reliable confidential informant nor did it substantiate that he in fact was who he purported to be. Nor did it disclose whether this confidential informant was paid by the network for the interview. His appearance increased the discord against Vick and eventually aroused the suspicions of the federal government. In Vick's indictment a confidential informant was cited as implicating him. Was it the same one who appeared on ESPN? On the same show the network interviewed John Goodwin, who as deputy manager for the Animal Cruelty Campaign of the Humane Society certainly appeared to be an expert on dog fighting. However, ESPN failed to tell its viewers that nearly four months prior to his appearance on *Outside the Lines,* Goodwin was discredited as an expert and not allowed to testify at a dog fighting trial in Dane County, Wisconsin.[86] During a pre-trial hearing, defense attorney Charles Giesen deduced from Goodwin that he never graduated from high school and had never been considered an expert on dog fighting in any court. The judge ruled that Goodwin had neither the "requisite expertise nor training" to be considered an expert on dog fighting and for that reason his opinion was not acceptable for testimony. Obviously, ESPN has a lower threshold for allowing a so-called expert to give his opinion on its show. Of course, this is the same network that gave Rush Limbaugh a platform as a studio analyst on its NFL pregame show. ESPN's tendency to let any "expert" appear on its network, no matter how unqualified, had not waned despite the potential harm to the public. Furthermore, ESPN never informed its viewers that Goodwin had a checkered background in the world of animal advocacy, which included affiliations with radicals and actions that suggested the same, including acts of arson and vandalism of fur retailers. He had previously pleaded guilty to misdemeanor vandalism and conceded to participating in "economic sabotage." Was his appearance on ESPN an attempt to commit "economic sabotage" against Michael Vick and other black athletes? Without qualification, Goodwin noted that a "subculture" of dog fighting exists among professional athletes. While the cases of Qyntel Woods of the NBA's Portland Trailblazers and LeShon Johnson of the New York Jets were mentioned, these instances hardly amounted to a bourgeoning subculture. Still, Goodwin continued, "You know, it's very interesting that we have got a whole roster of names of professional athletes that we know are involved in dog fighting" (Naqi, 2007). This inexpert sweeping generalization went unchecked by ESPN. The network was terribly wrong to give credence to such hyperbole from Goodwin, who was described

---

86 Retrieved from www.humanewatch.org/.../HSUS/expertise. "Humane 'Expertise' Slammed from the Bench."

by defense attorney Charles Giesen as a "faux expert," a self-proclaimed expert without expertise. Despite the court ruling, he was expert enough for ESPN to create a new profile of the dog fighter in the public's view that no longer reflected the prototypical white male in the back roads of southern towns. Instead, the profile became professional athletes who are black, wealthy, and resented for the huge sums of money they earn. Add on the fact that Vick was at the time the highest paid player in the history of the NFL and you have a recipe for the kind of "economic sabotage" that Goodwin was infamous for in his animal advocacy. Dog fighting would not only place Vick in criminal court but civil court as well. ESPN asked its confidential informant what he thought "people's reaction" would be to his implication of Vick as a dog fighter. The answer would be seen, heard, and felt as public outrage against Vick grew louder and more demonstrative.

With each passing day and every negative news report of the scandal, the demands for justice against Vick grew more intense. Protesters showed up at the Atlanta Falcons training camp as the vitriolic vengeance against the quarterback multiplied by the minute. When taken as a whole, these factors not only turned up the pressure on Vick, but on the NFL as well, as the informal sanctions of the public led to formal sanctions by the league and the law.

The NFL's Wait-and-See Approach

Realizing the tremendous commodity Vick had shown himself to be in his first five years in the NFL, Commissioner Goodell initially took a wait-and-see approach. After all, Vick had not only electrified the Atlanta Falcons' fan base, but increased its revenue as well. Additionally, he was a popular player who further enriched the entire NFL. Besides home games in the Georgia Dome, which were often sold out during Vick's time there, the dazzling quarterback filled up stadiums throughout the league. Because NFL teams split gate receipts 60/40, with the greater portion going to the home team, Vick was a revenue generator of the highest order. Furthermore, his exciting play became must-see television, which boosted ratings, which also equates to greater revenues for all NFL teams. So while Vick's economic value was known to the league, it depreciated markedly in the wake of his downfall.

Once the NFL realized that Vick's presence would have a negative effect on business given an angry public and the growing specter of dog fighting charges, they dropped him like a bad habit. The commissioner then flexed his muscles with the new conduct policy and suspended Vick for the year and for the foreseeable future. In what may have been the lowest blow, in July 2007, with Vick under federal indictment and the animus toward him at a fever pitch, the NFL published a photo on its website enjoining an angry and menacing public to "Kick Vick." Because of the potential revenue Vick was costing the league, in addition to the public relations nightmare, the NFL seemed resigned to seal his fate.

To further underscore the commissioner's disregard for the beleaguered quarterback, Goodell may have undermined his defense by disclosing details of Vick's legal thinking to the media. The press asked the commissioner to disclose the content of his conversations with Vick. Goodell conceded there were details he probably should not share. Then, oddly enough, he revealed that Vick was planning to plead guilty. In doing so, Goodell could have compromised Vick's defense, especially if his attorneys were intent on using his willingness to plead guilty as a bargaining chip for a lesser sentence. Instead, Goodell's admission seemed to have the effect of hardening the position of federal prosecutors. Not to be outdone, the mainstream media was unceasing in bringing down the crestfallen NFL star.

The inflammatory media coverage all but assured Vick was going to prison. Consequently, the sports media began providing dire forecasts of his football future in the NFL. Some publicly exclaimed that he should be banned for life. Others said Vick would never play quarterback again in the NFL. The assertions that he would never play quarterback again were consistent with the view of most, who had never wanted to see him playing quarterback anyway. Still most of the media's negative reaction was driven by a sense of resentment because of what Vick was supposed to mean to them: a dazzling football star who they could write about for his actions on the field rather than off of it. Because they were not able to talk about his extraordinary playmaking ability, it was no longer enough to criticize his passing skills, which often earned their ire. He had now tarnished the NFL's coveted shield, which many sports reporters hang their hats on as a career. Yet the role of the sports media and its coverage was a problem for Vick from the beginning.

On the one hand, the media coverage was framed by sports reporters who sought to enrage rather than enlighten the public. The problem with the overindulgence of sports reporters is that although Vick was a sports celebrity, the dog fighting scandal was not a sports story. For Vick, this misplay on the part of the mainstream media exacerbated his legal and social problems. Consequently, there was never any careful examination of the social contexts that may have explained how this extraordinary calamity occurred. Without any concern for why this disaster unfolded, Vick was ostracized, excommunicated, and convicted without any mitigating factors being considered, even though a range of social factors were involved and warranted explanation. Questions of this so-called culture of dog fighting that Vick spoke about were ignored by the media. His comments to the press about how the police in his neighborhood ignored dog fighting, an account he reiterated to the presiding judge in his case, went unheeded. The general public was less concerned about why it happened because sports reporters did not care about why it happened. Their primary concern was that Vick had derailed his career and stained the mighty amulet of the NFL.

When Vick attempted to show contrition for his misdeeds, he was ridiculed by the press. Rather than giving credence to his show of remorse during a press conference that he scheduled, the media questioned his sincerity and became fixated on what his prison sentence might be. In the end, the media seemed preoccupied with showing the public at large and Limbaugh in particular that the disproportionately decadent coverage of Vick's dog fighting dilemma was designed to dispel the idea that they cared about black quarterbacks in the NFL.

For all of the informal and formal sanctions against Vick, the most punitive and humiliating one was the federal prison sentence of nearly two years. The sentence was the final straw that capped this most unfortunate saga in Vick's relatively young life. His family, which included his fiancée and young children, were distraught over his imprisonment. Despite the ominous outlook of others, he vowed to resume his life and NFL career, notwithstanding the doubters. After nearly two years, Vick was given a supervised release from prison. In the time that he was away, anger and angst were still simmering, and death threats were still mounting. Consistent with his attempts to regain a measure of respect and restore his good name, Vick sought out the same animal rights organizations that fueled the outrage against him.

PETA was unrelenting and outright refused to acquiesce to Vick's offer to work with the organization to stem dog fighting. PETA not only declined to work with Vick, but warned the NFL that protests would follow if any league team signed him. On the other hand, the Humane Society was a bit more open-minded, although it appeared it was more interested in promoting its own name and cause rather than helping Vick restore his. Upon his release in 2009, the besieged quarterback was expected to reassure the larger community that he was remorseful and sincere about being an advocate. The Humane Society would be the collaborating conduit, or so it seemed.

The Inhumane Society's Late Hit on Vick

On the surface the organization's decision to work with Vick appeared to be aligned with its mission to advocate for animals and oppose dog fighting. But the Humane Society showed how much it cared about Michael Vick's attempts to rehabilitate his name when it partnered with Rush Limbaugh, who availed himself to record a public service announcement opposing dog fighting. The unlikely pair teamed up in April 2009, just one month before Vick was released from prison. The animal rights organization must have known that Limbaugh had derided black quarterbacks like Vick while on ESPN, which resulted in his being fired. In the recorded spot, Limbaugh wasted no time harping on the dog fighting theme while perpetuating the idea that the blood sport was primarily an issue involving urban street fighters. Consistent with his tendency to lump all black males together to illustrate a polarizing point, Limbaugh referred to street fighters of dogs derisively as "street toughs" and "people like Michael Vick." For the Humane Society to give Limbaugh a platform to pound Vick after agreeing to work with him was a sucker punch of the worst kind.

As a consequence, Limbaugh found a way to label Vick in a negative light despite his attempts to reclaim his name by turning a negative into a positive. Whereas before, Limbaugh had relabeled Vick and others of similar ilk as black quarterbacks, he now relabeled him as a street fighter of dogs. But at the time was Vick involved in dog fighting as a street fighter? There are indicators that suggest he was not. Ortiz (2010) found that some street fighters engage in the blood sport in abandoned apartment buildings or even in the trunks of cars, while professional fighters use more discretion, are highly secretive, and compete for large cash prizes. The latter description more aptly defines Vick's level of involvement, which helps to explain why the public and the law enforcement community were unaware of it. Limbaugh's attempts to associate Vick's actions with street fighters followed the tact of animal rights organizations, various state legislators, and the federal government. But labeling Vick as a street fighter was a misappropriation of reality that led to the passage of stronger laws that targeted street fighters, i.e., inner-city blacks. Limbaugh seemed to contribute to this skewered focus on blacks with his reference to "street toughs" who fight dogs as "people like Michael Vick." Chart 4.1 shows that in the seven years that preceded Limbaugh's PSA (2002-09), versus the three years that followed (2009-12), blacks saw their arrest rates for dog fighting increase, while whites and Hispanics saw their arrests rates decrease. Furthermore, Chart 4.1 shows, in the three years after Limbaugh's PSA, the number of blacks arrested for dog fighting surpassed those arrested in the seven years prior.[87]

---

87 Analysis based on arrest data by race, which was deduced from www.pet-abuse. com, using mug shots and photos of defendants and suspects to examine racial

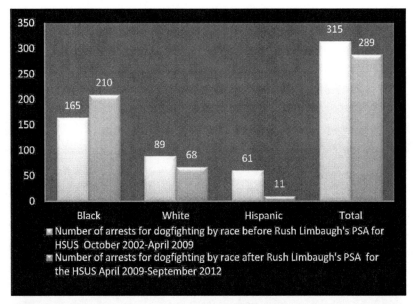

Chart 4.1 The analysis is based on arrest data as reported by www.pet-abuse.com. The period encompasses the seven years that preceded Rush Limbaugh's PSA on April 14, 2009, and the three years that followed.

Of the 289 defendants arrested for dog fighting in the aftermath of Limbaugh's comments, African-Americans accounted for 210 of them. In stark contrast, whites were only sixty-eight of the 289 defendants charged, while Hispanics, who are more often involved in cockfighting, were a mere eleven of those arrested from April 15, 2009 through September 29, 2012.

Of the 306 blacks who were arrested after Vick's property was raided on April 25, 2007, 210 were charged after Limbaugh's public service announcement in April 2009. Not only did Vick's bust lead to a greater number of blacks being targeted, but nearly seventy percent of those arrested occurred after Limbaugh's comments. Keep in mind, Limbaugh began his public service announcement by commenting on the alliance between the Humane Society and law enforcement in combat-

differences in arrests (search term "Fighting," pp.1-14.) Chart 4.1 shows actual arrest data for defendants by race.

ing dog fighting. To further underscore this concern of selective enforcement by race, African-Americans were the only group in the analysis that saw their arrest rates increase from the seven years prior. Chart 4.2 shows that in the three years following Limbaugh's PSA, African-Americans arrested for dog fighting outnumbered whites, by nearly 3-to-1.

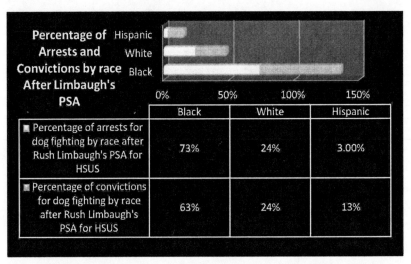

Percentage of Arrests and Convictions by race After Limbaugh's PSA	Black	White	Hispanic
■ Percentage of arrests for dog fighting by race after Rush Limbaugh's PSA for HSUS	73%	24%	3.00%
■ Percentage of convictions for dog fighting by race after Rush Limbaugh's PSA for HSUS	63%	24%	13%

Chart 4.2 Data deduced from arrest incidents and convictions by race with photos of defendants as reported by www.pet-abuse.com from April 15, 2009 through September 29, 2012 (search term "Fighting" pgs. 1-14.)

Beyond the arrest data by race, the percentage of convictions bore out much of the same. The analysis shows that following Limbaugh's PSA, African-Americans were sixty-three percent of those convicted for dog fighting. Furthermore, the number of African-Americans convicted was more than twice the number of whites, at twenty-four percent, and nearly five times that of Hispanics, at thirteen percent. The data analysis in these reports raises additional questions of selective enforcement by race in the enforcement of dog fighting laws. In addition, there appears to be an unequal distribution of the law, which has led to African-Americans having the highest rates of arrests and convictions when compared to whites and Hispanics. To presuppose that these increases that followed Limbaugh's comments are simply a by-product of a greater number of blacks being involved in dog fighting and whites' suddenly losing interest is to be terribly naïve. The Humane Society, among others, suggests that street fighters are upwards of 100,000 of all dog fighters. But where is the data to support such a number? The tremendous increase in the arrests and convictions of blacks following Limbaugh's statements seemed to reflect his influence on the greater attention to inner-city blacks by law enforcement officials nationwide. The Humane Society accorded Limbaugh a platform and lent its own name to his decision to label "people like Michael Vick" as the problem associated with dog fighting. His comments contributed to racial disparities in arrests and convictions of blacks. Even worse, Limbaugh's comments created the impression that dog fighters were the sum of animal cruelty.

Limbaugh opined there is much to argue about and added, "Indeed we must, but when it comes to dog fighting…there's no other side of the story."[88] I disagree emphatically! Such a distortion is a gross misrepresentation of reality. Limbaugh's assertion that there is no other side of the story negates any discussion of other forms of animal cruelty, which were never assailed. Consequently, he undermined the credibility of the Humane Society, which co-signed for his lunacy. Individuals abuse animals in no shortage of ways, which leads to other acts of violence.

Oddly enough, the Humane Society propagated Limbaugh's misguided meandering, despite that the organization produced a document titled *Fact Sheet: Bestiality and Other Violent Crime* (n.d.). According to their sheet, FBI researchers checked the backgrounds of serial homicidal rapists and found a history of sexual assaults against animals. Another study found that nearly forty percent of sexually violent juvenile offenders had a history of animal assaults; other data showed upwards of ninety-six percent of juvenile offenders who engaged in carnal relations with

---

88 Rush Limbaugh recorded public service announcement on dog fighting for the Humane Society, April 14, 2009.

animals were more likely to sexually assault human beings than their counterparts of the same age and race who had not sexually assaulted animals.

Conclusion

The decision by ESPN to hire Rush Limbaugh was a horrible mistake that had wide ranging implications beyond the 2003 season. Hence, the preceding discussion disavowed the suggestion that the media and NFL was ever desirous to see a black quarterback succeed. Just the opposite: Perspectives like the labeling theory and the hierarchy of naming showed that the notion of a black quarterback, as used in the media, has hindered African-Americans attempting to play the position in the NFL, historically and presently. As highlighted in the preceding chapter, subsequent to Limbaugh's unfortunate remarks there was a noticeably negative shift in the media coverage of African-American quarterbacks. This change was particularly observable in the succeeding NFL drafts, from 2004 through 2007. Of course, it was also in 2007 when the Michael Vick dog fighting scandal came to light. The revelations involving Vick had the misfortune of giving the NFL and the media a perfect opportunity to show that there was never any social concern for black quarterbacks.

On the other hand, the Humane Society was supposed to help Michael Vick in his quest for redemption, which included becoming an advocate to stem the problem of dog fighting. But, as this chapter has shown, the animal rights organization helped Rush Limbaugh skewer the focus of dog fighting to street fighters, whom he referred to as "people like Michael Vick." Consequently, data reported in this chapter showed that subsequent to Limbaugh's comments, racial disparities in arrests for dog fighting by race were exacerbated. African-Americans saw both their rates of arrests and convictions increase.

The next chapter will continue the discussion of differential treatment by race in examining the scandals involving quarterbacks Michael Vick and the dog fighting chronicle versus Ben Roethlisberger, who faced two separate allegations of rape involving two different women in two different states, in a span of nine months.

CHAPTER V

Labeling Versus De-labeling:

Vick, Roethlisberger, and Race

"Abuse your dog, and people howl. Smack around your girl-friend or face charges of sexually assaulting a woman, and people shake their heads and roll their eyes."
—Rick Morrissey (2007), *Chicago Tribune*

"(Roethlisberger) should have to speak to young kids about the fact that 'No means no.' He should, in other words, have to do everything Michael Vick has had to do to make amends."
—Dave Zirin (2010), *Edge of Sports*

In this chapter *labeling theory* will be used to explain the harmful effects of negative stereotypes (i.e., reckless, danger-ous, Bad Newz, Virginia) on Michael Vick's self-identity. Since labeling is a social process, these negative ideas seemed to not only shape a contorted self-image for Vick, but it also seemed to influence his choice of unsavory friends. These factors, among others, ultimately shaped his dire decision to finance an ille-gal dog fighting enterprise. In Chapter IV the labeling theory helped explain the injurious effects of the derogatory notion *black quarterback* in the NFL. As a consequence of such label-ing, African-Americans such as Marlin Briscoe, Elridge Dickey, and Joe Gilliam encountered racial barriers and were rejected as legitimate quarterbacking talents in the NFL. Not only did such disparaging labels lead to greater prejudice and racial discrimination, but all three battled drug addiction as a consequence of their shattered NFL careers (Briscoe, 2002).

The larger impact of the labeling process is that it can determine people's chances in life. Negative labeling usually involves casting the lesser others as deviants. At the heart of this process is the realization that deviance is not always an act but the label attached. As a consequence of being labeled as black quarterbacks, such players have been typecast as deviants in large measure because they deviated from the preferred white quarterback. Concomitantly, black quarterbacks were treated as outsiders in the NFL. Becker (1987) observed that social groups with power (i.e. the media, NFL teams, corporate sponsors, etc.), will not only define who are the deviants or outsiders, but will also establish the norms or rules that will govern their interactions with those who have the power to affix such labels. In the case of powerful groups like the NFL and the media, such norms and unwritten rules reflected widely held social beliefs that whites should be placed in leadership positions that require intelligence, like quarterback. Historically, blacks playing football had been labeled by the media as ignorant sambos who were devoid of the requisite intelligence to play NFL football, much less manage a starring role like quarterback.

Beyond such labeling on the field, the NFL and the media have been just as inclined to label them as deviants for off-the-field incidents as well. Indeed, black football players in the league have been overrepresented in such indiscretions that have resulted in a host of criminal charges and convictions in court (Benedict & Yaeger, 1998). Although quarterbacks who are black are a mere twenty percent of starters in the NFL, most have been law abiding. However, as this discussion will show, when there have been off-the-field incidents, including criminal charges or deviant conduct involving black quarterbacks, they have been treated more harshly by the NFL, the media, corporate sponsors, and the law. On the other hand, when white quarterbacks have been charged in criminal matters or cited for deviant conduct, there has been a greater willingness to forgive and forget. This differential treatment of blacks and whites as quarterbacks was clearly evident in the reaction of the NFL, media, corporate sponsors, and the politics of the state, to the respective acts of deviance involving Michael Vick and Ben Roethlisberger.

In 2010, both Vick and Roethlisberger staged incredible comebacks in the face of their scandal-plagued pasts. Michael Vick became a starting quarterback for the first time since his dog fighting downfall. Despite the odds against him, he would have his best season as a professional quarterback, earning All-Pro honors en route to being named NFL Comeback Player of the Year. On the other hand, after serving his four-game suspension, Ben Roethlisberger returned to the NFL amid swirling allegations that he sexually assaulted two women in nine months. Notwithstanding the disgraceful charges, he led the Pittsburgh Steelers back to the Super Bowl in 2010, a game they eventually lost. While the NFL and other powerful entities ensured that Vick would be labeled in perpetuity for his cruelty to dogs, these same forces helped to de-label Roethlisberger for his alleged acts of sexual deviance against women. Was race a factor in the differential treatment of Vick versus Roethlisberger in the social responses to their respective scandals? It was indeed. Furthermore, the difference in treatment was the difference between labeling versus de-labeling. To further underscore this point about labeling and the differential sanctions imposed by race, other negative incidents involving NFL quarterbacks who are white and black will be reviewed.

The Racial Impact of Labeling Black and White Quarterbacks in the NFL

In 2010 there was a spate of negative incidents involving NFL quarterbacks such as Michael Vick, JeMarcus Russell, Vince Young, Chris Simms, Brett Favre, and Ben Roethlisberger. While the first three quarterbacks are black, the latter three are white. Although all six players had a negative incident in 2010, which involved some measure of deviance or criminality, the negative sanctions were disproportionately greater for the blacks. The differential responses from the NFL, the media, and the law belie the racial impact of negative labeling.

Michael Vick Falls 2.0?

For all the downtrodden disappointment that plagued Michael Vick's life from 2007 to the time he was released from prison in 2009, it was universally agreed that he was fortunate to get another shot in the NFL. While Vick's acts of criminal deviance have been well documented, an incident in the summer of 2010 nearly cost him his comeback. With the American public still seething over his misdeeds, his career was once again in jeopardy. In the summer of 2010, Vick hosted a thirtieth birthday party for himself in his home state of Virginia. The party, which was open to the public, proved to be an unmitigated disaster. One of Vick's co-defendants, Quanis Phillips, showed up and reportedly attempted to rub cake in Vick's face. A fight broke out and Phillips was shot. This incident had the media once again encircling Vick like sharks as they attempted to have him ousted from the league. The media understood that NFL Commissioner Roger Goodell reinstated Michael Vick under strict parameters with no margin for error.

Although the party was indeed Vick's, police investigators repeatedly stated he was not a person of interest. But the media did everything it could to make him a suspect. A police spokesman told the media that Vick's name as a suspect only came up when reporters mentioned it (Mihoces, 2010). In July 2010 the police finally cleared the quarterback entirely as a suspect, yet the media relentlessly pressured the NFL and the Philadelphia Eagles organization to announce some punitive sanctions against him. There was even a published report by the Associated Press that the Eagles were planning to release him, which the organization denied.[89] Although the rumors

---

89 Retrieved from http://usatoday30.usatoday.com/sports/football/nfl/eagles/ 2010-07-03. Eagles deny AP report that team is considering cutting Michael Vick.

were later determined to be false, the press attempted to use its considerable influence to have Vick relabeled as a deviant. The consequences could have resulted in him being waived or banned from the NFL. Although Vick had certainly courted disaster, it was only the beginning for his 2010 season. While he was working hard to amend his reputation and the public's view of him, the birthday fiasco made the target on his back even larger. As this incident revealed, once you become a pariah in the eyes of the media, always a pariah, especially if you are black. He would also learn that as long as he provided the media with ammunition, they would certainly use it against him. While there is more to be said about the reaction from the NFL and media toward Vick, the question of race and the role of the media in typecasting other quarterbacks who are black as deviants was commonplace in 2010.

No Hustle in Russell

During the same summer of Vick's infamous birthday party, JeMarcus Russell, the former first overall pick of the Oakland Raiders in 2007, was arrested in July for possession of a controlled substance. His arrest came shortly after he was released by the Raiders. The release of Russell compounded the negative label of him as the greatest bust for a first overall pick in the history of the game. Russell had just three short years in the league. After his release, a former quarterback coach of the Raiders said the team did not surround Russell with enough support, and only Al Davis, the team's owner, wanted him on the club. Russell, who was expected to have a great NFL career, may never resume it after the arrest incident and the negative label of being a bust. The question of race in the media coverage of these respective incidents involving Vick and Russell is warranted when compared to the treatment of white quarterbacks who had incidents with the law. Chris Simms, who is white, was a quarterback with the Tennessee Titans when he was arrested in July for suspicion of driving while under the influence of drugs by New York City police.

"Simms to NYPD"

During a police sobriety checkpoint in Manhattan, Simms's car was stopped after it was observed by officers making an erratic turn. One of the approaching officers reported smelling the strong stench of marijuana, while the other officer reported that Simms looked to be in a "zombie" state. Consequently, he was arrested on charges of driving under the influence of drugs. According to the police report, Simms, who was transporting his pregnant wife of eight months and two other passengers, admitted he had been smoking marijuana.[90] Simms's lawyer argued in court that Simms never made such a statement to the police, yet his attempts to suppress the statements were overruled by the presiding judge. Despite the testimony of two reputable officers of the New York City Police Department, a jury acquitted Simms in 2011. The outcome in Simms's case underscored how racial bias in the media coverage seems to favor whites over blacks in America generally and the NFL in particular. It was fairly obvious that Simms benefitted from his father, Phil Simms, being the number one game analyst of the *NFL on CBS*. Additionally, the elder Simms is a former Super Bowl-winning quarterback with the New York Giants. It seems most of the sports reporting media ignored Simms's legal quandary out of consideration for his father, who was also a colleague. In every media account of the Simms case, his famous father was noted. Guys like Michael Vick and Je Marcus Russell were not fortunate enough to have a famous father who the media and the NFL would reference. Because Simms's trial was without the sensational media hyperbole that accompanies the arrest of black players in the NFL, it seemed to give the jurors the impression that there was not much public interest or concern. Minus the public clamor, Simms was acquitted despite the testimony of two police officers. Would a black quarterback have been acquitted on drug charges had two police officers testified about him driving while impaired on marijuana?

---

90 Retrieved from http://wwwusatoday.com/sports/football/nfl/2010-10-07-chris-simms. Ex-NFL QB Chris Simms pleads not guilty in drug case.

Contrary to the media's questioning the Eagles about releasing Vick after his ill-conceived party, there was no such question posed to Simms's team by the national media. Furthermore, the media never asked the NFL commissioner about Simms being suspended for violating the league's personal conduct policy as they had with Vick. The league's policy does not rely on the outcomes of criminal matters. The policy states in part, "It is not enough simply to avoid being found guilty of a crime" (Kriegel, 2010). The mere incident of police contact has been enough to prompt the commissioner to act unilaterally, particularly against black players who run afoul of the law. By contrast, Commissioner Goodell showed unusual restraint by not even meeting with Simms to get his version of events, like he typically does with blacks. Ironically enough, Simms's teammate, Vince Young, who is black, and whom he backed up at quarterback with the Tennessee Titans, was arrested on a misdemeanor charge after he got into a fight at a strip club in June of 2010. Goodell met with Young after the quarterback made it publicly known he was concerned about a potential meeting with the commissioner.

While Young was not suspended, he still had to meet with Goodell, which once again raises questions about race over the arbitrary and capricious enforcement of the league's conduct policy. On the contrary, the media did not question the commissioner or the Titans about whether Simms would be tested for drugs, especially in light of his refusal to take a drug test while in police custody. The league might argue that their restraint in Simms's case was the result of his arrest being drug-related, which falls under the rubric of their joint drug program for players with the NFL Players Association. This initiative is considered separate from the league's personal conduct policy. The confidentiality of the drug program notwithstanding, Simms was arrested for driving while intoxicated and did acquiesce to a blood screening for alcohol, which came back negative. But if he had not been smoking marijuana, why did he refuse to take a drug test? Simms should have been suspended by the NFL for the arrest incident. After all, while the drug program is primarily for those who fail drug tests, this consideration is distinct from the arrest incident, which should have fallen under the conduct policy because it was off the field. At the very least, Goodell should have met with Simms over the incident as he did with Young, whose transgression involved alcohol use. Since alcohol is abused by a greater number of Americans than illicit drugs, I would imagine that it would also fall under the league's drug program with the players union. Such differential treatment in how the media and the NFL downplayed Simms's incident while magnifying Young's underscores this problem of labeling versus de-labeling of black and white quarterbacks. The commissioner's differential treatment, which helped to de-label Simms versus negatively labeling Young, lends credence to the view that the autocratic rule and unbridled discretion of the league's commissioner can be biased and problematic. Goodell reserves the latitude to meet with a player and suspend him for any personal conduct viewed detrimental to the league. The disinterest shown by the media and the NFL in Simms's case seemed to shield him. The differences in the treatments of these quarterbacks by race reflects the differences between blacks being labeled as deviants versus whites, who are less often cast as deviants, and thus are easily de-labeled.

Also, 2010 brought to light allegations that All-Pro quarterback Brett Favre sent lewd photos of himself to a female employee of the New York Jets when he played there in 2008. Would the NFL commissioner suspend Favre, who is white, or show him favoritism?

Favoritism for Favre

The widespread allegations of a former employee of the New York Jets being sexually harassed by Brett Favre, who was one of the NFL's most popular players, were not good. Given the allegations of sexual misconduct against Ben Roethlisberger in March of 2010, the reports about Favre represented the second such case of a female alleging improper sexual conduct against a high-profile NFL quarterback in a year. In Favre's case, the complainant reported that the quarterback invited her to his hotel room. She also produced lewd photos, which she says were sent to her via text message by Favre. When asked by the press, Favre flat out refused to address the reports and was later fined $50,000 by the NFL for failing to cooperate with its investigation. Although he was fined, he was never suspended for violating the league's personal conduct policy, as a litany of African-American players had been. Nor did he have to meet with the commissioner. To further underscore the double standards existent with Goodell, in 2012 he suspended four New Orleans Saints players, three of whom were black, for failing to cooperate with his investigation of the so-called Bountygate scandal. The Saints players' lack of confidence in Commissioner Goodell's ability to be fair prompted them to seek a court injunction in furtherance of their collective bargaining agreement.

Ultimately, a three-member appeals panel overturned the suspensions and remanded the decision to Goodell to be re-determined. In the next round, the players argued vehemently that it was unfair for Goodell to preside as the appeals officer over his own decision. In response, the commissioner appointed his predecessor, former NFL Commissioner Paul Tagliabue, to serve as "appeals hearing officer."[91] Although Tagliabue upheld Goodell's general findings of misconduct among Saints players for their alleged involvement in a bounty program, he vacated their suspensions. Among the factors Tagliabue cited in rendering his decision was the lack of consistency and historical precedents. He found that in the past, the league had only fined NFL clubs a mere $25,000 (or less) for pay-for-performance programs, which has a longstanding history. Additionally, Tagliabue reasoned that there was no precedent for suspending players for failing to cooperate with the commissioner's investigation. In fact, consistent with this author's own analysis, Tagliabue cited Goodell's failure to suspend Favre, who did not cooperate with his investigation. Ironically enough, one of the players report-

---

91 Paul Tagliabue, December 11, 2012. In the Matter of New Orleans Saints Players Pay-for-Performance / "Bounty".

edly targeted by the Saints' bounty program was Brett Favre while a member of the Minnesota Vikings in 2009. Tagliabue was correct in questioning the double standard perpetuated by Goodell, given the failure to suspend Favre.

Goodell's attempts to suspend the Saints players, all but one of whom was black, while only fining Favre, once more evokes the issue of selective enforcement by race. Interestingly enough, on the question of race, Tagliabue's findings actually absolved Scott Fujita, the only white player among the four disciplined by Goodell, for his purported involvement in the bounty program. Tagliabue only affirmed Fujita's involvement in a pay-for-performance pool. Saints linebacker Jonathan Vilma had also argued that his participation was only in a pay-for-performance program rather than a bounty, but Tagliabue affirmed the commissioner's findings against him, Will Smith, and Anthony Hargrove, all of whom are black. Tagliabue's conclusions were especially questionable since he affirmed the league's position that a bounty program existed, based in part on the testimony of coaches, whom he chided for being inaccurate in their testimony. Tagliabue reasoned that he could not uphold the suspensions as the case against the players was "contaminated by the coaches and others in the Saints organization" (p. 3). If Tagliabue could not uphold the suspensions because of the denials and retractions by coaches and members of the Saints organization, why affirm Goodell's findings? Additionally, to exonerate the white player while further casting the black players as deviants for engaging in conduct detrimental to the league was hardly a consolation prize for Vilma, Smith, and Hargrove. These controversies over player discipline only raise additional questions about Commissioner Goodell's authoritarian rule in the NFL.

Independent of his differential treatment of Saints players, Goodell's failure to strongly punish Favre was especially surprising since the Jets team came under fire in 2010 for allegations of sexually harassing a female reporter. The journalist, of Mexican descent, was attempting to interview Jets quarterback Mark Sanchez in the team's locker room. Her presence aroused a raucous reaction from players and coaches. Additionally, it was reported that the head coach and assistant coaches began throwing footballs in her direction to draw additional attention to her presence. While the league supposedly conducted an investigation, no punitive action followed against the players, coaches, or the Jets organization. The league's passive dismissal was puzzling, given the back-to-back complaints of sexual misconduct against Pittsburgh Steelers quarterback Ben Roethlisberger in 2010. Given the wave of incidents involving women feeling violated and sexually harassed by NFL personnel, Favre should have been subject to stronger punitive sanctions from the league. Still, more negative incidents involving white quarterbacks would follow.

In July 2010, just months after escaping a rape charge, and with a civil lawsuit over another alleged sexual assault pending, Roethlisberger was in the media again. This time it was reported that while participating in a golf outing at a private course one of his associates urinated in public (Leahy, 2010).[92] No one in the media pressed Roethlisberger to explain how this incident, reported by a woman, seemed to conflict with his so-called commitment to maturing. Although Roethlisberger was not identified as the person demonstrating public indecency, you are only as good as the company you keep. While the media and the NFL monitored and advised Vick about his associates, no such concern was apparently conveyed to Roethlisberger. He was with an entourage when the Georgia rape complaint was filed in March 2010. Unlike with Vick and his birthday party fiasco, no one asked the NFL commissioner if he would review the incident to see if Roethlisberger had run afoul of his commitment to improve himself. Instead, the media seemed to rationalize that it was not Roethlisberger who had urinated in public and did not make an issue of the matter. Later that summer, when Commissioner Goodell visited the Steelers training camp in 2010, he indicated that Roethlisberger was doing everything asked of

---

92 Retrieved from http://content.usatoday.com/communities/thehuddle/post/2010/07/
police-in-ohio-investigated-ben-roethlisberger-golf-foursome-for-alleged-public-
urination/1. Sean Leahy, July 13, 2010.

him and more. So unlike in Vick's case, the commissioner was less concerned with Roethlisberger consorting with individuals demonstrating public lewdness. The differences in the way the media covered these NFL quarterbacks who were black and white reflected distinct differences by race, given these off-the-field incidents. These incidents reveal a disturbing pattern of disparate treatment of black versus white quarterbacks by the NFL and the media when they engaged in behavior that was criminogenic or perceived as deviant. These occurrences prompt the need for a broader discussion of the disparate treatment accorded to Vick versus Roethlisberger.

Ben-efit of the Doubt

The first complaint against Roethlisberger was filed in the summer of 2009 when an employee at a Las Vegas hotel indicated that Roethlisberger sexually assaulted her in his hotel room the previous year. While the woman never filed any criminal charges, she did pursue a civil lawsuit against the star quarterback (which was eventually settled in 2012). In March of 2010, a young college student from Milledgeville, Georgia, filed a sexual assault complaint against Roethlisberger, alleging that he raped her in the bathroom of a bar. Witnesses indicated that Roethlisberger took the woman to what was described in the police report as a "small dingy bathroom" (Kriegel, p. 2). Even more unsettling, the report indicated that while Roethlisberger had this young girl in the bathroom, his bodyguard, who happened to be an off-duty Pennsylvania state trooper, stood guard outside the door. When the young girl's friends attempted to check on her safety, the off-duty state trooper did not allow them access. Later, the young lady, who was admittedly drinking, was taken to a hospital where a rape kit was administered. The examination showed she suffered a laceration in the area of her vagina. Even though his DNA was sought, Roethlisberger's attorney did not allow him to provide it to investigators. Consequently, the district attorney decided not to pursue criminal charges, citing their inability to prosecute him beyond a reasonable doubt. In response to the district attorney's rationing, Dave Zirin, an attorney and critically acclaimed author, quipped, "And here I thought that was a judge and jury's job to determine whether a case could be proven beyond a reasonable doubt."[93] While the outcomes for Vick and Roethlisberger were as different as black and white, the issue of race emerges as a question in the media coverage and respective criminal probes of each.

The criminal justice system has long been cited as an institution that perpetuates racism and structural inequalities in the prosecution of blacks and whites. Blacks are more likely to be punished to a greater extent than whites for similar crimes. By contrast, whites are generally thought of as less criminogenic than are blacks (Becker, 1987, p. 11).

Media Coverage of Vick and Roethlisberger in Black and White

Although Vick was subject to the harshest forms of social sanctioning, Roethlisberger was not reviled, ridiculed, rebuked, or charged with a crime. It was documented that Roethlisberger not only served alcohol to minors, a criminally deviant act for which he was never charged, but he also disparaged them by pronouncing: "All you bitches take my shots." The difference in how Vick was treated versus how Roethlisberger was treated by powerful social entities was especially observable in the disparate news coverage of their respective scandals.

As a consequence of labeling, blacks in almost every segment of society, including spectator sports, are seen as a deviation from acceptable norms by virtue of being non-white and purportedly criminogenic. The effect of such differential labeling by race has resulted in African-Americans experiencing structural racism that has bred structural inequalities

---

93 Newsletter forwarded electronically from Ron Stewart, Ph.D., who subscribes to the "Edge of Sports" editorials of Dave Zirin. Sent to Kenneth N. Robinson, M.S., on April 20, 2010.

throughout nearly every sphere of their lives, including the distribution of justice. The NFL and its conduct policy of-a-cop in Commissioner Roger Goodell are no different. When white players have engaged in deviant conduct, the NFL and its media alliances have sought to de-label them more often. The process of de-labeling speaks to how individuals like Ben Roethlisberger can avoid being permanently labeled as a deviant despite the complaints of two women who claimed he raped them. How is it that Vick continues to suffer the long-term effects of being negatively labeled while Roethlisberger has been able to shed his? The same powerful social elites that can influence labeling can also influence de-labeling. It is through de-labeling that Roethlisberger was able to reemerge in the NFL after Commissioner Goodell pronounced him fit, after he complied with the league's edict that he undergoes clinical intervention. Rather than the psychological evaluation contributing to an unfavorable view of him, it actually created a more favorable view of Roethlisberger. It had the effect of removing the stigma of him being a deviant, just as a doctor can lose the stigma of being an alcoholic after a successful intervention and treatment. As a consequence of such a ringing endorsement by the league's commissioner, the media followed suit with their coverage, and Roethlisberger resumed his NFL career without the residual effects of the negative label, i.e., sexual deviant. The person who is de-labeled is often welcomed back with open arms and is received with kindness and consideration, devoid of any negative attention being accorded to their deviant actions. The media deliberately avoided any questions about the rather serious sexual assault allegations, which helped Roethlisberger, concentrate on football. Consequently, he was able lead the Pittsburgh Steelers back to the Super Bowl in 2010. By contrast, Vick was relabeled rather than de-labeled. He was not welcomed back into society or the NFL, less the baggage, as was Roethlisberger. The relabeling of Vick was apparent when he found himself answering questions about dog fighting in 2010, despite having been reinstated in 2009.

Labeling Versus De-labeling: Similarities and Dissimilarities

The most important distinction between labeling versus de-labeling is whether the deviant label becomes affixed to the individual as a part of their social identity.

In the respective scandals involving Michael Vick and Ben Roethlisberger, the former was stigmatized for his dog fighting; the latter was sanitized despite his purported sexual deviance toward women. No matter which social reaction follows the perceived deviant act, the individual must attempt to reenter society with the hope of shedding the deviant identity. The differential effects of harmful labeling will be discussed in the context of Howard Becker's *Sequential Model of Deviant Behavior*. The model will be used to examine the issue of race and the differential effects of being "perceived as a deviant" as Michael Vick was, versus "not being perceived" as a deviant, as was the case of Roethlisberger.

The Process of Labeling Vick

The primary form of labeling establishes a deviant identity for the person, which may also include some form of deviance. But it is the person's belief in such a deviant identity that spurs them to commit secondary acts of deviance. The secondary deviance takes effect when the individual has accepted the deviant label, given their norm-violating actions, and continues to act out accordingly. Hence, Vick seemed to buy into the unsavory suggestions about him and his neighborhood, which shaped his identity, decisions, and downfall. By contrast, Roethlisberger appeared to have had a more stable socialization with his upbringing in Findlay, Ohio.

Roethlisberger's Upbringing

Ben Roethlisberger is the product of a two-parent household, which is supposed to bear its own distinctive advantages. He did not have to contend with the perils of poverty nor the effects of pejorative labeling. Vick, who was raised primarily by his mother, is a member of the African-American community, a minority group that has been plagued by crushing stereotypes that lead to dysfunctional behavior. By contrast, Roethlisberger is a member of the dominant group of whites who are portrayed as law abiding, reliable, and giving in to conformity. Such individuals are less often suspected of being deviants and are therefore less likely to be seen as deviants. Although they may commit deviant acts, it can occur in secrecy, which allows them to avoid prosecution and the negative label. Does this phenomenon of Roethlisberger not being perceived as a deviant help to explain how he may have functioned with secrecy when these reported rape incidents occurred? Did this secrecy help him avoid criminal prosecution? For Roethlisberger, the benefit of not being perceived as a deviant not only helped him avoid being charged with a crime, but it enabled him to remove the stain associated with the alleged deviant conduct. He resumed his NFL career without ongoing media queries over his sexual encounters with women. Conversely, Vick, being an African-American, came into the world plagued by the perception of being flawed. As false as such perceptions of African-Americans are, Vick fulfilled such low expectations and had to bear the awful stigma of being a merciless dog fighter and a convicted felon who was both financially and morally bankrupt. He was abhorred by American society for his crimes. Consequently, he resumed his NFL career amid questions of whether he should ever be allowed to reenter the league.

Vick is Labeled

Throughout his NFL career, Vick has been plagued by a series of pejorative descriptors. Some have included uncomplimentary notions like black quarterback, running quarterback, or an athlete, as opposed to the more palatable mobile quarterback. While the latter reference is typically reserved for white quarterbacks with athleticism, the notion of a black quarterback is a racist relic used to bring attention to the quarterback's race rather than his talents. When Vick scrambled or left the pocket, as some white quarterbacks often do, the television announcers would always second-guess his decision making. Hence he was described as *having no patience, too quick to run, unable to read the defense,* or *not going through his progressions* (i.e., exhausting his sequence of options on passing plays). Conversely, when white quarterbacks like John Elway, Brett Favre, and even Ben Roethlisberger have used their running abilities, the media would remark that such quarterbacks were *going the extra mile, showing leadership,* or *doing everything they could to help their team win.* Furthermore, despite their propensity to run, the media never referred to whites as *running quarterbacks* as they do blacks. Instead, when Elway ran with the football he was described as playing "sandlot football all over again."

Quarterbacks who are white have always run with the football but were heralded in the annals of pro football history for their feats with their feet. It is worth noting that for all of the stereotypes about blacks being running quarterbacks, the all-time record for rushing yards by a quarterback was held by a white quarterback. Bobby Douglas of the Chicago Bears gained 968 yards in 1972 on 141 rushing attempts, a mark that stood for thirty-four years until Vick broke it in 2006 with 1,039 yards on 123 attempts. Even Roethlisberger, who will also run with the football, is referred to by the media in efficient terms like *mobile quarterback* rather than *running quarterback,* and is revered for his ability to "extend the play." (Although, he is never criticized for his tendencies to get sacked as often as he does when extending the play.) As a consequence of being labeled as a running quarterback or athlete, Vick's unique brand of productivity has often been obscured, overlooked, and largely distorted.

Is Vick a Running Quarterback or a Real Quarterback?

In 2010 *NFL Network* analyst and former NFL head coach Steve Mariucci told *USA Today* that with the Philadelphia Eagles, Vick went from "Nervous Ned" in Atlanta—yet another label—to becoming a "real quarterback" in Philadelphia (Bell, 2010). In his eleven games as a starting quarterback with the Philadelphia Eagles in 2010, Vick threw twenty-one touchdowns passes against six interceptions and amassed more than 3,000 yards passing while completing sixty-two percent of his passes. While most NFL analysts felt the 2010 season signaled his arrival as a quarterbacking talent, his growth in the position was actually observable in 2006, the season before the dog fighting debacle.

Prior to his outstanding comeback season in 2010 when he posted his best passing statistics in his career, Vick's tremendous quarterbacking production was largely undervalued by media pundits covering the NFL. In fact, Brian Burke (2009) of Advanced NFL Stats reported on Vick's veiled production that has often gone overlooked. For example, he found that in 2006, while Vick was often chided for his tendencies to run with the football, he averaged more yards on such plays running than most quarterbacks who opted to throw. As an indicator of his ability to be two-dimensional, Vick's average yards per pass completion was higher than the top thirty quarterbacks in the NFL. Moreover, his "air yards" (how far the ball travels in the air before reaching the receiver) was higher than nearly all the top quarterbacks in the NFL. This sort of production underscores the role of the media in distorting reality. But it's this kind of production that has allowed Michael Vick to win throughout his career. Through week eight of the 2012 season, his career record as a starter was 56-40-1, with only one losing season. Having won nearly sixty percent of his games, Vick has one of the highest winning percentages of any active quarterback in the NFL. The reason this sort of dominance has been obscured is due to the media's tendency to give a warped view of Vick's outstanding play-making abilities.

For example, in the same *USA Today* article that featured comments from Mariucci about Vick as "Nervous Ned," the headline stated that his arrival as a bona fide passing threat made him *dangerous*. While negative notions of Vick as a black quarterback and running quarterback were indeed unfavorable ideas, perhaps the most harmful label, which seemed to have the most deleterious influence on Vick's off-the-field conduct, was the media's suggestion that he was *dangerous*.

Vick is "Dangerous"

Vick's style of play, which involved disabling defenses with his speed and agility and by running on designed passing plays, made him a human highlight reel. Additionally, his outstanding plays from the pocket made him one of the most exciting and difficult players to defend in the NFL. As thrilling as his runs were, and as awesome as his passing skills became, rather than describe him as a multi-talented quarterback, who was multi-dimensional, the media would refer to him as *dangerous*. Was there any particular harm in the media describing Vick's play as dangerous? Did such references have any influence on his decision to risk his career in dog fighting? How does labeling theory help to explain the damaging effect of Vick being typecast as *dangerous*? It appears that the media's use of such a term in describing Vick on the football field seemed to make him dangerous off the field. His dangerousness came to light through revelations of his abuse and torture of dogs in furtherance of his illegal dog fighting activities.

Historically, black males in American society have had to contend with perceptions of them promulgated in the media and in the criminal justice system as prototypical members of the *dangerous* classes. In fact, such typecasting of blacks influenced the creation of drug and sentencing laws that have targeted them on the state and federal level. These laws created so-called mandatory minimum prison sentences that punished black males disproportionately when compared to whites and others and have caused the prison population to skyrocket in the last twenty-five years. Yet crime has consistently declined over the same period. These outcomes raise questions of selective enforcement by race and underscore the harm of being labeled. In Vick's case, it was not enough for him to be labeled as dangerous because he was black. He was also labeled as *dangerous* for his style of play as a black quarterback. Is it realistic to suppose that Vick being labeled by the media as *dangerous* on the football field might have actually influenced his dangerous behavior off the field?

When television commentators referred to Vick as *dangerous,* it was usually after he left the security of his passing pocket during games. On the other hand, Vick engaged in the dangerous practice of dog fighting when he left the "pocket" of his Atlanta Falcons team on his off days.

For those who doubt that the media's reference to Vick as dangerous might not have influenced his dog fighting behavior through labeling, consider this: Vick verified his susceptibility to being typecast when, in response to references to him as "Superman," given his mode of play he had the "Superman" insignia tattooed on the back of his right hand.

This example provides ample evidence of the impact of media labeling and how it influenced Vick's self-identity. If the media's reference to him as Superman for his football exploits influenced him to tattoo the Superman logo on the back of his right hand, is it not logical to surmise then, that references to him as *dangerous* on the field might have also influenced him to demonstrate dangerousness toward dogs? Becker found that the deviant is the one to whom the deviant label has been successfully attached (1987, p. 10). As Table 5.1 indicates, Becker's sequential model of deviance shows the difference between being perceived as a deviant, as Vick was, versus not being perceived as one, like Roethlisberger. The difference can influence the self-identity and the roles fulfilled, which can ultimately affect outcomes in response to actual deviant behaviors.

Becker's Sequential Model of Deviant Behavior

Perception of subject/actor	Obedient behavior (falsely accused)	Rule-breaking behavior
Michael Vick is a deviant	Black quarterback, running quarterback, outsider, deviant, dangerous, Bad Newz, Virginia	Pure deviant-dog-fighter, operates Bad Newz Kennels, arrested, indicted, convicted sentenced to federal prison
Ben Roethlisberger is not a deviant	Seen as a conformist; white quarterback; received behavioral counseling	Secret deviant-not arrested for rape

Table 5.1. Pfohl's "Types of Deviant Behavior" (1994). Adapted from Howard S. Becker's *Outsiders* (1963).

Table 5.1 is an adaptation of Becker's model of sequential deviance, which shows that such processes and impacts of labeling usually develop over time. As a result of Vick being affixed with a plethora of pejorative labels in the NFL, such as black quarterback, running quarterback, reckless, and dangerous, he demonstrated both deviance and dangerousness toward dogs. The labeling he suffered in the NFL is only a part of the problem. It was also in his home state of Virginia where Vick experienced the onset of labeling.

Primary and Secondary Deviance

Primary deviance is measured by the onset of deviant conduct or even the awareness that one is a deviant, given the perception. For Vick's part, growing up as a black male in the American South in public housing projects carried with it a negative stigma all its own. As much as he found football to be a refuge from the pangs of growing up relatively poor, the impoverished surroundings brought out more negative ideas. Aside from Bad News, his community was also known as Newport Nam, a not so subtle reference to Vietnam, given the war-torn zone of drugs and violence (Vick, 2012). These conditions placed him on a teeter-totter cycle of ups and downs that would come to define his life's experiences. As his book details, depending on his choice of friends on any given day, football was either a refuge or a subterfuge; a deceptive device to obscure his tendency to be deviant. Vick walked the fine line between his good friends who enjoined the game of football like him and bad friends who encouraged him to be deviant, such as committing petty thefts. This initial onset of primary deviance would also include his tendency to watch dog fighting as a youth, only to result in secondary deviance as an adult when he developed an appreciation for participating in it. Not even the bourgeoning prospects of NFL stardom could dissuade Vick from becoming fully immersed in dog fighting. How does an NFL quarterback, drafted first overall, with the potential of becoming one of the greatest players in the game, use his career earnings to develop a dog fighting enterprise? How did he mistakenly blur the lines between right and wrong in such a careless manner? To say that Vick learned the behavior in his youth as a form of primary deviance is true, but an oversimplification of what went wrong. On the other hand, just as Vick had experienced cycles of conformity and deviance based on his circle of friends and the impact of labeling, such behavioral patterns would resurface in the midst of his promising NFL career.

The emotional high of being the first African-American quarterback ever drafted first overall was somehow diminished by the low blow of being thought of first as a black quarterback. Vick was seen as a deviation from the preferred model of whites at the position, which ushered in the primary feelings of being an outsider. Other indices of this primary deviance was the aforementioned perception of him as dangerous given his style of play and his hometown being labeled *Bad News*, Virginia. The secondary deviance follows when the actor internalizes the negative ideation and acts on the perceptions of the primary labeling (Trice & Roman, 1987). Because Vick apparently believed these negative perceptions defined him, he acted accordingly. He created Bad Newz Kennels and played the part of the dangerous deviant that the media had fashioned of him. The end result of this secondary deviance was his law-breaking involvement in dog fighting. These outcomes lend credence to W.I. Thomas's perspective of the self-fulfilling prophecy of labeling. It holds that if you believe a situation is real, then it is real in its consequences. The effect of Vick being pejoratively labeled as a deviant, i.e., black quarterback, as well as being treated as an outsider, in addition to media references of him as dangerous, combined with his hometown being typecast as *Bad News*, Virginia, all contributed to his fatalistic self-image and his ill-fated criminal conduct. By contrast, Roethlisberger, like most white quarterbacks, was never perceived as a deviant. He was seen as a conformist who was ideal, loveable, embraceable, wholesome, and one whom everyone could appreciate. "Big Ben," as he is affectionately known, was seen as being no different than the kid next door.

Roethlisberger was seen as complying with normal social expectations. But did such considerations mean he was not inclined to commit deviance? Just the opposite, such sentimentalities and perceptions might have allowed Roethlisberger to act out his deviance more secretively, given the explanation of Becker's sequential behavioral model. Hence both incidents involving allegations of sexual assaults by women occurred in closed-door settings, involving just him and the alleged victims. But more importantly, unlike Vick, because Roethlisberger was not perceived as a deviant to begin with, his actions did not result in any criminal charges and consequently no deviant label.

Roethlisberger is De-labeled

While Vick was accosted by animal rights advocates, Roethlisberger did not face a barrage of women's rights advocates, feminists groups, opponents of date rape, or activists touting "No means no." Roethlisberger shooed away any attempt by the media to even question the allegations of rape when he returned from his four-game suspension in 2010, even though he still faced a civil lawsuit. The differences in how these quarterbacks were treated meant Vick was unceremoniously typecast as this deformed public figure while Roethlisberger was hailed ceremoniously as a reformed figure. Roethlisberger was showcased as a beneficiary of quality intervention. The informal sanctions against him were relatively mild compared to what Vick endured. Most of the strong social reaction, which resulted in informal sanctions against Roethlisberger, came from Steelers fans, such as the decision to remove his image from the Pittsburgh Zoo. But nationally, there was not much outcry.

It also helped Roethlisberger that the only formal sanctions against him came from the NFL through the league's conduct policy. He was never charged with rape in either Nevada or Georgia. Additionally, neither Congress, nor the Georgia and Nevada state legislatures issued public rebukes. Neither state adopted new legislation in response to Roethlisberger's alleged criminal acts, nor did they question why existing laws were not enforced. In the Milledgeville incident, neither Congress nor the Georgia state legislature questioned why Roethlisberger was not arrested for serving alcohol to minors. Not even his reported pronounce-ment, "All you bitches take my shots," was enough to prompt any formal and punitive sanctions against him. In stark contrast, Vick's misconduct prompted Congress to amend the Animal Wel-fare Act, which increased the prison sentence from three to five years. In light of these indices of disparate treatment accorded to Vick versus Roethlisberger by a host of dominant entities, the following analysis will look specifically at how Roethlisberger was welcomed back with open arms following his scandals. The consequence of course is that he was de-labeled, which effectively removed the stigma of him as a sexual predator.

The NFL and the media were intent on de-labeling Roethlis-berger after his second allegation of rape for a number of reasons. On the one hand, the NFL and the media know that franchise quarterbacks, particularly those who are white, stimulate ratings, readers, and revenues. These respective powers were intent on reestablishing Roethlisberger as an acceptable personality and player in the NFL. The Steelers fans, who love their team, had grown weary of Roethlisberger and openly suggested the team get rid of him. Even worse, the Rooney family, which owns the Pittsburgh Steelers, strongly considered trading him. To further underscore how disappointed the Rooney family was in their fran-chise quarterback, Congressman Tom Rooney (R-FL), grandson to the Steelers' original owner and patriarch, Art Rooney, derided Roethlisberger publicly as an idiot (Leahy, 2010). The social reaction was so strong, that as noted, Pittsburgh patrons ordered that Roethlisberger's picture be taken down at the Pittsburgh Zoo (Leahy, 2010). Such a wide range of disparaging responses from the public was the sort of informal social sanctions that prompted the NFL and the media to de-label *Big Ben*.

De-labeling

De-labeling is the process where an individual who is labeled a deviant is able to shed the negative label and rejoin society anew (Trice & Roman, 1987). Often times, individu-als who served a prison sentence seek to be de-labeled to gain reentry as an acceptable member of society. Vick attempted to do so, only to learn that much of the anger toward him had yet to subside when he was released from prison. Much of the general public and animal advocacy groups like PETA flat out refused to accept his offer of contrition and reform. He still bears the label of a dog fighter despite over twenty speeches to young high school students in urban communities. Other examples of de-labeling as a process include individuals who are on the pathway to sobriety from an addiction to drugs or alcohol. Their successful completion of a substance abuse program may result in a ceremony of sorts and the deviant label of an addict is shed.

It should be noted that groups like Alcoholics Anonymous are viewed as "mutual aid organizations" that were created and sustained by people of high-ranking status, such as medical physicians to foster de-labeling (Trice and Roman, 1987, p. 372). The import of such organizations like Narcotics Anonymous is that they can de-label the addict by typecasting their addiction as a disease. Such an interpretation of alcoholism and drug addiction as a disease requiring social and clinical intervention was instrumental in reducing or eliminating the stigma attached to individuals needing treatment. This process is consistent with the role of dominant elites who are able to define who the deviants are and what constitutes deviance.

For Roethlisberger's part, the NFL took steps to de-label him by recommending behavioral counseling for him in 2010 after a second allegation of rape surfaced in less than a year. It may have seemed humiliating for Roethlisberger to go through a counseling evaluation, but in actuality the league's decision seemed to be a contrived attempt to de-label him. The NFL needed to institute some form of punitive sanctioning to reassure the public that it viewed his alleged sexual misconduct as serious. The league suggested that Roethlisberger get behavioral counseling after Commissioner Goodell met with him. It was after Goodell formulated his own impressions of Roethlisberger in their meeting that he recommended counseling. Roethlisberger emerged from his meeting with Commissioner Goodell very upbeat and indicated the meeting was very productive. The commissioner himself had to believe that the clinical results of a psychological evaluation would show that Roethlisberger was normal and therefore would diminish the view that he posed a sexual threat to women. While the results of this behavioral counseling were never made public, all indicators suggest that Roethlisberger was deemed fit and normal.

For the league's part, this was predictable. The results had the desired effect of de-labeling Roethlisberger. The league commissioner set the stage for his reentry into the league's circle and the community by pronouncing him fit and backing it up with the clinical evaluation, which created the impression he was harmless. By contrast, although Vick participated in animal sensitivity training and apologized for his abuse of the dogs and paid $1 million for their rehabilitative care, the commissioner required him to show remorse after his release from prison. In addition, Goodell was reticent to proclaim Vick fit to return to the NFL and instead expressed reservations. Even worse, the commissioner never mandated counseling for Vick.

The league's interest in de-labeling Roethlisberger was necessary for a couple of reasons. The league has always sought to preserve whites as franchise quarterbacks, which is the bread and butter position of the league. In the 1970s, NFL Commissioner Pete Rozelle ordered New York Jets star quarterback Joe Namath to divest his interest in a nightclub after it was revealed that organized crime figures were associated with the establishment. Namath initially refused and retired from the game, only to rescind and return to the NFL. Secondly, Dan Rooney, owner of the Pittsburgh Steelers, was among the biggest supporters of Roger Goodell as the replacement for Paul Tagliabue as NFL commissioner. De-labeling Roethlisberger was also important to the NFL's business interests, given that women are a big part of the NFL's viewing audience. Women are the fastest-growing segment of the NFL's fan base and are also the hubs of football families.

In addition, the league and its television network partners depend heavily upon the millions in revenues generated through the marketing nexus involving the *boys,* the *beers,* and the *babes.*

These commercials are usually set in bars. Therefore, the idea of a star NFL quarterback being charged with raping a college student in a bar was not a storyline that the NFL, the television networks, or beer sponsors wanted to face. Most beer commercials that are shown during NFL games feature barroom scenarios of men pursuing women with their favorite beer in hand with the underlying inference of a good-natured sexual conquest in progress. As noted earlier, in the fall of 2010 a Latina reporter was reportedly harassed by members of the New York Jets staff, including players and coaches. Aside from players responding lasciviously to her appearance in the locker room, when she was on the practice field, footballs were deliberately thrown in her direction. What happened next underscores the intermingling influence of NFL football and the nexus between *the boys*, *the beers*, and *the babes*. After the widely reported incident at the Jets facility, Corona, the beer manufacturer, which advertises on television during NFL games, developed a commercial showing a couple of women on the beach having footballs thrown to land near them.

In furtherance of this strong relationship between beer advertisement and football, beer companies such as Coors and Budweiser will pay hundreds of millions of dollars annually to be the official beer of the NFL. For other beer companies who do not gain the distinction of being the official beer of the NFL, they will pay television networks millions to advertise during games. Of course, the millions in beer advertising revenue help to explain why the attention to the scandalous behavior of Roethlisberger was minimized in 2010. In an apparent attempt to support their business interests with beer sponsors and the television networks, the league and the media sought to de-label Roethlisberger.

Stigmatized Versus Sanitized: How the Dominant Elites Treated Vick Versus Roethlisberger

As for the NFL's reaction to the Michael Vick dog fighting allegations, the league's commissioner was swift in addressing the question of the quarterback's involvement in the illegal enterprise. On the other hand, when the revelations of the rape allegations against Roethlisberger came to light in 2010, Commissioner Goodell indicated he would meet with Roethlisberger in due time (Wilson, 2010). That the league's commissioner demonstrated such moderation raised questions of differential treatment of players by race. Especially since, he addressed the allegations against Vick and other black players with deliberate speed. While most of the press chose to ignore this double standard by the league's commissioner, writers like Jemele Hill of ESPN.com (2010) and Allen Wilson of the *Buffalo News* (2010), both of whom are African-Americans, wondered aloud about the differential treatment accorded to Vick versus Roethlisberger. Further evidence of differential treatment being accorded to Vick versus Roethlisberger, by the league, was their reaction to the respective investigations by law enforcement officials.

Criminal and Civil Investigations of Vick Versus Roethlisberger

As noted, when reports emerged that Michael Vick was the subject of a criminal probe by state and federal law enforcement entities over dog fighting, the NFL publicly announced that it was dispatching its security team to *assist* investigators. The league's decision to send its security personnel to assist with the criminal probe against Vick was unusual for a couple of reasons. On the one hand, the NFL does not typically send its security personnel to *assist* with criminal investigations of its football players. Rather, the league will use its security personnel to fact-find for internal purposes, namely to be informed and to enforce its conduct policy. Thus, the decision by the NFL to extend unsolicited assistance to investigators in the Michael Vick dog fighting scandal was without precedent. Conversely, in neither of the two separate allegations of rape involving Roethlisberger, in two different states, involving two different women, did the NFL report sending its security personnel to *assist* investigators. Still of greater importance is that the differences in the NFL's reaction to Vick's and Roethlisberger's legal predicaments seemed to influence the different outcomes of the respective investigations.

The detective who should have been investigating the sexual assault complaint was so star-struck by Roethlisberger that he posed for a picture with him. Instead of exercising due diligence, the detective disparaged the young woman and consequently he later resigned. With so much unwarranted and unethical support from criminal justice personnel at Roethlisberger's disposal, the prosecutor seemed intent to spare the law enforcement community further embarrassment by ending the probe. These disparate outcomes reflect the larger issue of racial indifference on the part of the NFL and the media and selective enforcement of the law.

The league, much like the criminal justice system, seemed to place a higher value on the reputation and livelihood of Ben Roethlisberger, who is white, than it did Michael Vick, who is black. Of course the NFL has a history of according preferential treatment to white quarterbacks over black quarterbacks. Even more disconcerting, the NFL sent a very unfortunate message to women in our society. By not assisting investigators probing Roethlisberger as they did with Vick and the dogs, the league seemed to devalue the issue of sexual violence against women. Left open for interpretation, the message is that the NFL cared more about how one star quarterback mistreated dogs, than how another star quarterback allegedly mistreated women. The interesting irony of it all is that while Vick admittedly abused dogs and was vilified for it, in Roethlisberger's Georgia incident, he treated the female college students like dogs when he gave them alcohol and declared, "All you bitches take my shots" (Kriegel, p. 3). The league and the media never addressed Roethlisberger's comments about women being *bitches*. NFL football has become so popular among women that reportedly more of them watch the sport on television than those who watch soap operas. Furthermore, it is not lost on the league how their game has grown in popularity with women. The league markets products to women with commercials promoting NFL ladies apparel. While the NFL and media were up in arms about animal rights given Vick's abuse of dogs, Roethlisberger's conduct never became an issue of women's rights, nor was Roethlisberger required to speak to causes of preventing sexual violence against women the way Vick has had to speak out against violence against dogs.

Vick Needs to Show More Remorse

After Vick was released from federal prison following his near two-year sentence, he was told by the league commissioner that he needed to show "remorse" to the *"larger community"* before he would be reinstated (Bell, 2009). As for this need to show remorse, Vick did that abundantly before he went to prison. He stood before a throng of media with much contrition and apologized for his actions. In addition, he participated in animal sensitivity training and paid a king's ransom ($1 million) to rehabilitate the dogs that he harmed. Still, it was not enough for the NFL commissioner or the white male-dominated media. Alex Marvez (2009) of FoxSports.com stated, "The only clause Goodell forgot was the one forcing Vick to sit, beg, and roll over on command" (p. 1). On the other hand, Roethlisberger made one statement where he apologized, but for nothing in particular. It was deemed enough by the league commissioner and the white male-dominated media, which did not insist that he show more remorse. So of the two, Vick was more sincere and pointed about what he was sorry about given the greater social harm associated with such conduct. By contrast, Roethlisberger seemed superficial and was less forthcoming about his deviant conduct or its wider implications in society. To many objective observers, the failure of the NFL to impose similar requirements on Roethlisberger was a classical double standard. According to Zirin (2010), "He (Roethlisberger) should have to speak to young kids about the fact that 'No means no.' He should, in other words, have to do everything Michael Vick has had to do to make amends."[94] Incidents of sexual violence against women when alcohol is involved are an increasing social problem in America, particularly among

---

94 Dave Zirin, *Edge of Sports* is a weekly column transmitted via email. This editorial, "Ben Roethlisberger: No Justice, No play?", was sent to Ron Stewart, Ph.D., on April 20, 2010 at Buffalo State College, who forwarded it to Kenneth N. Robinson.

college students. Therefore the failure of the NFL to demand more from Roethlisberger sent the wrong message.

But there were a couple of problems associated with Commissioner Goodell's suggestion of Vick needing to show remorse to the *larger community*. The mandate was hardly inconsequential. This requirement by the commissioner meant that the negative labeling of Vick would only be perpetuated, especially throughout the media.

> According to Trice and Roman (1987): If these labelers see fit "officially" to classify the actor as a type of deviant, a labeling process occurs which eventuates in (1) self concept changes on the part of the actor and (2) changes in the definitions of him held by his immediate significant others, as well as the larger community (p. 371).

Rather than Vick being welcomed back from prison through a process of de-labeling, which would have shed the deviant label, his self-concept once more became that of the deviant dog fighter/ex-con who needed to placate the larger community, which labeled him in the first place. Because he was subject to greater labeling by the NFL and the media, definitions of him remained negative, especially in the face of the *larger community*. The effect exacerbated the animus toward him. Despite his showing remorse, he was continuously voted the most hated player in sports. One study of Vick's dog fighting dilemma found that whites more than non-whites felt that his prison sentence was too soft and believed that he should not be reinstated by the NFL.[95] The results of this study, which surveyed 400 adults, seemed to reflect the attitudes of many white fans and patrons of the game. Such attitudes seemed to not only influence the thinking of Goodell but also lent credence to the view that the term *larger community* referred to whites. Thus Commissioner Goodell was essentially telling Vick before he would be reinstated in the NFL that he had to genuflect before whites in

---

95 Piquero, Piquero, Gertz, Baker, Batton, and Barnes, 2011.

this country, the most influential of whom were angry with him and had already labeled him a deviant.

Who is the Larger Community?

There were other indicators that the commissioner's use of the phrase *larger community* was a direct reference to whites. It was fairly obvious that this concept did not include blacks in America, the one group that supported Vick throughout. In fact, despite his dog fighting crimes, most African-Americans acknowledged his wrongs but had forgiven him before he went to prison. Furthermore, many African-American players in the NFL spoke up in support of Michael Vick both before he pled guilty and again after he was released. Other prominent African-Americans who spoke up for Vick included Academy Award-winning actress and television talk show personality Whoopi Goldberg. Other advocates included heroines and heroes of the civil rights movement such as Juanita Abernathy, widow of the late Reverend Ralph Abernathy, and the Reverend Joseph C. Lowery of the Southern Christian Leadership Council (SCLC). There was also the support of the NAACP of Atlanta, most notably Reverend R.L. White, who called for justice, fairness, and due process in the investigation. Beyond civil rights icons and institutions, there was support from former professional athletes of prominence who are African-Americans. Many expressed their support for Vick in writing before he was sentenced. Among them were Major League Baseball Hall of Fame great and home run king Hank Aaron and former heavyweight boxing champion George Foreman. Other prominent African-Americans such as Shirley Pratt, mayor of Atlanta, forwarded a letter of support for Vick. Despite the advocacy of such luminaries who appealed to Judge Henry Hudson for leniency in the court's sentencing, Vick received the longest prison sentence of any of his co-defendants. While none of these individuals or groups sought to diminish what Michael Vick did, each tried to assuage the public vitriol with a bigger perspective. That bigger picture of course involved a reminder to the *larger community* that the legal process needed to unfold and that Vick had done a lot of good in his life, and these crimes involved the destruction of animals, not human beings.

The Relabeling of Vick

As a consequence of the league's differential treatment, Vick had to once more face the music of a media-orchestrated symphony of cynicism over his misdeeds. In 2009 he reentered the NFL amid questions of whether he should be allowed the privilege of playing. In keeping with this theme of differential treatment by race (Vick versus Roethlisberger; labeling versus de-labeling), questions by the media about whether Vick should be readmitted into the NFL helped to obscure the first allegations of rape against Roethlisberger over the Las Vegas hotel incident, which emerged in the summer of '09. By the summer of 2010, the NFL and the media offered the public reassurances that despite two sex scandals involving Roethlisberger, he had become a better person. The influence of the NFL on the media's coverage of these respective quarterbacks also contributed to the differential social reaction to both. Because the league treated Roethlisberger with more regard than Vick, the media and the general public seemed to followed suit.

The Media and Its Differential Treatment of Vick Versus Roethlisberger

One of the consequences of the NFL mandate that Vick show remorse was that it played perfectly into the hands of the mainstream media. Vick was ripped mercilessly by the same media in 2007 when he was tarred and feathered for his animal abuse crimes. Because the league's commissioner commanded Vick to display compunction, he could not decline to discuss the dog fighting crimes with the media as Roethlisberger had done with the allegations of rape. Had Vick declined to discuss the dog fighting malaise as late as 2010, the season of his NFL rebirth, he would have been criticized for failing to show contrition. As a consequence, the media preyed on Vick with questions about the dog fighting scandal that had him reliving the nightmarish details over and over. In May 2007, ESPN was among the first to break the story of an informant who indicated Vick was one of the "heavyweights" in illegal dog fighting. Conversely, in 2009, ESPN was reluctant to even report on the first rape allegation against Roethlisberger. (Note: The network had previously refrained from reporting on a civil lawsuit filed against Michael Vick by a woman, although rather than rape, the woman claimed she contracted a sexually transmitted disease from him). Despite the stunning allegations against Roethlisberger, which came to light just months after he led the Pittsburgh Steelers to a Super Bowl championship in '09, the media let it go. Instead they focused on Vick, who was seeking to be reinstated and thus had to take questions from the media. Consequently, Vick's dog fighting scandal from 2007 was used by the media to shield Roethlisberger from the allegations of sexual misconduct both in 2009, when the Vegas incident was first reported, and then again in 2010 when Roethlisberger returned from his suspension after the second allegation. Although Vick's management team may have thought it was advantageous for the quarterback to discuss the dog fighting debacle with the media, just the opposite occurred.

As a result of Vick providing so many interviews in the 2009 and 2010 seasons, he was permanently labeled a dog fighter/ex-con. Several reporters remarked of Vick that no matter what happened with the rest of his NFL career, he would forever be known as a dog fighter (Gleason, 2009; Saraceno, 2007). Even more disconcerting for him, instead of his interviews with the media improving the public's view of him, it actually worsened. The persistent questions about the dog fighting debacle contributed to Vick being voted the most hated player in sports in 2008, 2009, and 2010, despite his outstanding season in 2010, when he was named NFL Comeback Player of the Year and was runner-up for NFL MVP. He also lost out in a popular vote among fans who decided which player would appear on the cover of EA's (Electronic Arts) *Madden 2011* edition. Vick was out-voted by a finalist whose first name is Peyton. But rather than All-Pro, NFL MVP, Super Bowl-winning quarterback *Peyton Manning*, which would have made more sense, fans chose the unheralded, unremarkable, unheard of Peyton Hillis, running back for the Cleveland Browns. Such fan voting underscored the depths of rancor and enmity still harbored toward Vick, which was further inflamed by protestations from PETA, which spoke out against him appearing on the cover of EA Sports' NFL Madden game (*PETA wants Vick off Madden tourney*, 2011).[96] These unfortunate distinctions reflected the wide-ranging effects of Vick being stigmatized as the face of animal cruelty. Moreover, it was the NFL, the media, and the animal rights advocates like PETA that sought to permanently label Vick as a dog fighter, which contributed to his unpopularity and obscured his extraordinary reclamation season in 2010.

By contrast, Roethlisberger rode the wave of support and cooperation he received from the NFL and the media, which ensured his alleged misdeeds with women, would be non-issues when the 2010 season began. As early as August 2010, while Vick was being hammered by the media for his ill-begotten birthday party, news reports of Ben Roethlisberger were becoming more favorable. In light of his highly anticipated arrival at the Pittsburgh Steelers summer training camp and speculation over his March 2010 bar incident, coupled with the commissioner's decision to suspend him, and a pending lawsuit over an alleged sexual assault, renewed focus was centered on Big Ben.

Stigmatize Versus Sanitize

The 2010 NFL training camp was full of intrigue. Roethlisberger's second rape allegation in less than a year captured headlines, at least initially, and raised the ire of concern for the NFL. The big question posed by the media centered on how Big Ben would be received by fans at training camp. Additionally,

---

96 Retrieved from http://www.yardbarker.com/nfl/articles/peta_asks_ea_sports_to_remove_michael_vick.

there was interest in how Roethlisberger's teammates would react to him, since he never addressed them about the off-season incident in Georgia.

Despite the questions, the Steelers faithful greeted Roethlisberger warmly. It also helped Roethlisberger that wide receiver Hines Ward, one of the more popular players on the team, offered to accompany him when he took the field for the first time in camp. As the Steelers' camp commenced, more evidence of the media de-labeling Roethlisberger was apparent. An example of this phenomenon is observable in the *USA Today* newspaper's disparate coverage of the respective training camps of Vick's Falcons team in 2007 and Roethlisberger's Steelers team in 2010.

In covering Roethlisberger's much anticipated return to the Steelers in 2010, amidst two separate allegations of rape, *USA Today* inexplicably published a photo of the quarterback posing for a picture with two smiling women (Mihoces, 2010). The newspaper's decision to show two women happily posing with Roethlisberger seemed contrived and had the effect of lessening the stigma of him as a sexual threat to women. Yet the decision of *USA Today* to show this snapshot was far from coincidental. Instead it coincided with the thinking of NFL Commissioner Roger Goodell, who had reassured the public that Roethlisberger was fine. The judgment by *USA Today* to publish a cheerful caption of Roethlisberger with the two smiling women was particularly galling since he still faced a civil lawsuit in the Las Vegas incident.

By contrast, at the height of Vick's scandal in 2007, *USA Today Sports* published a picture of angry women holding signs at the Falcons training camp, protesting against Vick and calling for his suspension.[97] There were no women's rights groups protesting Roethlisberger, nor was there inflammatory media coverage of him in 2010. Instead, the storyline became that most Steelers fans welcomed him back, and so too did his team-

---

97 Colston, C. (2007). *Vick protests dominate opener of Falcons camp*. Retrieved from www.usatoday.com/sports/ football/nfl/falcons/2007-07-26-camp-scene_N.htm.

mates. Consequently, these media outlets ensured the public that Roethlisberger would not become the face of sexual violence against women among athletes, the way Vick became the face of animal cruelty against dogs.

Roethlisberger's methods in both alleged incidents of rape were described as very similar. Zirin (2010) stated that details in both complaints against Roethlisberger were "so similar, patterned and damning," that one must conclude that either the Milledgeville college student was a "sociopathic genius" or that Roethlisberger has a *modus operandi* when sexually assaulting women.[98] Apparently, *USA Today* did not care enough about the alleged victims in either case. The newspaper identified two women, Brielle Leinweber, twenty, and Amber Mechling, twenty-seven, who posed for a picture with Roethlisberger at the Steelers camp. Leinweber, who at the time, was the same age of the Milledgeville victim, seemed to sum up the feelings of most fans when she said, "We don't really care what he does in his personal life. As long as he plays good on the field, we're happy" (Mihoces, 2010, p. 1). In another article, Mihoces (2010) quotes a thirty-year-old woman and Steelers fan who stated the purported victims of these rapes were "full of crap." Of all the media outlets to provide disparate coverage of the Vick and Roethlisberger scandals, the television networks that partner with the NFL were the most blatant. The pre-season ended with the commissioner reducing Roethlisberger's suspension from six to four games, which also helped to de-label him. While Roethlisberger's 2010 pre-season quickly gave way to him serving the four-game suspension imposed by the league, Vick's season took flight as he was thrust into duty as the starting quarterback of the Philadelphia Eagles on opening Sunday.

The 2010 season began with these quarterbacks at polar opposites. The media would oblige with coverage that continued to stigmatize Vick and further sanitize Roethlisberger. Whereas

---

98 Dave Zirin, Edge of Sports is a weekly column transmitted via email. This editorial, "Ben Roethlisberger: No Justice, No play?", was sent to Ron Stewart, Ph.D., on April 20, 2010 at Buffalo State College, who forwarded it to Kenneth N. Robinson on same day.

Kenneth N. Robinson, MS

Vick was persistently peppered with questions about his dog fighting debacle, which was now three years old, Roethlisberger's more recent incidents received little or no attention. In fact, Roethlisberger forbade the press to even broach the rape complaint(s), and they complied. By contrast, Vick did national interviews with the likes of Jim Mora, Jr., his former head coach in Atlanta, turned analyst for *NFL Network*; Bob Costas of NBC's *Sunday Night Football*; and Chris Berman of ESPN. In each interview, Vick recounted his repulsive crimes, which had already been addressed on numerous occasions. Reiterating as much only perpetuated the view of him as an ex-con/dog fighter, thus perpetuating derogatory distinctions that overshadowed his extraordinary story of redemption.

A-Mora-l: "Isn't Vick a Coach Killer?"

In each of the nationally televised interviews that Vick acquiesced to in 2010, he relived the horrors of his dog fighting deeds, despite the fact he was already one year into his reinstatement. With the exception of his 2009 interview with James Brown of CBS's *60 Minutes*, no national interviewers deduced anything unique from Vick. It was Brown's probing questions that reached Vick's innermost thoughts, prompting him to reveal that his involvement in dog fighting was influenced by a *so-called culture*. As meaningful as this concession was to become, most in the media and some in academia misappropriated this so-called culture to mean hip-hop's gangsta rap culture. Rather, research presented in this work reveals that this culture is actually a centuries-old parent culture of dog fighting. Beyond Brown's insightful discussion, neither the NFL Network nor NBC nor ESPN accorded Vick a nationally televised feature interview when he was a non-story, third-string quarterback in 2009. Unfortunately, these networks waited for Vick to reemerge in 2010 as a primetime player in the NFL before rehashing a host of disparaging questions, which stigmatized him further in the eyes of the public. Conversely, neither the NFL Network, NBC, ESPN, nor any other major media outlet interviewed Roethlisberger upon his return with such uneasy questions about the rape allegations. This is especially notable since Roethlisberger played the entire 2010 season with the outstanding question of sexual misconduct involving the college student on the periphery, and a pending civil lawsuit from the Las Vegas incident in front of him.

Mora or Less?

Among the first national interviews of Vick during his 2010 comeback season was one with the NFL Network's Jim Mora, Jr., Vick's former head coach with the Atlanta Falcons. Oddly enough, Mora asked Vick why he had not told the truth about his dog fighting since America is such a "forgiving nation." As best as he may, Vick, who has certainly been maligned in the media, tries to tell the press what he believes they want to hear. Hence he responded that he did not tell the truth because his whole life had been a lie. While that may be in large part true, had Vick been more truthful he could have told Mora more than he expected. Unbeknownst to the public, another reason why Vick initially lied about his involvement in dog fighting was that his life was being threatened by lynching. Even worse, if the nation was so forgiving, as Mora pointed out, why was Vick still the subject of death threats? If the nation was so forgiving, why was Vick voted the most hated player in sports three years in a row? If the nation was so forgiving, why were people like Tucker Carlson of Fox News saying he should have been executed for his crimes? Why would Matt Buehrle of the Chicago White Sox later say both he and his wife wished he had gotten hurt in his successful comeback season? If the nation is so forgiving, why was the animal rights advocacy group PETA still hounding him? Even more disparaging, who was Mora to be raising questions about honesty, when he went on public radio lobbying for the head coaching job at the University at Washington in his last season of coaching Vick in Atlanta in 2006?

Mora not only lobbied for the head coaching job at his alma mater, but indicated that he would leave the Atlanta Falcons in the middle of the playoffs if offered the job. He would later say his comments were said in jest, but they derailed Vick and the team. The Falcons not only failed to make the playoffs, but 2006 became Vick's first losing season of his illustrious NFL career. If Mora cared anything about Vick like he said during the interview, he would have offered the quarterback an apology on behalf of his father, Jim Mora, Sr. It was also during the 2006 season that Mora Sr. was asked on public radio if Vick was a coach killer, and he agreed. Had Mora Jr. been any kind of interviewer, he would have brought this up during his discussion with Vick. Mora Jr., then asked, in a very self-serving way, if there was anything else he (as head coach) could have done. How about standing up for Vick after your father derogatorily labeled him a coach killer? How about having the decency to admit his failures as a head coach when he became a huge distraction to Vick and the team in his selfish attempts to land another head coaching job at his alma mater in 2006? Mora's bizarre radio interview became a huge story in the NFL, which overshadowed Michael Vick's most outstanding season to date. He had career highs in passing and broke the single-season rushing yards record for a quarterback. Still, Mora was not alone in using an interview to further perpetuate the image of Vick as a dog fighter/ex-con.

NBC: No Balanced Coverage of Vick and Roethlisberger

On November 21, 2010, during halftime of a nationally televised game between the Philadelphia Eagles and the New York Giants, NBC broadcasted a previously recorded interview of Vick by Bob Costas. Initially, the interview highlighted Vick's outstanding exploits as a passer up to that point in the season. But such currency soon gave way to more questions about the dog fighting scandal and his imprisonment, which quickly overshadowed his amazing comeback story. Rather than focus strictly on his football season as the media did with Roethlisberger, Costas asked Vick as many as six questions related to his dog fighting case, from his crimes, to his imprisonment, to being on parole, etc. Such questions did more to debase Vick as an ex-con rather than a quarterback who was once again excelling in the NFL. More evidence of such unconstructive typecasting in the media coverage of Vick came from comments made by *Sunday Night Football's* color commentator Chris Collingsworth.

During the December 12 game between the Eagles and the Dallas Cowboys, NBC's play-by-play man Al Michaels shared that when the team travels, Vick receives a positive response from the public, according to his head coach Andy Reid. Then Collingsworth derisively retorted, "There must be some very forgiving people out there, because I will never forget what he did." [99] Despite Vick establishing himself as one of the premier quarterbacks in the NFL, the dog fighter/convict identity was still being treated as his master status (Pfhol, 1994, p. 353). The disdainful distinction superseded other descriptors of him as a once-again elite performer in the NFL. But there was more evidence of racism in the media's differential coverage of Vick versus Roethlisberger.

On December 5, 2010, NBC's *Sunday Night Football* featured Ben Roethlisberger and his Pittsburgh Steelers against the Baltimore Ravens. But unlike NBC's interview with Vick, Costas did not interview Roethlisberger about his aberrant conduct. The absence of a halftime interview of Roethlisberger by Costas was indicative of a double standard by race in the media. The decision to not interview Roethlisberger was questionable since newer allegations of sexual assault had occurred in 2010. In addition, he had been suspended for the first four games of the season. Plus, he was the subject of a pending civil lawsuit from one of the incidents. So why would NBC and Bob Costas interview Vick about his dog fighting scandal and prison sentence from 2007 but not interview Roethlisberger to discuss allegations of rape from 2009 and 2010?

One explanation is that the media has always portrayed blacks as criminogenic. The decision by NBC and Costas to interview Vick about his issues and not Roethlisberger perpetuated stereo-

---

99 The NBC Sunday Night Football NFL Philadelphia Eagles versus Dallas Cowboys, December 12, 2010.

types of black males as inherently deviant while whites are not. But more attempts to sanitize Roethlisberger would follow.

"Side-lie"

In his introductory comments for the December 5 *Sunday Night Football* game between the Steelers and Ravens on NBC, Al Michaels noted that in the previous meeting between the two teams on October 3, Roethlisberger had been "sidelined." This statement by Michaels was misleading and of course amounted to a side-lie. To say that Roethlisberger was sidelined suggested he was unavailable because of an injury. Roethlisberger was not sidelined in the earlier contest between the two teams. He was actually serving his four-game suspension imposed by the league in response to successive complaints of sexual assault against him. As a consequence of being suspended by the NFL, he was forbidden from any interaction with the team, including being on the Steelers sidelines. So why did Michaels distort the truth about Roethlisberger's conspicuous absence in the first meeting between the Steelers and Ravens?

Clearly, NBC's Michaels and Costas followed the NFL's lead and sought to sanitize Roethlisberger in spite of his deviant conduct. These efforts demonstrate the harm associated with a media industry dominated by white males. These same media outlets had no problem piling on Vick about his deviant conduct. The NFL Network and NBC were not alone. ESPN, whose report on Vick's involvement in dog fighting seemed to spur the federal probe, exacerbated the disparate treatment in the coverage of Vick when compared to Roethlisberger.

NY Daily News Piece on ESPN

ESPN was no different in its differential treatment of the two quarterbacks, by race. Chris Berman, the Emmy Award-winning host of ESPN's flagship NFL pre-game show, *Sunday NFL Countdown,* interviewed Michael Vick on December 20 and rehashed some of the same questions about his dog fighting, including a discussion of his imprisonment. For good measure, Berman even brought up the infamous birthday party that Vick threw for himself in the summer of 2010. But, like the other networks, ESPN did not interview Roethlisberger about his off-the-field, seedy conduct. That Roethlisberger was not asked such negative questions during the 2010 season contributed to his ability to lead his team to the Super Bowl, despite his four-game suspension. Even more evidentiary of this deliberate attempt to de-label Roethlisberger were comments made by Berman and his co-host on ESPN, Tom Jackson, after the Steelers won the AFC Championship game and advanced to the Super Bowl.

Raissman (2011), of the *New York Daily News,* stated that ESPN's Berman and Jackson "Twinkied up the story" about Roethlisberger advancing to the Super Bowl. Consistent with the deliberate attempt to avoid mentioning Roethlisberger's reported transgressions against women, Berman proffered, "Whatever happened or did not happen, everybody knows the story of why he didn't play the first four weeks of the season" (Raissman, 2011, para. 5). The writer could readily sense the reluctance of Berman to address Roethlisberger's transgressions. Raissman observed, "Maybe Berman didn't want to present the facts, but he should not have assumed everyone watching knew the allegations that led Roger Goodell to suspend the quarter-back (Roethlisberger) (para. 6)." But Berman, who leads these discussions for ESPN's NFL programming, seemed so intent to de-label Roethlisberger that in addressing his travails, he, like Al Michaels, refused to use the word "suspension." Instead, Berman simply noted that the quarterback did not play the first four weeks. Berman then made a wholly subjective observation in noting that Roethlisberger's emotional reaction to winning the AFC Championship, in which he knelt down and covered his face, showed he was a "changed man" and a "better person." Such comments amounted to unsubstantiated, fallacious hyper-bole, designed to sanitize Roethlisberger in the eyes of fans. When compared to Berman's discussion of the Vick scandal, such differential treatments are a double standard. His partner Jackson was equally inclined to forgo commentary on Big Ben's scandalous incidents. He too observed that Roethlisberger was a changed man and noted that the quarterback took his *medicine* from the commissioner's office. Didn't Vick take his medicine from the commissioner's office? He was suspended indefinitely when the revelations of his dog fighting came to light in 2007. Then he served another four-game suspension after he was released from prison and reinstated. Moreover, he was only reinstated after the commissioner insisted that he show remorse. On the other hand, Jackson's suggestion that Roethlisberger took his medicine from the commissioner is consistent with the process of de-labeling.

Both alcoholics and drug addicts often undergo clinical intervention that includes medication in recovery. Because their social problem is seen as an ailment or illness, the affected person is seen as one who needs treatment rather than punishment. The medicine in this case, as Jackson alluded to, was the meeting with Commissioner Goodell in his office, where he mandated that Roethlisberger receive a "professional behavioral evaluation," the results of which culminated in Roethlisberger being pronounced fit for football by the commissioner, which influenced the way the media covered him. These processes had the effect of eliminating the stigma associated with Roethlisberger's behavior. Consequently he was de-labeled. In a rather twisted irony, ESPN's disparate coverage of Vick versus Roethlisberger reaffirmed the results of a study, the network reported on just weeks before the Super Bowl. During a National Town Hall Meeting at the New Ebenezer Baptist Church, to commemorate the national holiday in honor of Dr. Martin Luther King Jr., Bob Ley of ESPN's *Outside The Lines* reported that media coverage of the Vick scandal was the least kind, while the coverage of Roethlisberger's scandal(s) was the most kind.[100]

This disparate treatment of Vick versus Roethlisberger surfaced once again in preparation for the 2010 Super Bowl. While Vick's Eagles were eliminated in the first round, Roethlisberger

---

100 ESPN's *Outside The Lines*, town hall meeting at the New Ebenezer Baptist Church, in Atlanta, GA., January 15, 2011.

would be competing in his third Super Bowl in five years. Since the media had complied with Roethlisberger's edict that he would not discuss the allegations of rape during the regular season, it would be interesting to see how the press would react now that he was in the Super Bowl. Mike Lombardi of NFL Network reflected the approach of most in the media when he lofted this soft volley: "Ben, how does it feel to be going back to the Super Bowl after everything you've gone through this year?"[101] This very vague question reflected the widespread practice of the media, which was designed to insulate Roethlisberger by avoiding specific mentioning of the actual allegations of rape. Instead, the public was left to infer what happened in Roethlisberger's offseason rather than those issues being reported as the media did continuously with Vick.

During the season Roethlisberger told the press he would discuss these sexual assault complaints when the season was over. Now during Super Bowl week he had a new response. He would deflect media questions about the rape allegations with this: "That's a reflective question." Put another way, Roethlisberger was telling the press he would not reflect on nor discuss the rape allegations. The media obliged. Conversely, despite being a spectator during the run-up to the Super Bowl, somehow the media found a way to use Vick for more fodder. There were several media stories that underscored how much residual dislike the public harbored for Vick. First there was controversy when Dwaine Caraway, the city of Dallas's mayor pro tem, awarded Vick the key to the city, which drew a sharp rebuke from the media and animal rights groups. Then there were reports of a dog owner who adopted one of the dogs from Vick's Bad Newz Kennels, and who approached Vick in public but was ignored. Yet, the most stunning example of differential media coverage during Super Bowl week occurred when a story broke that a party in Michael Vick's honor would be hosted in Arlington, Texas.

---

101 Mike Lombardi, of the NFL Network, interviewing Ben Roethlisberger in the Steelers locker room after the AFC Championship, January 23, 2011.

While it certainly would have been ill-advised for Vick to have his name associated with a Super Bowl party, still it was shocking to see the amount of media attention this report garnered. It was so bad that the commissioner was questioned about it following his State of the League address. Goodell remarked that he had spoken to Vick several times about his schedule during Super Bowl week in the host city. Why is it that the commissioner seemed more preoccupied with Vick's activities during the Super Bowl week than Roethlisberger's? This is an especially important question when you consider Vick was not playing in the game, but Roethlisberger was. While every conceivable issue confronting Vick, from receiving the key to a city to a dog owner approaching him to rumors circulating that his name was associated with a party, drew greater media scrutiny, Roethlisberger was left alone. Such differential perceptions conjured up Becker's *Sequential Model of Deviant Behavior.* While Vick was perceived as bad, Roethlisberger was not. Because Roethlisberger was perceived as conforming, as the model suggests, he would be more likely to engage in deviance discreetly.

During Super Bowl week, TMZ obtained video of Roethlisberger, who along with some of his offensive linemen, was running up an $800 bar tab. Unlike rumors of Vick's name being associated with a party, there was visual evidence of Roethlisberger laughing with his teammates while drinking alcohol. Additionally, the idea of Roethlisberger being in a bar with a group of large men too closely resembled the 2010 scenario that nearly resulted in him being arrested for an alleged rape. Where was the media concern that his use of alcohol in a bar might have negative consequences given the issue with him and women? Apparently, none of these questions were seen as important to ask the commissioner, as they did about Vick. Even worse, following the Super Bowl, which the Steelers lost to the Green Bay Packers, Roethlisberger's drinking during the week was never questioned as a potential factor in his relatively poor play. He threw two interceptions that helped spell defeat for his team in the biggest game of the season. The latter example once more demonstrated how Vick and Roethlisberger were treated

differently by the NFL and the media. Roethlisberger was portrayed as a changed man according to the likes of the NFL and
ESPN's Chris Berman. If he was such a changed man as Berman
asserted, why would he be in a bar running up an $800 tab in
a setting that was not so different from where an alleged rape
occurred? If he was such a better person, why drink so much
during the week in which he would be playing in the biggest
game of the season? Incidentally, on Super Bowl Sunday, the
story of Roethlisberger's drinking was discussed by Berman's
colleagues on *Sunday NFL Countdown.*

While Berman did not have much to say about it, despite
his premature promotion of Roethlisberger as a better person,
his colleague, ESPN analyst Keyshawn Johnson, did. Johnson,
a former NFL player, noted that Roethlisberger's drinking in a
bar should have been an issue given his previous conduct issues.
While Mike Ditka, who is also an analyst on ESPN, disagreed,
Johnson aptly noted that if Michael Vick was seen walking
down the street with a dog, it would certainly have been an issue
of concern. Johnson was absolutely correct. Not one member of
ESPN's panel disagreed with him. Still, Johnson was a rarity in
his ability to objectively juxtapose the differences between how
Roethlisberger was treated by the media versus Vick.

There were other examples of how the media and American
society treated the quarterbacks differently. When Vick released
his reality series that attempted to give the public insight into
what went wrong in his life in 2010, it was noted that he became
engaged to his longtime girlfriend. But the mainstream media
ignored this development as a potential sign of his ongoing
maturation. On the other hand, in 2011, when it was revealed
that Roethlisberger was engaged to marry, it was given favorable
media attention by major news agencies such as *USA Today,*
ESPN, and others. Additionally, Roethlisberger indicated he
wanted to become a role model, and the press spoke about his
not-for-profit organization and charitable work. By contrast,
when it came to Michael Vick, his charitable works were treated
as irrelevant by the mainstream media. Despite Vick's Grateful
to Give Back Foundation giving toys away to children during

the holidays and distributing free turkeys during Thanksgiving, his good works were ignored. Furthermore, Vick contributed to the delivery of upwards of $100,000 to aid victims of Hurricane Katrina, none of which was brought up when he was attempting to rehabilitate his reputation.

The most decisive demonstration of differential treatment accorded to Vick and Roethlisberger was that of the law enforcement community. Vick was charged, convicted and imprisoned for his criminal misdeeds. By contrast Roethlisberger was never charged for his alleged acts of sexual assault. The arm of the law is an extension of the politics of the state, which exercises considerable influence in defining, who is a deviant and what constitutes criminal deviance.

Conclusion

The preceding chapter addressed the differential effects of labeling versus de-labeling given the social reaction to deviant conduct involving Michael Vick and Ben Roethlisberger. While both of these quarterbacks were cited for conduct that was not only seen as deviant, but also criminogenic, Vick bore the brunt of negative media coverage. Although Vick was stigmatized for his conduct, Roethlisberger was sanitized. The chapter highlighted the manner in which labeling led to both primary and secondary deviance on the part of Vick. Throughout his life, he has been plagued by pejorative references to him that have shaped his self-identity and seemingly his conduct. Vick grew up with a host of negative reflections of himself and his community.

In light of these disparate developments, the NFL and the NFLPA (National Football League Players Association) should provide more counseling to all players, but particularly African-Americans, given the history of pejorative labeling in the sports reporting media that covers it. This is especially important given the greater proportion of African-American players in the NFL having problems with arrest incidents. In addition, the NFLPA should push for greater mentoring support and counseling for

African-Americans playing quarterback given the history of structural racism that the NFL has fostered at this position, and that the media has perpetuated. In addition, Congress should take a closer look at the unbridled authority that the NFL commissioner has in dispensing punitive sanctions. Questions have been raised about the commissioner's tendency to treat black and white players differently, and the Vick and Roethlisberger scandals added credence to this view.

CHAPTER VI

Vick Versus Boudreaux
in Black and White:

Was Race the Case?

"When it's a Vick versus a Boudreaux, it's no contest."
                              - Earl Ofari Hutchinson, 2007[102]

Throughout the Michael Vick dog fighting narrative of 2007, there was a strong sense, particularly in the African-American community that the mainstream media contributed mightily to his criminal prosecution. It became rather clear that the sensational reporting of Vick's legal dilemma created the false impression that dog fighting as a social problem was somehow unique to black males as street fighters. The very opposite is true. Historically, and even presently, white males loom large in the underworld sphere of dog fighting. Dog fighting as a form of animal combat is a centuries-old artifact of European culture that was transplanted to America. But, the Vick scandal recast dog fighting as a social problem primarily confined to urban areas among gang members, drug dealers, and others with a host of criminogenic behaviors. Yet there is evidence that whites throughout America remain actively involved in dog fighting at the highest levels.

---

102 Earl Ofari Hutchinson wrote a commentary titled "Vick versus Boudreaux: A Tale of Hypocrisy." It appeared in the Huffington Post, August 27, 2007.

In 2003, prosecutors in New York State nabbed James Fricchione, who is known as the "Al Capone" of dog fighting. Fricchione's involvement included publishing magazines on the blood sport that were distributed worldwide (Weir, 2007). Police raided his apartment and found an electrocution chamber for dogs that did not perform well. That Fricchione had a device for executing dogs underscores how errant the media was in skewing the view of this primitive practice as if it were somehow unique to Vick. These wretched behaviors are centuries-old conduct norms that remain as central tenets of the dog fighting culture. The benefit of reexamining Vick's depraved indifference toward dogs is that it gives additional credence to the assertion that a parent culture of dog fighting influenced his conduct. Although Vick pleaded guilty and served nearly two years for dog fighting, Fricchione was sentenced to two to seven years in prison for animal cruelty.[103]

In another high-profile case involving dog man David Tant, who is white, police discovered his dog fighting operation in the worst way. A state surveyor was wounded after tripping a booby trapped shotgun set by the notorious dog fighter. Tant, of Charleston, South Carolina, was convicted in 2004 and later sentenced to forty years in prison. Despite his status as a world-renowned dog fighter and breeder (whose dogs were reportedly sold as far away as Asia and eastern Germany), his sentence was reduced to thirty years. But in 2010, a parole board voted five to two to release him after serving a mere five years and ten months.[104] The high-profile arrests of Fricchione and Tant represent examples of white males' continuous involvement in dog fighting. Evans, Forsyth, and Gauthier (1998), of the University of Louisiana at Lafayette, studied a subculture of dog fighting and found that ninety percent of the participants were rural working-class whites.

---

103 Tom Weir, *USA Today Sports*, 2007: "Vick's case sheds light on dark world of dog fighting."
104 Retrieved from http://www.postandcourier.com/article/20100908/PC1602/309089938. Yvonne Wenger, 2010.

The researchers examined dog fighting as a "symbolic expression of white masculinity" in the South. That these researchers emanated from the city of Lafayette is not so ironic, considering the parish has remained a fertile breeding ground for the blood sport. Lafayette, whose population is seventy-three percent white, is the fourth largest city in Louisiana and is regarded as the center of Cajun culture. Beyond this unique distinction, Lafayette remains an epicenter for animal combat generally, and dog fighting in particular. The parish has produced legendary dog men such as Lafayette Police Chief Gaboon Trahan and his comrade in canine combat, the "don" of dog fighting, Floyd Boudreaux. A dog man is one who is particularly adept at breeding and training dogs for animal warfare. Trahan and Boudreaux were among the most renowned, and each contributed much to the lore and lure of the blood sport throughout America and the world. In 1950, Trahan invented the Cajun rules of dog fighting. As noted, these rules are still used today in dog fighting matches from America to Afghanistan. But the most infamous dog man from Louisiana, whose legend only grows with time, is the aforementioned, internationally renowned Floyd Boudreaux.

Boudreaux is considered royalty in the dog fighting game. His bloodline of fighting dogs was among the most sought after in the world. Some estimates suggest his litters have fetched more than $10,000 a pup from buyers as far away as Mexico and Japan.[105] The sheer breadth of Boudreaux's international sales of dogs caught the attention of U.S. Customs officials in the Department of Homeland Security. Their surveillance of his property, along with evidence uncovered by state investigators and animal rights advocates, culminated in the arrests of both Floyd and his son Guy in March 2005. Their arrests on forty-eight counts of dog fighting occurred two years prior to Michael Vick's bust. By the time the Boudreauxs went to trial in October 2008, Vick was already serving a near two-year federal prison sentence. Although the state of Virginia and the federal

---

105 Retrieved from http://www.pet-abuse.com/cases/3994/LA/US/.

government charged Vick, only the state of Louisiana charged Boudreaux and his son. The failure of the federal government to charge the Boudreauxs was surprising. Floyd had a prior arrest on dog fighting charges and has a world-renowned reputation for dog fighting. Additionally, the failure of the federal government to charge the Boudreauxs as they did Vick was especially galling given the latitude of the amended Animal Welfare Act of 2007.

This chapter will review details of the state of Louisiana's investigation and the arrests of Boudreaux and his son, as well as factors that influenced the outcome of the trial. It will examine the question of why the federal government did not use the Animal Fighting Prohibition Enforcement Act of 2007 to prosecute Boudreaux. Included in this discussion will be a review of the differential treatments accorded to Vick versus Boudreaux by the media, animal rights organizations, and the federal government. The dissimilarities were especially observable in the disparate outcomes of their criminal cases. While Vick was convicted on over fifty counts of dog fighting and sentenced to federal prison for nearly two years in 2007, Boudreaux and his son were acquitted on all state charges in 2008.

Vick's guilty plea was largely driven by his co-defendants and their willingness to testify against him. By contrast, the Boudreauxs chose a non-jury trial in their home parish of Lafayette, Louisiana, where a presiding judge decided their fates. Although the Boudreauxs were tried together, the bulk of this chapter's focus will be on Floyd rather than his son Guy. The father is the renowned dog fighting legend and was the focal point of the criminal investigation. Despite the differential results, a host of important questions warrant reflection. Given the national attention that Vick's case brought to dog fighting as a social problem, why did the national media ignore the Boudreaux trial? Why were national animal rights organizations such as PETA and the Humane Society so visible during Vick's legal drama but were practically invisible at Boudreaux's trial? Was race a factor in the differential treatment accorded to these respective defendants by the federal government? Did the inaction of the federal government in the case of the Boudreauxs reflect the tradition of states' rights? Given the differential treatment accorded to Vick versus Boudreaux, the chapter will discuss the import of equal protection of the law. Additionally, in an attempt to better explain the disparate consideration accorded to Vick versus Boudreaux, both the labeling theory and the subculture of violence perspective will be discussed. This chapter will explore the preceding questions in depth, while inculcating race as an interceding variable.

Climatic Change

As for why the federal government did not get involved in the Boudreaux case, the inattention by the national media and national animal rights advocates certainly contributed. During the investigation of Vick, the national leaders of PETA and the Humane Society used the media to inflame public sentiment. Their leaders did media interviews and distributed protest signs to the public. The signs showed disturbing pictures of dogs with injuries that were apparently related to dog fighting. These provocative images spurred angry protests throughout the country and especially outside the Falcons training camp in Flowery Branch, Georgia. The heated demonstrations continued outside the federal courthouse in Virginia whenever Vick appeared. Such actions were not only inflammatory, but achieved the desired effect of stoking the fires of the American public, which also alerted elected officials on Capitol Hill. Consequently, the federal government launched an independent probe that led to Vick being indicted. Such a retributive reaction, undoubtedly spurred by the media and animal rights activists, prompted Congress to pass an amendment to the AWA, making dog fighting a federal felony in 2007. The national animal rights leaders who were vociferous in their vilification of Vick were missing in action in the media coverage of the Boudreauxs' trial. Instead of high-profile national advocates like Wayne Pacelle and John Goodwin of the Humane Society, low-profile representatives from the Humane Society of New Orleans and the Louisiana SPCA were interviewed in the press. Because the Boudreaux case only received attention from local animal rights advocates, the media coverage remained local as well.

The decidedly local press coverage lessened the prospect of the federal government becoming involved with the amended Animal Welfare Law of 2007. Moreover, the inaction on the part of the federal government in the Boudreauxs' trial is especially questionable since he and his son did not go to trial until October 2008. Furthermore, the evidence against them came from U.S. Customs agents from the Department of Homeland Security.

Boudreaux is Raided

In March 2005, authorities in Louisiana raided Boudreaux's property and found a plethora of evidence to suggest a dog fighting operation existed. Incidentally, the scene police and animal rights activists encountered was not dramatically different than what investigators found at Vick's property. At Boudreaux's place, police discovered fifty-seven pit bulls that bore visible scars commonly associated with dog fighting. The evidence recovered included videos, steroids, treadmills, pictures, a sawed-off shotgun, and other indices of a well-developed dog fighting enterprise. Whereas Vick's involvement in dog fighting was largely unknown to authorities, Boudreaux was renowned as a legendary dog man. Louisiana state police and other animal rights advocates were not surprised at what they uncovered at his home. They found dogs latched to heavy chains in orderly aligned huts, which harbored some of the most well-known fighting dogs in the world. The ardent desire to bring Boudreaux to justice was so fervent that Jeff Dorson of the Humane Society of New Orleans went undercover. Dorson was so intent on toppling the don of dog fighting that he undertook a dangerous clandestine investigation, known as Operation Dog-Bite.

Operation Dog-Bite

Dorson's role became pivotal to getting state investigators to launch their own probe of Boudreaux. Given the secret and seemingly impenetrable world of a purported professional dog fighter, Dorson concocted an investigatory scheme that would have impressed FBI Director J. Edgar Hoover. He went undercover, posing as a dog food salesman. This placed him face to face with some of the more notorious dog fighters, trainers, and breeders in the state of Louisiana. But it also placed him in demand, as dog fighters were paging him around the clock. Dorson reported that one name continued to come up during his operation, no matter who he spoke with. That name was Floyd Boudreaux. Dorson pursued those leads and gained a window of opportunity to obtain evidence on Boudreaux, the most reputed dog man in the blood sport. Any meaningful evidence developed by Dorson was expected to be useful given the latitude of Louisiana's laws against dog fighting, which allows for inferable circumstantial evidence. Operation Dog-Bite procured both audio and video recordings at Boudreaux's home. The evidence of a dog fighting operation seemed reliable enough to prompt the state police chief into action, with help from the U.S. Department of Homeland Security. Dorson's investigation found that Boudreaux was at the top of the dog fighting pyramid and had clientele that reached as far as Japan.

It was the international trail that prompted the state police to entreaty the federal government. As a consequence, U.S. Customs agents from the Department of Homeland Security shot aerial footage of the Boudreaux property. The aerial pictures of the myriad dog houses reflected the same indices of a dog fighting operation that convicted others, including Michael Vick. After two years of undercover work, and evidence procured by the Humane Society of New Orleans, and an additional two months of aerial surveillance from Homeland Security, the state police along with the Louisiana SPCA raided Boudreaux's property in March 2005. As noted, evidence seized included home videos, dog fighting magazines, treadmills, anabolic steroids, computer records, break sticks, and a sawed-off shotgun. Investigators also found fifty-seven pit bulls, bound by six-foot heavy chains, whose habitat was a circumference of confinement. The Louisiana SPCA was on hand so that the dogs could be examined for evidence of scarring or other injuries associated with dog fighting. The dogs were determined to have been involved in dog fighting. Consequently, fifty-seven were put down per state law, which requires officials to euthanize dogs that were used for fighting. Given the evidence seized, authorities charged both Floyd, then seventy, and his son Guy, then forty, with nearly fifty counts of dog fighting.

The Boudreaux Case

After being postponed in January 2008, the Boudreauxs' trial began in October of that year and was full of intrigue. Taking center stage was Floyd, the family patriarch, with nearly a half-century of experience in animal combat. By his own admission, Floyd's passion for the blood sport was honed over fifty years under the tutelage of his father. Floyd expected that this dog fighting tradition would continue uninterrupted with his son Guy, who authorities believed was groomed to be a third-generation dog man. Louisiana charged the father and son as co-defendants. The outcome of the trial would hinge on the question of whether Floyd was still involved in the blood sport and whether his son Guy was an accomplice.

The Boudreauxs were represented by defense attorney Jason Robideaux. In an apparent legal stratagem, the defendants waived their right to a jury trial. Their fates would be left up to a state judge, duly elected by the people. From a legal standpoint, the non-jury trial turned out to be a risks-rewards proposition that would eventually pay off. Rather than the burden of raising a reasonable doubt in the minds of twelve jurors, the Boudreauxs needed only to do so for Judge Kristian Earls of the 15th Judicial District Court. The other advantage of the non-jury trial was that after the state rested its case, the defense could file a motion to acquit over lack of evidence. The prosecution's case, being presented by Ronald Pauterive, was largely circumstantial. It was based on evidence obtained by state and federal investigators as well as animal rights advocates in Louisiana. All told, nearly 100 pieces of evidence were collected. Despite

an abundance of indicators that suggested a dog fighting operation existed, there were no eyewitnesses who testified. Inexplicably, Jeff Dorson of the Humane Society of New Orleans,
who developed the tape and video recordings that implicated
the Boudreauxs, was apparently never called to testify. Hence,
the defense attorneys saw the evidence as mere inferences of
a dog fighting operation rather than actual indicators of direct
involvement. On the other hand, a case based largely on circumstantial evidence would seemingly benefit the prosecution,
especially since Louisiana state law allows inferable evidence
such as pictures, videos, treadmills, magazines, videos, etc., to
establish culpability in dog fighting cases. But during the trial,
the defense seemed to do a better job of diminishing the circumstantial evidence than the prosecution did in developing it. The
undoing of the prosecution's supposedly iron-clad case occurred
in several stunning ways.

Guy's attorney argued that rather than fighting, the dogs
were used for hunting and weight-pulling competitions, none
of which is illegal in Louisiana. Interestingly enough, Dorson
found that many dog fighters used weight-pulling competitions
to strengthen dogs for fighting. This was an important point that
prosecutors could have deduced from a witness like Dorson.
His undercover work gave him greater insight into the different
methods used to cultivate gameness in dogs. Dogs considered
"game" are primed and prepared for animal combat. As for the
steroids found, the defense argued they were used for roosters
that the family raised for cockfighting, which Louisiana law
does not prohibit. However, in the dog fighting culture, steroids
are used to add muscle and mass to fighting dogs. There was no
shortage of experts from animal rights organizations in Louisiana that could have given such key testimony. Although the
defense conceded that the family was involved in cockfighting,
videotaped evidence presented in court only showed dogs fighting, something the prosecution failed to adequately address.
When confronted by the question of the videotape evidence of
dog fighting, the defense argued that neither of the defendants

could be seen participating in these acts. As for the bite marks on the break sticks used to pry open the mouths of fighting dogs, the defense argued that they were barely noticeable. Even more disconcerting, the prosecution brought in Wendy Wolfson, an instructor at the School of Veterinary Medicine at Louisiana State University.

As a veterinarian and instructor of shelter medicine, Wolfson examined the dogs seized following the raid of Boudreaux's home. She determined that the scar tissue found on the animals was consistent with dog fighting, which was sufficient to euthanize them all, per state law. Despite her examination and expertise, the defense deduced a simple admission from Wolfson that the scarring could have been from some other cause. This concession raised more than a reasonable doubt about the case. It also raised eyebrows, as Boudreaux's lawyer pried away at the prosecution's case. As if matters could not have worsened, another significant blow to the prosecution's case occurred on the third day of the trial.

In a shocking development, Judge Earles upheld a defense motion that disallowed Kathy Strouse from testifying as an expert for the prosecution. Strouse, a supervisor with the Chesapeake Bay Animal Control Unit in Virginia, has over twenty years of experience investigating animal abuse cases including dog fighting. She has testified in other dog fighting cases where defendants were convicted. In a rather twisted irony, Strouse's expertise was instrumental in getting a conviction of Michael Vick in 2007. A year later, her testimony was considered unreliable in a state trial against the Boudreauxs.

The judge agreed with the defense attorney's assertion that Strouse was not an expert since she was testifying in a trial against a defendant that she had not investigated. Additionally, the attorneys discounted her expertise by noting that she had never published a book on dog fighting. That Judge Earles acquiesced to this motion was astonishing, given that other animal rights experts on dog fighting have testified at trials of similar import without such prerequisites. For example, Sandy

Christiansen, president of the Humane Society of Spartanburg, South Carolina, has reportedly served as a consultant for law enforcement agencies in several states. He has participated in upwards of thirty raids of suspected dog fighting operations and testified as a government witness at a number of trials (Weir, 2007). The denial of Strouse's expertise in the Boudreauxs' trial because she had not actually investigated the case seemed without precedent.

The judge's decision on Strouse spelled the end of the prosecutor's case. Despite ninety-five pieces of evidence, the judge acquitted the defendants. While a defense attorney has the responsibility of raising a reasonable doubt as to the guilt of their client, which the Boudreauxs' attorney sought to do, the judge's decision was questionable when you consider the weight of evidence and letter of the law. As noted, Louisiana's dog fighting laws allow for deducible evidence like videos, etc. as evidentiary in establishing the existence of a dog fighting operation. Ann Zorilla, chief executive officer of the Louisiana SPCA, stated, "What we found on the scene was a how-to on dog fighting, and this verdict (was) tantamount to ignoring a mountain of evidence."[106] The judge's decision to discount the validity of such evidence seemed to underscore how politically popular and powerful Boudreaux is in Lafayette. Even the prosecution seemed wary of the potential political fallout of prosecuting the elderly Boudreaux and his son, who are beloved in Lafayette. One of the factors that delayed the trial was that a prosecution witness was not able to testify. Moreover, Jeff Dorson, who risked his own life to get Boudreaux by posing as a dog food salesman, never emerged as the prosecution's star witness. How intent was the prosecution in gaining a conviction against Boudreaux without edifying Dorson as an unimpeachable witness given his undercover role? Even more revealing, no U.S. Customs agents from Homeland Security were called to testify. The judge's decision seemed to reflect the greater tolerance of dog fighting as an endemic

---

106 Retrieved from http://www.pet-abuse.com/cases/3994/LA/US/.

part of Cajun culture in Lafayette. Boudreaux's case seemed to benefit from the lack of inflammatory media coverage that engulfed Vick. The same can be said of the relative calm of national animal rights advocates from PETA and the Humane Society, who seemed far less concerned about Boudreaux than they were with Vick. In contrast to Vick's court appearances, there were no protestors or picketers with placards outside the court when the Boudreauxs arrived (Hutchinson, 2007). The aforementioned institutions, including the federal government, seemed resigned to the idea that it was enough to get Vick, the big catch. The general public followed suit.

But are there other factors that help to explain the differential outcomes of Vick's case when compared to Boudreaux's? It can certainly be argued that Vick pleaded guilty, but Boudreaux went to trial and was acquitted. Vick's guilty plea was induced by the decision of his co-defendants to testify against him. On the other hand, Boudreaux's co-defendant was his son, who did not testify against him. Although Vick and his co-defendants' cases were split up, the Boudreauxs were tried together. Another significant point to consider is that many law enforcement officials in the South see dog fighting as a less serious act of criminality, as Vick himself observed in his youth. It is worth reiterating that then-Lafayette Police Chief Gaboon Trahan was himself a famous dog man. Could these factors have influenced Judge Earles's view of the case, especially since he is a former officer of the Acadia Parish Sheriff's Department? Did the judge harbor an affinity for dog fighting as many officers of the law have shown? Was he somehow concerned about the potential political fallout of convicting a local legend from Lafayette Parish, where dog fighting is revered? In the end, Judge Earles's decision to acquit Floyd Boudreaux was especially surprising since he had a previous arrest for dog fighting. But the most important distinction between Vick's case versus the Boudreauxs' is that the federal government never launched an independent investigation of Floyd, whereas both the state of Virginia and the federal government charged Vick. This disparity is questionable for several reasons:

1. Agents from the United States Customs office of the Department of Homeland Security participated in the investigation against Boudreaux, providing aerial surveillance of his home where the evidence procured led to his arrest.
2. All three branches of the federal government (executive, legislative, and judicial), exacted a measure of retribution against Vick, prompted by passage of the amended Animal Welfare Act of 2007.
3. The failure of the federal government to pursue an independent investigation against Boudreaux as it did with Vick raises questions of selective enforcement by race and broader questions of equal protection of the law, pursuant to the Fifth Amendment.
4. The failure of the federal government to independently charge the Boudreauxs resonated as an issue of states' rights. Historically, states' rights proved to be an Achilles heel for African-Americans seeking equal treatment in the South.

Federal Government

Inexplicably, the federal government showed no interest in an independent investigation of Boudreaux, despite the latitude of the amended AWA of 2007. As stated, the failure of the federal government to lodge charges against Boudreaux was especially galling, since federal officials from Homeland Security contributed to the investigation that led to his arrest. Similarly, television broadcasts from news station KATC3 of Louisiana showed Boudreaux's property with a plethora of dog houses, which gave every appearance of a dog fighting operation (2005).[107] Not so ironically, the artifacts associated with dog fighting found at Boudreaux's property very much resembled what investigators

---

107 From a KATC3 television report from the property of Floyd Boudreaux, March 12, 2005.

routinely find at the properties of other defendants charged with dog fighting.

The inaction on the part of the federal government against Boudreaux is also questionable in light of the Commerce Clause. This article allows the federal government to regulate economic industries in this country and punish those that operate illegally. The three forms of economic affairs that are under the clause include interstate commerce, Indian commerce, and foreign commerce. Indian commerce, which is not a part of this discussion, allows Congress to regulate the economic affairs of Native American communities that exist as sovereign nations. Interstate commerce involves the regulation of economic activity across state lines and provides strong teeth for the AWA. Because Vick's dog fighting occurred across state lines, the federal government charged him with conspiracy in the course of interstate commerce.

Congress also regulates American companies engaged in international trade. Because dog fighting is a global phenomenon, which includes the international sale of puppies from prized fighting bloodlines, the amended AWA of 2007 covers foreign commerce as well. Given the latitude of the federal AWA and its coverage of both interstate and foreign commerce, it is fair to ask whether Boudreaux's purported involvement in dog fighting rose to these levels. The next section will examine the question of whether the federal government could have used provisions of the Commerce Clause in the AWA to charge Boudreaux as they did with Vick.

The Commerce Clause and Dog Fighting

The intent of the Animal Fighting Prohibition Enforcement Act of 2007, which amended the AWA, is to prevent the spread of dog fighting in America and the world. Thus the act prohibits any person to knowingly engage in an "animal fighting venture" with an animal who may have been moved in either interstate or foreign commerce (Ortiz, 2010). Boudreaux, the "don" of dog fighting, has a history of engaging in interstate dog fighting.

Even more revealing of his legacy is the dynasty of champions from his line of fighting dogs. The names *Eli*, *Eli Jr.*, and *Blind Billy* are among the world-famous canine combatants whose legacies are as well-known as their celebrated owner. Despite the renown of both the defendant and his dogs, the secrecy of professional dog fighters like Boudreaux greatly diminished the odds of a conviction. Given the limitations of state prosecutors in trying their case, would the federal government have been successful in prosecuting Boudreaux?

The possibility seems tenable for several reasons. On the one hand, the Justice Department has greater financial and legal resources to try a case like Boudreaux's. Although Louisiana's laws against dog fighting permits the use of circumstantial evidence, the federal statute is more far-reaching. As noted, the AWA gives federal authorities the ability to arrest and convict defendants for engaging in dog fighting on the basis of interstate and foreign commerce. Conversely, the state of Louisiana was confined to addressing Boudreaux's involvement in dog fight-ing as a local matter. Given the seemingly impenetrable nature of the professional dog fighting culture, the state was unable to crack the apparent wall of silence surrounding Boudreaux, despite that many of Boudreaux's neighbors conceded his involvement in dog fighting. In fact, many were surprised that it took investigators so long to arrest him. On the other hand, the federal government not only had the AWA, but as noted, Con-gress increased the prison sentence for dog fighting from three years to five. Such sentencing guidelines might have enabled federal prosecutors to increase the charges and secure a plea bargain deal with the Boudreauxs in exchange for a guilty plea, as they did with Vick. Because both father and son were willing to stand trial together, federal prosecutors could have used the threat of a long prison sentence for the aging father, given his prior arrest for dog fighting, to persuade either or both defen-dants to take a plea deal. While the state case seemed hamstrung by the defense's rebuttals, the legal provisions of the AWA may have allowed a seasoned federal prosecutor to satisfy the burden of proof, given the evidence.

Why the AWA May Have Mattered

The AWA prohibits "any event" that involves at least two animals in an animal fighting venture, whether conducted as sport, for gambling, or simply for entertainment (Ortiz, 2010, p. 22). Given the latitude of this stipulation, the federal government could have made a stronger argument with the evidence than the state. In the state's case, the defense argued that although video tapes showed two dogs fighting, the defendants were not seen in the videos. Although Boudreaux and his son were not seen in the video, the dog fighting was on their property. Additionally, there was no shortage of corroborating evidence found at the property, which should have made the video a smoking gun. There was no videotaped evidence of Vick. His initial reaction was that he was rarely at the property where the dogs were found. That Vick's cousin was arrested and used his address was enough for the police to suspect him immediately. When they arrived at the property in Surry County and saw what appeared to be a dog fighting operation, it gave them enough to secure a conviction. In addition, it appears that the state of Louisiana's prosecutors did not use the inferable evidence well enough. The discovery of computer records, treadmills, doghouses, and steroids would have allowed a federal prosecutor to substantiate such evidence with other indicators. Perhaps the most striking development that signaled the need for a federal investigation was a remarkable concession by the defense that may have implicated the Boudreauxs on animal fighting charges. After the Boudreauxs were arrested, their defense attorneys explained publicly that steroids found at the property were used "for the dozens of roosters the family raised for cockfighting."[108] While cockfighting was not illegal in Louisiana at the time, it became punishable as a federal crime in the 2007 AWA (if a defendant knows the bird is being used in an animal fighting venture, as a part of interstate or foreign commerce). The admission by the defense that the defendants used roosters for cockfighting could have amounted to lawyerly mal-

---

108 Retrieved from http://lovinpitts.blogspot.com/2008/10/louisiana-v-floyd-boudreaux-who-are.html.

practice. Except at the time those comments were made in 2005, the federal AWA had not been amended to make cockfighting a potential federal crime. Still, by the time the Boudreauxs went to trial, the amended law was in effect, so pursuing federal charges was doable. Similarly, the amended AWA was not in effect when Vick was initially implicated on state charges. But it did not stop the federal government from charging him with with the AWA. The federal government's failure to investigate and charge the Boudreauxs, despite the incriminating concession by Boudreaux's defense that the family was involved in cockfighting, was but another example of differential treatment by race. Furthermore, the inaction of the federal government in the case of the Boudreauxs raises questions of equal protection of the law, by race, pursuant to the Fifth Amendment.

Additionally, a federal case could have drawn from the successful prosecutions of dog fighters such as David Tant in South Carolina and James Fricchione in New York. A federal prosecutor could have used the Tant and Fricchione convictions as relevant case law, although both were tried at the state level. The similarities in the evidence procured could have been foundational in establishing that Boudreaux headed a dog fighting operation. Without the longer arm of the federal law, Boudreaux's case remained decidedly local, which is how it was prosecuted. The Justice Department would not have failed to utilize the testimony of Jeff Dorson of the Humane Society of New Orleans, who had both audio and video recordings of his undercover investigation of Boudreaux.

A federal prosecutor would have made greater use of incriminating evidence, including the surveillance conducted by U.S. Customs agents from the Department of Homeland Security. By contrast, there were no reports of state prosecutors even calling U.S. Customs agents to testify as witnesses, which of course benefitted Boudreaux's defense. Furthermore, the federal government would have had more cause to convict the defendants given the discovery of his international sale of puppies from his famous bloodline of fighters in furtherance of foreign commerce.

Foreign Commerce

The federal government could have sought charges using the AWA, pursuant to the Foreign Commerce Clause. The language of the amended AWA is explicit on this point. The law strictly forbids the "knowing placement" of a dog in either interstate or foreign commerce if the reason or purpose is to have the dog participate in an animal fighting venture (Ortiz, p. 22). The latter stipulations are important given the renown of Boudreaux, whose legendary bloodline of fighting dogs have reportedly attracted buyers the world over. To be sure, international buyers would not come to Lafayette, Louisiana, to buy puppies from ferocious dog fighting bloodlines to become household pets. In fact, it was this sort of realization that aroused the suspicion of U.S. Customs officials initially. Therefore, the federal government's decision to not charge Boudreaux using provisions of the AWA in furtherance of either foreign or interstate commerce poses additional questions of unequal distribution of the law.

It can be argued that the differential treatment by animal rights advocates, the media, and the Justice Department was seemingly influenced by Vick being black and Boudreaux being white. The end result of their respective court cases also bore out these distinctions. Vick pled guilty, while Boudreaux and his son were acquitted at trial. Although Vick agreed to plead guilty, it was the pressure of the federal government and the real threat of a superseding indictment that contributed to his decision. There is nothing to say Boudreaux would not have pleaded guilty had the federal government charged and tried both him and his son. The failure of the federal government to charge Boudreaux as they did Vick, given the evidence of dog fighting deduced from each defendants' property, and the advent of the amended AWA, raises questions of equal protection of the law.

Equal Protection of the Law

Both the Fifth and Fourteenth Amendments to the constitution have requirements that establish equal protection of the law for all citizens independent of race. While the Fourteenth Amendment gives American citizens protections against states, the Fifth Amendment is binding upon the federal government. The Fourteenth Amendment was initially passed to extend equal protections to blacks following their emancipation from slavery. The manner in which the federal government superseded the state of Virginia's investigation of Vick and indicted him, while failing to do the same in the state of Louisiana in Boudreaux's case, is a question of equal protection and due process. Equal protection of the law, as the Fifth Amendment guarantees, has the binding expectation of equal enforcement of the law. Given this constitutional provision, what explains the federal government's use of the AWA against Vick but not against Boudreaux? Several congressmen went on record lambasting Vick for his deeds, but were conspicuously silent during the Boudreaux case. The same members of Congress seemed to follow the Justice Department's tact by deferring to local investigators. The effect not only perpetuated the idea that blacks are more criminally deviant than are whites, but such disparate treatment conjured up the notion of states' rights. The latter refers to the reluctance of the federal government to intervene in local matters of policy and law involving blacks by instead deferring to local states of the South. Although none of the branches of the federal government asserted the notion of "states' rights" to explain their failure to independently investigate and charge the Boudreauxs, history suggests it is hardly implausible.

States' Rights

As a vestige of the American Civil War, the federal government often failed to address the concerns of African-Americans in the post-bellum South over equal protection. Instead, in an attempt to soothe the residual resentments of southern states, the federal government acquiesced to their mistreatment of blacks as a matter of states' rights. (Of course, this very same issue was at the core of southern states' attempts to maintain slavery and secede from the Union.) Therefore, in order to preserve the Union, the federal government did not intervene when southern states implemented Jim Crow segregation in the post-bellum

South. Did the failure of the federal government to charge the Boudreauxs using the AWA, as it did with Vick, reflect this issue of states' rights? Was there a feeling in the Bush Administration that the state of Louisiana should be left to deal with its *own* in Boudreaux? While one side of the South's claims to states' rights focused on their ability to handle *their* blacks without federal intrusion, it also reflected their ability to shield whites from criminal prosecution. When it came to whites being tried for alleged crimes against blacks, they were essentially immune from prosecution in the South. Left open for interpretation, the federal government's lack of interest in launching its own investigation of Boudreaux seemed to be another indicator of unequal justice by race in the name of states' rights.

The Issue of States' Rights: Vick vs. Boudreaux

As for Michael Vick's case, states' rights were clearly not an issue, as all three branches of the federal government joined forces to topple him in 2007. To wit, the federal government launched an independent investigation of his involvement; Congress passed an amendment to the Animal Welfare Act making it a felony to fight dogs; and President George W. Bush signed the amendment into law. With the strength of all three branches of the federal government lined up against him, Vick was convicted in federal court and sentenced to prison for nearly two years. By contrast, in the case of Boudreaux, no branch of the federal government showed any interest in prosecuting him. While states' rights may help to explain why the federal government did not charge Boudreaux, who is white, it seems rather obvious that Vick's race was also a factor in his being exposed, excoriated, and expelled from society for his involvement in dog fighting.

Differential Treatment by Race and Dog Fighting Types

The media coverage of Vick's legal dilemma was so incriminating that civil rights leaders and groups such as the NAACP wondered aloud if his due process rights were being compromised. While Surry County Attorney Gerald Poindexter from the Commonwealth of Virginia launched his own investigation of Vick initially, he questioned whether the federal government's probe was motivated by his celebrity and race. The federal government's decision to forgo its own investigation of Boudreaux certainly gives credence to the suggestion.

It can be argued that because Vick was an NFL superstar, the extraordinary reaction by the media, animal rights advocates, and federal authorities was altogether warranted. But Boudreaux is a celebrity superstar in the dog fighting game. He has been featured in dog fighting magazines, on the Internet, and in books on the blood sport. It is reasonable to assert that the Boudreauxs of the world made dog fighting appealing to the Michael Vicks of the world. Moreover, the suggestion that Vick's renown, and race contributed to his conviction seems plausible when you consider that other professional athletes who are African-Americans were arrested and convicted for their involvement in dog fighting.

It's worth reiterating that both Qyntel Woods of the NBA's Portland Trailblazers and LeShon Johnson of the New York Jets were arrested for participating in the blood sport. In 2004, Woods pled guilty to first-degree animal abuse for hosting dog fights in his home in Portland, Oregon (Frias, 2007). One year later, Johnson received a five-year deferred sentence after officials confiscated 200 dogs from his operation—four times the number of dogs in Vick's case. Yet neither of the cases evoked the raucous public outcry that Vick's yielded, and neither Johnson nor Woods was sent to prison, despite their convictions. Still, Woods, Johnson, and Vick had several factors in common: All were professional athletes who are also African-Americans, and all were found guilty on charges of dog fighting. Aside from the observable indices of differential treatment, there were also indicators of race-baiting in the discussion of dog fighting as a social problem following Vick's emergence as a criminal suspect.

Law enforcement's attention turned toward African-Americans from urban communities, who, by default, became the prototypical street fighters. However, a closer examination of dog fighting types reveals Vick's involvement was actually on the plane of a professional fighter. Ortiz (pp.14-16) found that there are three types of dog fighters: professionals, hobbyists, and street fighters.

Of the three types, hobbyists are the least involved. They often participate as a hobby to supplement their income. Professionals are the upper echelon of dog men who not only train and fight dogs but breed them as well. Keep in mind that Vick was a licensed dog breeder, which was another indicator that he was not a street fighter. Additionally, professionals operate with extreme secrecy. This helps to explain why Vick could be among the most recognizable NFL players yet no one outside of the dog fighting underworld knew of his involvement. Yet there are several distinguishing characteristics of the street fighter which makes it clearer that associating Vick with this sort, rather than a professional, was a misappropriation of reality. Street fighters are the lowest on the totem pole and revert to the lowest forms of the blood sport.

For example, "trunking" involves placing two dogs in the trunk of a car and letting them fight until one emerges alive as the winner. Other methods involve starving as many as three dogs and placing them in an abandoned apartment and letting them fight and kill one another for one bag of food. Street fighters also commingle their involvement in dog fighting with other criminally deviant behaviors. They not only use dogs for fighting, but also to guard the stash houses of gang members and drug dealers as well as to alert them to the presence of the police. Given the perilous pitfalls of their multi-variant criminal lifestyles, street fighters rarely ascend to the top as professional dog fighters. Hence, the reaction to Vick's case, which put the focus on street fighters, was a gross distortion of the facts. All of which seemed deliberately designed to make dog fighting a crime of urban inner-city blacks. If having prior arrests and other convictions for violent crimes is typical of the street fighter, then including Michael Vick in this discussion is especially incongruent. Prior to this dog fighting case, Vick indicated that his only negative sanction from the law was a traffic violation. The use of his high-profile case and conviction not only swayed public sentiment against street fighters, but there are data that suggest selective enforcement by race followed.

Members of Congress who supported the amended AWA of 2007 cited the multi-dimensional criminality of street fighters as the main reason for the amendment. But Vick indicated that he attended his first "real" dog fight in Smithfield, Virginia, a rural community. Not so ironically, it was in this town that Vick developed his dog fighting enterprise. His home in Smithfield, at 1915 Moonlight Road, became a house of horrors where Bad Newz Kennels flourished and later floundered. That Smithfield is not in an urban inner city debunks the idea that Vick was a street fighter and also exposes the ensuing racialism that followed. The decision of powerful and influential groups to focus primarily on street fighters had the negative effect of skewing the discussion, which added to the problem. This greater attention on the lower rung of the dog fighting echelon shielded professional dog fighters like Boudreaux. After being released from prison in 2009, the Humane Society used Michael Vick to lobby on Capitol Hill for tougher laws against dog fighting. Included in these newer laws were harsher penalties for individuals who might simply attend dog fighting matches and those who would bring children. The creation of new laws against dog fighting seemed warranted. On the other hand, the overemphasis on street fighters predictably resulted in a higher number of blacks being arrested and convicted of dog fighting. Despite all the attention accorded to dog fighting following Vick's legal dilemma, hardly any attention has been accorded to the racial disparities in arrests and convictions that have followed. Interestingly enough, the disparate outcomes in the cases of Vick versus Boudreaux serves as a microcosm of the differential treatment of defendants by race that is now more observable. How can Wolfgang's theory be helpful in explaining such differences?

The subculture of violence theory provides a useful framework in examining the disparities in the cases of Vick versus Boudreaux. This perspective explains how the parent culture of dog fighting influenced Vick's involvement as a subcultural phenomenon. Were the disparate outcomes in the cases of Boudreaux's versus Vick's a reflection of the former being aligned with the parent culture, while the latter subject reflected the subculture? Dr. Marvin Wolfgang, who co-authored the subculture of violence perspective, held that young blacks in inner-city Philadelphia often used violence to express their toughness and strength (Wolfgang & Ferracuti, p.153). He observed that the violence exhibited by blacks was only partly different from the parent culture of violence. While the subculture of violence perspective studied interpersonal violence among human beings, the theory is also meaningful in explaining human beings committing violence using dogs. This conduct has been observable historically among whites and blacks, particularly in the South, a fertile ground for violence through animal combat.

Theory: The Parent Culture Versus the Subculture

An observable parent culture of dog fighting has been a part of Floyd Boudreaux's life for upwards of fifty years. Dog fighting and other forms of animal combat have been described as a "family affair" for the Boudreauxs. Renowned as a second-generation dog man, Floyd's father acculturated him in dog fighting while in grade school. It was presumed that his son Guy would continue the legacy. (Not so ironically, Guy was also charged and tried on forty-eight counts of dog fighting along with his father in 2005.) Other indices of this parent culture of dog fighting involving Boudreaux include the fact that his father worked with the bulldog breed for forty years. That Floyd is renowned for fighting the pit bull, whose ancestry is traceable to the bulldog, only bolsters the assertion of a preceding parent culture. His half-century of involvement in training, fighting, and breeding combative dogs has produced a contemporary parent culture of dog fighting. This development influenced subcultural offspring like Michael Vick. As stated, Wolfgang noted that the violence exhibited by blacks is only partly different from the parent culture of violence, particularly in the South (p.145). Just as dog fighting flourished among working class rural whites, it also thrived in impoverished urban areas like the Ridley projects, where Vick was raised.

The Subculture of the Blood Sport

Clinton Portis, a running back for the Washington Redskins, publicly defended Vick in the wake of his dog fighting charges. In commenting on how widespread dog fighting is in the South, Portis noted that where he was from, in Laurel, Mississippi, you can see a good dog fight in any backyard. Historically, this subculture of dog fighting in the South has been more widespread among whites than blacks. Researchers found that white participants often engage in dog fighting as a compensatory show of masculinity (Evans, et al., 1998). The power and strength of the dog is supposed to reflect on the owner accordingly. This metaphoric matching of human beings to dogs is true of what dog fighting came to reflect in European culture centuries ago. Wolfgang's theory held that individuals used violence as an expression of their masculinity given their marginal social status (p.153). This much is observable in the tendencies of inner-city blacks to commit acts of interpersonal violence toward one another. Thus interpersonal violence became a way for them to express the power and dominance that they lacked socially. Historically, whites in the rural South committed interpersonal violence against blacks not merely because of racism, but because they were as poor and in some cases poorer than blacks and resented them because of it. Although one factor that brought poor whites and blacks together was dog fighting. Wolfgang's theory is just as useful in explaining how these poor groups in both rural and urban settings used dogs to commit violence.

But whether examining poor rural whites or poor inner-city blacks, what is remarkable for this discussion is Wolfgang's summation that the violence exhibited by subcultures is only partly different from the parent culture. Interestingly enough, Evans et al. noted that the dog fighting violence exhibited by working class whites was similar to working class athletes who express aggression in sports like boxing and football (Evans, Gauthier, and Forsyth, 1998: p. 212; Ortiz, p. 12). Perhaps not so ironically, NFL superstar quarterback Michael Vick, who excelled in football while growing up, was also exposed to dog fighting as a child in public housing projects. These important connections were ignored by the mainstream media and academia. Although both Vick and Boudreaux were first exposed to dog fighting as young children, and both grew up relatively poor in the South, they were still viewed differently by the law it seems.

Individuals like Boudreaux are seen as reflecting the parent culture. Consequently, they are better insulated from prosecution than individuals like Vick, who reflect the subculture. That Vick was seen through the lens of the subculture of dog fighting is evidenced by the inordinate amount of discussion accorded to street fighters after his criminal probe and conviction. It followed that a greater number of African-Americans were arrested for and convicted of dog fighting than whites. Additionally, because of the extra-criminogenic conduct that typifies street fighters, including drug trafficking and gang activity, these offenders are especially targeted by law enforcement, rather than breeders of fighting dogs. But many professional dog fighters are also breeders. The greater focus on street fighters rather than professional fighters is analogous to the law focusing more on street dealers in the war on drugs. The strength of the law has targeted them as opposed to interdiction efforts against major traffickers. When taken as a whole, society's differential view of the parent culture, which is largely ignored, versus the subculture of dog fighting, which includes street fighters who are more often targeted by the law, helps to explain why Vick was convicted and Boudreaux was acquitted.

Of course, the creation of laws and their enforcement is greatly influenced by the social reaction to any social problem, whether perceived or real. Much of the public's social reaction will be influenced by powerful entities who label others as deviant as they see fit. In the respective criminal cases of Vick and Boudreaux, social reaction and perception emerged as important factors in the respective legal outcomes.

Vick vs. Boudreaux: The Sequential Model of Deviance

Because it is believed that social behavior occurs with some measure of order, Howard Becker found that deviant conduct follows a social sequence (Becker, 1987). Becker's Sequential Model of Deviance, which was used to explain the differential treatment of Vick versus Roethlisberger, is also meaningful in explaining the differential treatment of Vick versus Boudreaux. Becker measured "obedient behavior" and "rule-breaking behavior" against whether individuals were perceived as deviant or not. Thus, for an individual who is perceived as a deviant (i.e., Michael Vick), he could be "falsely accused" yet still become a "true deviant." A false accusation might suggest that because Vick is black, he is inherently deviant. In the latter scenario, the individual so labeled can be victimized by a fatalistic self-fulfilling prophecy. He or she will act out the behavior that reflects the deviant label. Conversely, the person who is not perceived as a deviant can be seen as a conformist (i.e., Floyd Boudreaux), and as such any charges of deviance can be dismissed as false. Consequently, the perceived conformist is able to engage in deviance secretly and avoid being negatively labeled. Table 6.1 below shows how Becker's sequential model of deviance helps to explain the differences in the way Vick was perceived versus Boudreaux.

In hearkening back to the example of Michael Vick being falsely accused as a deviant because of his race, this susceptibility is greater given his identity as an African-American male. Part of the legacy of racism in America generally and the

Becker's Sequential Model of Deviant Behavior

Perception of subject/actor	Obedient behavior (falsely accused)	Rule-breaking behavior
Michael Vick is a deviant	Black quarterback, running quarterback, outsider, deviant, dangerous, Bad Newz, Virginia	Pure deviant-dog-fighter; operates Bad Newz Kennels; arrested, indicted, convicted sentenced to federal prison
Floyd Boudreaux is not a deviant	Seen as a conformist; white male southerner, "former" dog fighter	Secret deviant-acquitted of dog-fighting in 2008

Table 6.1. Pfohl's "Types of Deviant Behavior" (1994). Adapted from Howard S. Becker's *Outsiders* (1963).

232

criminal justice system in particular is that African-Americans, males in particular, are suspected for being criminally deviant. Because this label was initially applied to Vick solely by virtue of his race, it also meant he was "falsely" accused. Additionally, despite being one of the most talented and exciting football players in the NFL, Vick was pejoratively labeled as a "black quarterback." Since this position has always been dominated by whites, he was perceived as an *outsider*, a deviation from the preferred norm. His style of quarterback play, which includes running when necessary, has often been derided as dangerous and even reckless. Such labeling, like the reference to Vick's hometown as *Bad News* (rather than Newport News), had the negative effect of shaping an unfortunate self-fulfilling prophecy in his life. When taken as a whole, such negative descriptors attached to Vick, along with his upbringing in the Ridley projects, ultimately led him to become a true deviant as a consequence of his rule-breaking behavior.

Conversely, Floyd Boudreaux was not perceived as a deviant, despite his significant renown as a legendary dog fighter. Such absolution was not only attributable to his being a white male from the South, but also his celebrity in Lafayette, Louisiana, a hotbed for dog fighting. While the police in Vick's community gave him the impression dog fighting was not a serious crime, the head of the police in Boudreaux's community of Lafayette was a principal in dog fighting's culture. How criminally deviant could dog fighting have been in Boudreaux's mind when one of his comrades in animal combat, Police Chief Trahan, developed rules for dog fighting? In fact, rule nineteen of the current Cajun rules stipulates that if the police interfere with a match, the referee is to schedule the next meeting place (Gibson, 2005). Given the uniqueness of a police chief inventing the original Cajun rules, it is reasonable to suspect that the enforcement of dog fighting laws might be more relaxed in the parish of Lafayette. Moreover, Boudreaux's ability to escape prosecution seemed to be aided by Lafayette's distinction as a bastion for dog fighting. The advantage of Boudreaux not being perceived as a deviant despite his legend in dog fighting and ample evidence of a dog fighting operation was that he and his son were acquitted in October 2008.

Boudreaux was able to avoid being labeled, despite a prior arrest, by exclaiming that he only used dogs for weight-pulling contests, which suggested he was conforming to existing laws. Furthermore, his lawyers claimed the steroids found on the property were used for the family's roosters, which were used for cockfighting. Did Boudreaux use this explanation of cockfighting to hide his involvement in dog fighting? Oritz (2010) found that professional dogfighters operate with considerable caution. While Vick also fought dogs as a professional fighter, his secrecy was blown by the arrest of his cousin and after being implicated by his co-defendants. That Boudreaux was not convicted by the state nor charged by the federal government seemed to reflect the view that Vick and blacks were prototypical dog fighters.

In conclusion, Becker's sequential model of deviance helps to explain how Vick and Boudreaux were treated differently in their respective legal cases based on whether they were perceived as deviant or not. Just as there is no doubt that Vick was involved in dog fighting, there is no doubting that Floyd Boudreaux has fought dogs and is a mythical legend in the world of dog fighting. In addition, his infamous bloodline of fighting dogs has garnered him international acclaim. Did the presiding judge in the Boudreaux case know that dog fighting is a part of the lure and lore of Lafayette, Louisiana's back roads culture? Did the judge know that Boudreaux and the town's former police chief were comrades in the dog fighting world? Did these realities influence his decision to acquit Boudreaux? The disparate outcomes of Vick's case versus Boudreaux's are as distinct as black and white. By virtue of being black, Vick was perceived as a deviant and labeled accordingly. Conversely, by virtue of being white, Boudreaux was perceived as a conformist, rather than a deviant, despite a prior arrest for dog fighting and nearly 100 pieces of evidence presented at trial. The differences in how these men were labeled by powerful and influential organizations helps to explain the differences in the outcomes of their respective criminal cases.

Lastly, that the federal government used the AWA, with its specific prohibitions against dog fighting to prosecute Vick, but not Boudreaux raises questions of equal protection of the law, pursuant to the Fifth Amendment. Moreover, the inaction of federal prosecutors in the Boudreaux case was especially surprising, given the role of the Department of Homeland Security, which was a part of the investigation that led to the arrest of Floyd and his son Guy.

CHAPTER VII

Redemption:

The Fall and Rise of Michael Vick

"Old pirates, yes they rob I/Sold I to the merchant ships/Minutes after they took I/From the bottomless pit./But my hand was made strong/By the hand of the Almighty./We forward in this generation/Triumphantly./Won't you help to sing/These songs of freedom/'Cause all I ever have:/Redemption songs."
—Bob Marley, "Redemption Songs"

The fall and rise of Michael Vick is the tale of two lives enmeshed into one conflicted soul. What makes Vick's story so compelling is that his life and NFL career are viewable through a prism of dualities. Having been raised in the Ridley Place housing projects of East Newport News, Virginia, Vick rose from the lower rung of society to become the highest paid player in the NFL. His dual threat to run and to pass made him a human highlight reel that became must-see TV. The southpaw sensation possesses a rocket for an arm. His whip-like throwing motion launches air-tight lasers, unleashing some of the more beautiful passes in the game. His passing prowess notwithstanding, Vick is equally equipped with quickness, speed, and agility, making his running ability a treasured art form in the game. The recent emergence and widespread acceptance of young African-American quarterbacks like Cam Newton, Robert Griffin III, Russell Wilson, and Colin Kaepernick is a testament of Michael Vick redefining the position in the NFL. No other quarterback

236

in the league better demonstrated the unique ability to run or throw for sixty yards on any given passing play than Vick. These combined talents have made him one of the most dynamic NFL players in the history of the game. Rather than being celebrated as the rarest of skilled players, media critics have questioned whether he is a legitimate quarterback. Although Vick has sought to answer his critics resoundingly with his play, he has been unable to silence them.

His Record Should Speak For Itself

As a starting quarterback in the NFL, Michael Vick has finished with a winning record in seven of his ten seasons (he went 1-1 as a rookie). For all the question marks surrounding his competencies, he has only had two losing seasons as a starting quarterback, going 56-44-1 through 2012. But rather than calling him a winning quarterback, the insatiable media calls him a running quarterback. He is a four-time All-Pro player who in 2006 broke the single-season rushing record for a quarterback with over 1,000 yards. Yet in 2004, Vick's distinction as a winning quarterback and the most exciting playmaker in the game made him the highest paid player in the league. He signed a ten-year, $130 million contract that should have made him an Atlanta Falcon for the rest of his career. With such early success, it was hard to imagine anything going wrong that would imperil his growing legacy. Of course, that was before the stunning revelations of 2007.

How is it that one of the most visible and viable talents in the NFL could be leading such a double life? How did his social environment in Newport News influence his interest in dog fighting? Which underlying factors contributed most to Vick's precipitous downfall, despite his celebrity and wealth? While some found it inexplicable that Vick would have two lives, brandish two faces, and demonstrate two personalities, it is far from implausible. As I will show, from the days of his youth through adulthood, Michael Vick has been plagued by a good heart and bad judgment. Consequently, he has not always discerned between good and bad influences. The inability to distinguish between the two has not only rendered him conflicted, but extremely vulnerable to sacrificing his better judgment to his own detriment. Still, his stunning ascension from the Ridley Place projects to the lofty perch of the NFL's elite suggests he made good choices more often. Yet the residual effects of some bad influences, like the friends who taught him dog fighting, would come back to haunt him. Some would believe a bourgeoning NFL career would be sufficient to ward off negative influences. Rather than ameliorating internal struggles, Vick's professional stardom complicated them. Because Vick's style of play deviated from long-held conventions of white quarterbacks, he was cast as a deviant. As a consequence of being treated as an outsider, he acted out the role of a deviant outsider. This in part helps to explain his deep-seated involvement in dog fighting. Although his style of play on the field was daring, the media called him dangerous. Is it surprising then that after being called dangerous on Sundays that he would fly home to Virginia on Tuesdays, his day off, and behave dangerously toward dogs? Other maltreatment from the press included pejorative notions of him as a running quarterback or a black quarterback. These disdainful descriptors can have a depreciating effect on black quarterbacks so-labeled, often affecting their self-identity. It seems Vick's inability to gain total acceptance as a unique quarterbacking talent outside the traditional quarterbacking model beleaguered him. Despite being able to achieve considerable success as an NFL quarterback, the pundits pummeled him. No matter how good he performed, the sports reporting media colored him bad, so bad that he risked his NFL career by creating Bad Newz Kennels, his illegal dog fighting enterprise, which led to his demise.

Absent in the discussion of Vick's dog fighting scandal was an exploration of factors that contributed to his misguided belief that he could be a professional football player and a professional dog fighter. Rather than his NFL stardom alleviating the pangs of a duplicitous self-identity, the disparate media coverage led to greater ambivalence. Vick was held to the standards of conventional quarterbacks, most of whom are white. While a quarterback's success is supposed to be measured by wins and losses, somehow a different metric is used for Michael Vick. Despite owning a winning record as an NFL quarterback he is still considered illegitimate. A study of Vick's life reveals a running anthology of duplicity that goes back to early childhood. It would be this unresolved tendency to acquiesce to good and bad influences that contributed to his demise.

Seeds of Duplicity

From his impressionable years as a youth, Vick discovered good friends and bad, and he interacted with both. While his good friends played the game of football with him, the bad friends engaged in various levels of deviance. Accordingly, Vick demonstrated both sets of behaviors (Vick, 2012). Throughout his life, he has attempted a delicate balancing act of being true to himself versus acceding to the interests of others. The inability to balance his priorities has resulted in Vick experiencing role conflict on several fronts. His desire to assent to a wide range of people has plagued him in nearly every sphere of social interaction. Whether in his youth, within his own family, or later in the NFL, Vick has had trouble establishing the importance of meeting his own interests versus those of others.

Even when he believed a matter was a win-win, the outcomes were too often win-lose. He found himself at a loss for why his good intentions resulted in bad consequences. This ongoing duality helps to explain how Vick went from one of the most famous players in the NFL to one of the most infamous. While his inability to put his own interests first was at the heart of his downfall, his unwavering desire to reverse this curse has been the cornerstone of his comeback. But can Vick sustain this drive to convert a major stumbling block into a stepping stone? Will his rise continue, or is his next fall inevitable? Most people are unsure of what to make of Michael Vick and his prospects for continued success. Some are reluctant to give him the benefit of the doubt. They are struggling with the question: Who is the real Michael Vick? Is he the person who fell from grace by operating an illegal dog fighting operation? Or is he someone who lost his way, only to rediscover his greater purpose on the way to redemption?

Will the Real Michael Vick Please Stand?

As many will attest, Michael Vick has a heart of gold. His charities include Grateful to Give Back, which gives toys to underprivileged children during Christmas and free turkeys to families during Thanksgiving in his hometown of Newport News, Virginia, and in Atlanta, Georgia.[109] Vick's charitableness enabled the Give Life Foundation of Herndon, Virginia, to deliver $100,000 in supplies to aid the victims of Hurricane Katrina in 2005.[110] In 2012, despite his finances still being in recovery over his 2007 bankruptcy, Vick donated $50,000 to the victims of Hurricane Sandy in the New Jersey area. In September 2012, Vick donated $200,000 for a new football field for an inner-city youth team in the city of Philadelphia. As much as such generosity should carry more social meaning in the public's eye, those deeds have been obscured by his unseemly contributions to animal cruelty. A read of Vick's life offers a glimpse into a young man confounded by a complex web of associations. These social ties that have caused him setbacks have varied from friends and family who extracted whatever good they could muster from him to corporate elites, like Nike and the NFL, who also sought to benefit from Michael Vick the product. While there is enough blame to go around, Vick himself is far from blameless.

As the dog fighting debacle revealed, Vick willingly sacrificed his own livelihood in developing an illegal enterprise which benefitted his so-called friends more than himself. In the end, these so-called friends who Vick fostered and whose leisurely lifestyles he financed all implicated him to federal investigators. While there is no shortage of people who sought

---

109 Copy of handwritten letter from Michael Vick to Judge Henry Hudson before he was sentenced (n.d.).
110 Letter of support for Michael Vick: From Patrick J. Hughes, Pres and CEO of Give Life Foundation, to Judge Henry Hudson. December 7, 2007.

out Michael Vick for selfish gain, sadly enough, some of those individuals were from his own family.

Although he undoubtedly has family that care about him as a person, others seemed to care more about what Vick could do for them. For example, the significant event that led police to Vick's home at 1915 Moonlight Road and the discovery of Bad Newz Kennels was the arrest of his cousin, Davon Boddie, who gave police the address of his famous cousin. In addition, while facing state and federal dog fighting charges, Vick's own father implicated him as a dog fighter; this during a time in which he was reportedly paying his father's rent. Besides family members and so-called friends, others shamelessly used Vick to advance their own causes. These include animal rights organizations, corporate sponsors, the media, the politics of the state, and even the NFL. Each of the aforementioned took advantage of Michael Vick the *product* at the expense of Michael Vick the *person*. Even worse, Vick the person also exploited *Michael Vick* the product. With so many people attempting to benefit from the revenue-generating celebrity football headliner, it is no wonder that Michael Vick the person became confused and ultimately confined in prison.

At his core, Michael Vick has an innocence about him that makes him exceptional. On the other hand, it also renders him exploitable. This is significant to not only help the public understand how the fall and rise of Michael Vick occurred, but to also help Vick as well. The frames of his life are like a photo essay of triumph and tragedy. A replay of these scenes may prove useful to better interpret his life's experiences as he continues to reconcile the wrongs in his quest for redemption.

The Fall and Rise of Michael Vick

Michael Vick's meteoric ascent to the top of the NFL as an All-Pro quarterback, where he became the highest paid player in the game, was an extraordinary journey from the relative poverty of East Newport News, Virginia. For Vick, experiencing such polar opposite worlds in one lifetime certainly defied the odds of social mobility. Yet the odds were stacked even higher that he would not maintain his wealth, fame, and promising NFL career. Despite taking flight like the falcon bird, which symbolizes the Atlanta Falcons team that drafted him, the high-soaring All-Pro quarterback had his wings clipped after six years in the NFL. Consistent with a dualism that has narrated his life, the dog fighting scandal threatened Vick's social freedom and financial security. The double trouble of the criminal probe and its wide-ranging economic consequences landed him in both criminal and civil court.

Despite signing a ten-year, $130 million contract with the Atlanta Falcons in 2004, the dog fighting charges rendered Vick unemployable in the NFL. As if the impending criminal case were not worrisome enough, Vick's loss of corporate sponsorships and his NFL career left him with $20 million in debts, overriding $16 million in assets. Given the enormous debt load, which exacerbated his social collapse, Vick filed for Chapter 11 bankruptcy to protect his assets. In filing for protection from his creditors, Vick saw his ability to emerge from bankruptcy as central to his goal of emerging from prison and the key to resuming his NFL career. In negotiating terms for the bankruptcy, Vick assured the court and the creditors that he would pay the money back once he returned to the NFL. He offered this reassurance without any indicator from the league that he would be allowed to return. So not only did Vick forecast a path of redemption, but his decision to file for Chapter 11 was, in his mind, a way to restore a measure of honor to his name. So while a prison term became an acceptable context to pay his debt to society, bankruptcy became the framework to pay his creditors. But before he could resume his NFL career and satisfy his outstanding debts, justice would have to be served in his criminal case.

While the majority of Americans wanted Vick locked up for his harm to dogs, another segment wanted him dead. Still a significant number of others, mainly African-Americans, felt prison was not warranted. But after serving his near two-year prison sentence, the rancorous debate raged on. Some respected his quest for redemption, while others felt he was incorrigible and therefore unfit for reentry into the NFL. In the midst of these ranging sentiments, Vick was challenged to show that he had the mental fortitude to regain his moral compass. This would also mean charting a meaningful course toward social repentance. Vick needed to be convinced, and at the same time be convincing, that as horrible as his crimes were, he could actually become a model citizen. His ability to regain a measure of dignity and respect, and more importantly, his NFL career, would mean showing people that given another chance he would be better than ever. In Vick's mind, the pain that he caused himself and others would reap a significant gain in the end. As much as the public acrimony made it seem, unfathomable that Vick could ever resurface in the NFL, much less as a top performer, he felt otherwise. It has been said that the road to success is always under construction. In Vick's case, he had built a road to success only to swerve out of control. But in the aftermath of his downfall, he had to build the road to redemption.

Vick's Road to Redemption

The most important factor that will determine whether Vick succeeds or fails at redemption will be his ability to dismantle the deep-seated dualism that has defined and defeated him. Will he revert back to the Michael Vick who loved animals as a boy, or is he still the Michael Vick who committed horrific acts against dogs? Is he the Michael Vick who quickly rose to the top of the NFL, or the Michael Vick who fell even faster to the bottom? Is he the Vick who gave charitably of his wealth to the needy, or the Vick who misappropriated and squandered his wealth in a criminal enterprise? Is he the Vick who was sincere enough to concede his mistakes and paid his debt to society, or the deceiving Vick who lied to everyone to protect his lucrative career? Will he have the wherewithal to recognize those who might want to exploit him for their selfish interests as they have in the past?

As Vick has learned rather painfully, when you become a wealthy celebrity quarterback in the NFL, your platform becomes a grand stage for all to see. The expansive audience will consist of those who will cheer you and those who will jeer you. The spectators will include those wishing you well versus those waiting for your downfall. Throughout Vick's life he has been mostly celebrated by fans for his football greatness. But after becoming a prosperous NFL quarterback, he miscalculated an important reality: when you reach the top, it only makes you an easier target.

Given this drama of the Michael Vick saga, it will be meaningful to review some of the significant scenes in his life that contributed to his ruin. Because this ongoing narrative involves a cast of so many characters, this conversation will include a reflection on Erving Goffman's dramaturgical theory. This perspective is especially useful since the storyline of Vick's life involves his attempts to please whichever social audience he appears in front of. The theory will provide a conceptual framework for discussing factors that seemed to influence the fall and ultimate rise of Michael Vick.

Dramaturgy

Erving Goffman's dramaturgical perspective is among the branches of symbolic interaction theories. It holds that life is an ostentatious stage. The perspective suggests that we are all actors and actresses, attempting to fulfill socially scripted roles. These scripts become guidelines and expectations for us to fulfill in our various spheres of social interaction. Additionally, these scripted roles will vary as much as the stages on which we appear vary. Hence, the audiences will vary from home life to schooling to our neighborhoods to religious communities to business organizations or sports institutions; from the media to peer groups and even to public authorities. When we succeed at fulfilling these expectations of *generalized others*, we are applauded accordingly. Conversely, when we fail to meet previously held expectations in any of these associations, we can be booed accordingly. No matter the social reaction, as individuals we attempt to refine ourselves to ensure we will be applauded. This social adaptability constitutes what Goffman referred to as *impression management* (Aaronson and Kimmel, 2011).

This social challenge of balancing different roles and priorities is universal for all human beings. However, in Vick's case, Goffman's dramaturgy perspective is especially valuable given the multitude of people that Vick encountered throughout his life. While he has sought the adulation of others in the course of these human connections, his inability to satisfy everyone's expectations has been a source of *role conflict* for him. Depending on the stage he has found himself on, Vick has been revered and reviled alike. Consequently, he has utilized impression management more than most NFL players in his attempts to placate the various entities, given their social reaction to him, good or bad. Despite scaling the heights of the most popular spectator sport in America, a dream Vick harbored since early childhood, he would receive a rude awakening. As much as his style of play had been celebrated from little league to the big league, media pundits covering the NFL criticized Vick incessantly.

Sports reporters and broadcasters did not always appreciate his tendency to make plays running with the ball in addition to passing with it. Consequently, his remarkable production at quarterback in the NFL was trashed more than it was treasured. This ongoing conflict between Vick being cheered for his play versus being jeered by his critics contributed to a host of negative labeling.

Vick: Should He Be Cheered or Jeered?

Despite being drafted as a quarterback out of Virginia Tech, the media has often referred to Vick dismissively as an athlete or a running quarterback. Oddly enough, this notion of a running quarterback has become a racially charged pseudonym for black quarterback in the NFL. Although historically, running quarterbacks in the NFL were not only the standard, but were invariably white. But, rather than being berated, they were celebrated. "Automatic" Otto Graham, the Hall of Fame quarterback, was formerly a running back at Northwestern University. But Paul Brown made him a quarterback with the Cleveland Browns. Graham was converted because "athletic" quarterbacks who could run were the norm rather than the exception in professional football. Moreover, in the often imitated T-formation of the 1940s and '50s, white quarterbacks like Sid Luckman of the Chicago Bears and Bobby Lane of the Detroit Lions continued the tradition of quarterbacks being dual threats with both the pass and the run. By contrast, the great Norm Van Brocklin was thought of as an anomaly at quarterback in the '50s because he was not a running quarterback. This tolerance of running quarterbacks continued in the 1970s with the likes of Fran "The Scrambler" Tarkenton and Roger "The Dodger" Staubach, and even the lesser heralded Bobby Douglass. Incidentally, when Michael Vick broke the NFL's single-season rushing record for a quarterback in 2006, a mark which had stood for thirty-four years, not many people knew that the previous record holder, Bobby Douglass, was white.

Even more evidentiary of the term running quarterback having racial implications for blacks is the recent emergence of quarterback Tim Tebow as an NFL folk hero. Tebow, who is white, has made an NFL career out of running the football from the wildcat formation and the read-option offense. But rather than call him a running quarterback, like the media has for Vick and other blacks at the position, Tebow is seen as a throwback to the days of old. That race is clearly a factor in how quarterbacks like Michael Vick are perceived is evident from the racially charged remarks from the likes of Rush Limbaugh. During his brief stint as an analyst on ESPN, Limbaugh relabeled African-Americans like Vick as black quarterbacks. Such media maligning has historically been designed to undermine quarterbacks who are black. In light of such racially charged labeling, Vick's career has been plagued by questions of whether he is a legitimate quarterback. His successes have often been marginalized by the media, which preferred to cast him as a misfit at quarterback in the NFL.

The *labeling theory*, as noted, is also a branch of the symbolic interactionist perspectives. It holds that individuals who are in positions of power and influence, such as the media, will label others as they see fit. Such labeling will determine the relations between the labeler and the person or persons so labeled. Hence, Vick has had a mostly tetchy relationship with the sports media. Moreover, the power of media labeling can also influence how the general public perceives the person so-labeled. In Vick's case, the mainstream media greatly distorted and diminished his value from the outset of his NFL career. Consequently, he has been both applauded and assailed in the NFL, despite his greater successes.

The sports reporting media often mischaracterizes Vick's productivity as abhorrent when there is much good. The negative portrayals, often based on perception, have morphed into a false reality. The biggest identity crisis that Vick has had to contend with, which was imposed on him by the media, is whether he is a legitimate quarterback (whatever that means) or simply a gifted athlete.

Vick's Not a Quarterback, He's an Athlete

Most NFL analysts felt that Vick's All-Pro season with the Philadelphia Eagles in 2010 signaled his arrival as a legitimate quarterbacking talent. However, his growth in the position was actually observable before the dog fighting debacle of 2007. Prior to his outstanding comeback season with the Eagles, when he posted the best passing statistics in his career, Vick's tremendous quarterbacking production was undervalued by media pundits. Brian Burke of Advanced NFL Stats reported on Vick's veiled production, which has been greatly understated.[111]

Numbers Don't Lie

Part of what has made Vick the subject of so much media criticism for his play in the NFL has been his tendency to run with the football on passing plays. Burke concedes that Vick is certainly an *unconventional* quarterback given his penchant for running. He points out that through 2006, his last season before the scandal, most of his 529 career runs came on passing

---

111 Brian Burke, Advanced NFL stats. *Vick as a quarterback? He's Underrated*, 2009.

plays. Therefore, an argument can be made that Vick was more productive on passing plays than most quarterbacks in the NFL, given that he averaged 7.1 yards when he ran, while the average passing play netted 5.1 yards. But Vick has been paid big money to throw the football, not run with it, right? Yet when it came to downfield passing, Burke found that Vick once again distinguished himself from other top quarterbacks in the NFL. In 2006 (his last season in Atlanta), the top thirty quarterbacks in the NFL averaged 11.4 yards per pass; Vick averaged 12.1 yards per pass completed, albeit inconspicuously. For all of the complaints about his tendency to run first on passing plays, in 2006 his "air yards" (the distance the ball travels from the line of scrimmage to the receiver) averaged 7.7, while the top thirty quarterbacks in the NFL averaged 6.3 yards. For all of the talk about Vick experiencing a renaissance as an NFL quarterback in the 2010 season, he actually picked up where his performance left off in 2006 with the Atlanta Falcons.

That year, Vick threw twenty touchdowns against thirteen interceptions while amassing 2,474 passing yards, which were career bests. In addition, he set a record in becoming the first NFL quarterback to rush for 1,000 yards in a season. This breakout year for Vick as a passer was overshadowed by his team's failure to make the playoffs and by his NFL record for single-season rushing yards by a quarterback. In light of this broader perspective on Vick's production, why was he criticized so much in the media for his play at NFL quarterback through 2006? During this span, he appeared in three Pro Bowls and led the Atlanta Falcons to the playoffs, including an NFC South division crown and a 2004 appearance in the NFC Championship game. Was race a factor in what amounted to a deliberate disregard for such successes? Historically, the tendencies of quarterbacks who are black to be more productive using their abilities to run and pass has been underappreciated in the league, and particularly in the mainstream press.

Blacks as quarterbacks are still underrepresented, despite their greater production and higher passing efficiencies in college, and their tendencies to lead teams to the playoffs. Most NFL teams still prefer to have whites as starting quarterbacks.

Today, whites are upwards of eighty percent of all starting quarterbacks, and those drafted high in the first round can expect NFL teams to be patient with their development.

Differential Treatment in Black and White

Conventional wisdom in the NFL held that a franchise quarterback needed about five years to arrive. Today, though, quarterbacks have to show and prove themselves in a much shorter time. A black quarterback must demonstrate his prowess even sooner. Cam Newton came out in 2011 and set rookie passing marks, including a single season record for rushing touchdowns by a quarterback, en route to a Pro Bowl berth. In 2012, the emergence of rookies Robert Griffin III (RGIII), Russell Wilson, and second-year pro, Colin Kaepernick, signaled a new era in qualified quarterbacks who are gifted and black. While Russell and Griffin had playoff seasons as rookies, Kaepernick led his team to the Super Bowl. Like Vick and other African-American quarterbacks, each had to overcome questions about their abilities as starting quarterbacks. In Vick's case, despite being drafted first overall in 2001, he was second-guessed about his readiness, size, lack of footwork, and accuracy. These criticisms notwithstanding, he was voted to the Pro Bowl in three of his first four years as a starter (in 2003 he missed most of the season with a leg injury). As if these Pro Bowl seasons were not validation enough, his 2006 performance showed the arrival of a quarterback ahead of his time, given the five-year window that white quarterbacks have generally been allowed. As noted, Vick's success in Atlanta was obscured by the media labeling him a running quarterback rather than a leader at quarterback. For all of the criticisms of his style of play, Vick had just one losing season in his career with the Falcons, where he posted an impressive 38-28-1 record as a starting quarterback.

To further underscore this point about racial double standards, Doug Flutie, who is white, was also renowned for his running abilities as a quarterback. He enjoyed success in the NFL without gaudy passing statistics. But the media would say of him "just throw away the statistics, all he does is win games." Vick was held to a different standard. Rather than throwing away the statistics as the media suggested with Flutie, the numbers were thrown in his face. Yet, when Flutie retired from the NFL in 2006, his career record was 38-28, virtually identical to Vick's 38-28-1, when his career in Atlanta concluded in 2007. Such differential social reaction by the media to quarterbacks with similar styles of play like Vick and Flutie underlines the variance in media coverage of quarterbacks who are black and white. Although Vick returned to NFL prominence in 2010 with a Pro Bowl season and being named NFL Comeback Player of the Year, the media continued the pejorative labeling.

For example, everyone knows that injuries are a part of the game, and quarterbacks are especially susceptible. When Vick becomes injured, the media blames him and his style of play. When Ben Roethlisberger suffers a twisted ankle, a broken nose, or broken ribs, his injuries are attributed to his fighting to make things happen. In 2011, the Houston Texans lost their first- and second-string quarterbacks in successive weeks due to injuries sustained in the pocket. Yet no one questioned their style of play or criticized them for not getting rid of the ball sooner. With Vick, no matter how he is injured, he gets criticized.

With so much criticism from the sports reporting media, which has included descriptions of him as reckless and dangerous on the field, is it any wonder that Vick's life off the field became reckless and dangerous as well? Given the media-induced fatalistic identity of Vick as a black quarterback, which has historically carried a plethora of problematic connotations, might such negative labeling have influenced his self-destruction? The term *black quarterback* is an overt suggestion that such quarterbacks are *outsiders* who deviate from the prototypical white quarterback in the NFL. Rather than being revered as a special quarterbacking talent, the way he had been in high school and college, Vick has been reviled for it in the NFL. Consequently, like actors generally do, he attempted to revise his role to win the applause of others.

For Vick, no matter how successful he was in winning games, his critics seemed to always drown out the good he produced. Perhaps this helps to explain why he kept friends of questionable repute near him during his time with the Atlanta Falcons. While his *friends* may have been disagreeable characters, it may have been that he was insecure about the perceptions held of his quarterbacking talents in the NFL. After all, his skills were universally appreciated back home, so why not have friends from the neighborhood nearby to reassure him in the NFL? When the press battered him for his style of play, his friends would applaud him just the same. Could it be that their applause in contrast to the media assailing him pushed Vick further in the wrong direction? Is it a coincidence then that Vick would fly back home to Virginia on Tuesdays, his days off, to carry out the affairs of Bad Newz Kennels?

In the movie *Red Tails*, which is the story of the Tuskegee Airmen, an all-black regiment of U.S. Air Force fighter pilots who fought in World War II, there is a famous line that states: *"Experience is a cruel teacher. It gives the exam first, then the lesson."*[112] For Vick, life became a very cruel teacher, both in the neighborhood and later in the NFL. In his hometown of East End of Newport News, also known as Bad News, he made unsavory friends who taught him dog fighting. In the NFL, there were more cruel teachers, particularly in the media, as Vick would learn. The ongoing struggle to be respected as an NFL quarterback, while being negatively labeled as a black quarterback was the cruelest of teachers. But as unkind as these teachers have been in Vick's life, the exam would be tougher. Without any textbook to study from, Vick's ability to handle success as an NFL quarterback would be sorely tested. Another significant test would be his ability to follow the rules and obey the laws of the land. But the biggest test of all would be how well Vick could balance his professional life in the NFL versus his private life off the field. Battling this duality would be tough and provide him with his most important lessons. Both the fall and rise

---

112 *Red Tails*, the Lucas film, was released by 20th Century Fox on January 20, 2012.

of Michael Vick is owing to an ongoing dichotomy, including the overriding need to control for the dualities in his life.

Duality That Has Defined Vick

The duality that has defined Michael Vick's life is a narrative on being split in twos. In high school he attended Ferguson High School for two years and Warwick High School for another two. At both high schools he excelled under Coach Tommy Reamon before heading to Virginia Tech University (Vick, 2012). In his youth, Vick had wholesome friends whom he interacted with, but he also had unwholesome friends who had the potential to break the law. While Vick's good friends played football in the neighborhood with him, the wayward friends influenced him to commit petty thefts, and others introduced him to dog fighting.

Paradoxically, as much as the dog fighting scandal cast Vick as the face of animal cruelty, he actually professed a love for animals in his youth. He noted owning two parakeets, gerbils, and a dog that he loved named "Midnight." Notwithstanding his love for animals, he ultimately became a dog fighter who hurt animals. Moreover, he reportedly used smaller family pets as bait for his pit bulls. Despite his growing appreciation for dog fighting in his youthful years, Vick conceded that he never fought his dog Midnight. He also admitted being terribly fearful of dogs that he did not know. Yet he participated in dog fights nonetheless. Vick's foray into dog fighting seemed to be a reflection of his tendency to seek the adulation of his peers. Such imbalanced reasoning was an example of how he sacrificed his better judgment in acquiescing to the interests of others. While he observed his first dog fight at age eight, it did not propel him into dog fighting as a participant. It would be later in life, when an older friend in his neighborhood named Tony introduced him to the blood sport. He enjoined Vick to let him know when he wanted a "real dog" (Vick, p. 98). Vick's inability to discern what was meant by a *real dog* is but another indicator of this duality that would ultimately contribute to his downfall.

Consistent with this tendency to seek applause from generalized others, Vick followed Tony's lead and attended a *real*
dog fighting match while home from college at Virginia Tech
(Vick, p. 99). In a rather twisted irony, Vick attended his first
real dog fight in Smithfield, Virginia, the same town where
he would later buy the house at 1915 Moonlight Road, which
became home to Bad Newz Kennels. Through his interactions
with Tony, Vick ultimately developed a love for pit bulls and
the blood sport of dog fighting. Even so, he concedes that his
initial impression of dog fighting was that it was violent and
inhumane. Yet he ignored his better instincts and gave in to the
camaraderie associated with the underground culture of animal
combat. As an indicator of how divided Vick was becoming, his
passion for dog fighting was increasing as his college career
at Virginia Tech was winding down. Vick notes that in March
2001, one month before the NFL draft, he saw Tony outside
of a barbershop in a notorious section of Newport News. Vick
expressed an interest in purchasing dogs for fighting. Despite
this very pivotal time, his duplicitous mindset was being further honed as he was preparing for the NFL draft. Such a
significant development as a bourgeoning NFL career should
have prompted Vick to resist the temptation of engaging in dog
fighting. Instead, these distinctly different worlds were becoming entangled. Vick the professional football player would help
create Vick the professional dog fighter. While the former edition of Vick led the Atlanta Falcons back to winning football
and playoff competition, the latter *Vick* led Bad Newz Kennels.
As quarterback of the Falcons, his outstanding play would take
him to the doorstep of the *Big Show*—the Super Bowl—before
losing the 2004 NFC Championship to the Philadelphia Eagles.
Conversely, his participation in dog fighting would, in 2007,
land him in the *Big House* — the Leavenworth Federal Prison.

A big part of this perplexing paradox that has undermined
Vick is this sense of ambivalence about being in the shadows
of others. While in high school, despite being an outstanding
quarterbacking talent, Vick was always overshadowed by cross-
town quarterback rival Ronald Curry. He noted that Curry was

always at the center of media coverage of high school football in Virginia. No matter how hard he tried, Curry, who had won national awards as a high school quarterback, was always seen as better than him. In his senior year, the star high school quarterbacks met on the field, with Vick in a position to secure a scholarship to attend Virginia Tech. Although his team would suffer a lopsided 34-16 loss, Vick outdid Curry statistically. In defeat, Vick won over Virginia Tech by throwing for more than 300 yards and one touchdown, with another 40 yards rushing. While Vick took flight to lead the Hokies football team, Curry went to the University of North Carolina. Although Curry was hobbled by injuries in college, he was eventually drafted by the Oakland Raiders. But, like so many African-American quarterbacks historically, he was asked to change his position to wide receiver in the NFL. Although Michael Vick had lived his high school years in Curry's shadow, at the 2001 NFL Draft he found himself front and center as the most coveted player on the board.

From a Hokie to a Falcon

In 2001, Vick was finally number one. As the first overall pick, he was drafted by the Atlanta Falcons. For the young man from East End of Newport News, it was a significant development. Still, it appeared that Vick did not fully understand all that came with it. Although there was a high distinction in being the number one overall pick, there were also lingering doubts. Vick was not merely a quarterback, but in the minds of critics and cynics alike, he was a running quarterback; an athletic quarterback; a *black quarterback*. The NFL sports culture had always maintained a caste system at this position. This view was held by NFL owners, coaches, and the media. Rush Limbaugh simply had the audacity or stupidity to say on ESPN what has always been said behind closed doors. In reflecting on the day in which he was drafted and lauded by most, Vick was miffed when Bill Walsh, widely viewed as the dean of offense and quarterbacking in the NFL, said Vick probably would not be ready to start for three years (Vick, p. 55). That Vick was surprised suggests he was unaware that *black quarterbacks* were still perceived as requiring more development before they could start in the NFL. Still, Vick outdid Walsh's low expectations. Rather than having to wait three years to play, within that time span, and as a starter, Vick became a two-time All-Pro, with two playoff seasons, including a victory in the 2003 wild card game against the Green Bay Packers. The defeat was the first-ever playoff loss at home for the storied Packers at venerable Lambeau Field.

In 2004, Vick led the Falcons to the NFC Championship game, where they lost to Donovan McNabb and the Philadelphia Eagles. While these outcomes were significant indicators of Vick getting better as an NFL quarterback, he was actually getting better at living a double life.

While such applause for playoffs and Pro Bowl seasons should have been enough to ward off the wrong influences, Vick continued seeking the association of his deviant friends back home, many of whom had lesser ambitions than he, but his success also meant their success. Following this script, Vick ignored the ominous signs and urgings of others about the company he was keeping. Like so many African-American professional athletes, he became conflicted between enjoying success he earned as an individual versus remaining "true" to his friends back home. Often, this staying "true" has meant sharing the success and rewards of their labor. This commitment entails not just buying them gifts, but becoming their surrogates. Vick took this bait and used resources from his NFL contract to purchase 1915 Moonlight Road in Surry County, Virginia. The place that became a house of horrors for the dogs of Bad Newz Kennels was also the house that brought down Michael Vick. Instead of using his wealth to invest in his friends and family by helping to pay for their college education or to develop meaningful enterprises, he created a flop house for friends and family who were clinging to his wealth and well-being. The beginning of the end of Vick's initial ascent in the NFL occurred with the arrest of his cousin Davon Boddie in 2007. It triggered a chain reaction that would send Vick on his precipitous plunge. Upon being arrested on drug possession charges, Boddie used Vick's Moonlight house address, which aroused the suspicions of police.

To further underscore how Vick was being exploited by friends and family, according to him, two weeks before the property was raided a neighbor came to the home, while Vick was not there, with a stunning revelation. The state police wanted permission to place a surveillance camera on his property to monitor traffic to and from Vick's place. Realizing that an unlawful dog fighting operation was being housed there, and that the property was owned by Vick, whose NFL career was at its height, someone among the friends and family members living there should have informed him. But they never did. According to Vick, he was only informed after the raid, but had he been told, he would have shut down Bad Newz Kennels. Unfortunately for him, state and federal agents would shut it down, and in the process put Michael Vick's dog fighting operation out of business. He would be indicted, convicted, and later sentenced to prison for his guilty plea of operating an illegal dog fighting enterprise in furtherance of interstate commerce.

This latter scenario underscores how Vick's attempts to win the respect and acceptance of his so-called friends and family members caused him to fail the biggest test of all: How do you handle success, fame, and high-end wealth? The friends who he sheltered not only failed to alert him that police were investigating his property, but they later gave statements to investigators implicating him as the financier of Bad Newz Kennels. The dog fighting debacle not only placed him in the national headlines, but he also faced justice in both criminal and civil court.

Vick had to pay a debt to society with nearly two years of imprisonment handed down in federal court. He was also ordered in civil court to pay $20 million to creditors. Because he only had $16 million in assets, Vick was forced to file for Chapter 11 bankruptcy. Despite his legal woes, it was hard to imagine that with a $130 million contract, Vick could have more debt than liquid cash. In his book, he indicated that he was paying monthly bills of $30,000 and $40,000 for multiple homes and payments on fourteen cars (Vick, p. 164). He also said that a bevy of financial advisors misappropriated his funds, some of which were never recovered. Other advisors doubled as his business partners on real estate deals. According to Vick, when he asked an advisor/business partner to sell real estate that he invested upwards of $6.5 million in and which would have helped him avoid bankruptcy, the advisor/partner refused. Given these accounts, it did not matter whether Vick was trusting neighborhood friends or financial advisors; his confidence in these individuals caused him troubles legally and financially. As a consequence, Vick learned another important lesson about friends and finances. Although the bottom fell out under him financially, he would descend to a bottomless pit in his criminal case. As a consequence of his friends agreeing to give statements against him as the principal financier of the dog fighting enterprise, Vick would go to prison. But in a strange way, prison would actually be a refuge from the widespread anger and angst that was feverish following his criminal probe and conviction on dog fighting charges. Despite the hard lessons learned through the actions of so-called friends, financial advisors, family members, and the myriad of life's tests that he failed, prison would accord him an opportunity to learn lessons for the rest of his life. The cheers of an NFL career had been drowned out by the jeers of protesters being led by animal rights advocates. Moreover, the media had a field day, publishing stories that excoriated Vick to no end. While prison life is not supposed to be promising, Vick promised himself that rather than being bitter about his downfall, he would be better because of it.

Two Years, Two Habits, and Two Visitors on the Path to Redemption

Consistent with his life unfurling in twos, Vick would serve nearly two years of a federal prison sentence. While imprisoned, he allowed two habits to shape his experience and pass the time. He became a voracious reader and a writer. As a reader, he delved into works like the renowned Chinese classic, *The Art of War*, which is widely regarded as a blueprint for a successful military expedition. Among its precepts is the idea of striking first in battle. Perhaps Vick was preparing himself for the battle of his next life, once released from prison, a battle that would entail learning how to satisfy his own interests first, rather addressing the interests of others. In addition, he read *The 48 Laws of Power* and a Christian novel titled *The Shack*. Vick's commitment to reclaim a sensible balance between faith and family undoubtedly influenced such study. In addition, he seemed recommitted to reading the Bible as he had done in his teens. He also reported reading a book of 480 pages in two days.

Another habit that formed his new-found sense of self was the 27,000 letters he reportedly received while imprisoned. He indicated that he read every one. Much to his surprise, only six or seven were hate-filled. The letters seemed to affect him profoundly as they showed how much people cared about him, despite his egregious errors. Before his downfall, he seemed unable to distinguish between people who cared more about Michael Vick the person versus Michael Vick the product. Hence he was often exploited by friends, advisors, sponsors, and others, given his wealth and celebrity. But while in prison, he was bankrupt, so the letters reflected widespread concern about Michael Vick the person. Of course, the other significant habit that truly seemed to empower Vick was writing his memoir, *Michael Vick: Finally Free*.

According to him, his ability to tell his side of his story would be impossible through interviews with the press. That Vick decided to write his own book showed that although life had been a cruel teacher, he was intent to learn from the lessons. Whatever Vick learned behind prison walls would become manifest in his actions once released. His incarceration only emboldened him to resume his life and NFL career. Throughout his imprisonment, Vick watched NFL football with other inmates and longed for the day of his eventual return. While on the one hand he was confident he could play again at a high level, he also feared that no team would give him another chance. As Vick wrestled with this ambivalence about his NFL future, two visitors gave him cause for optimism. One was

Wayne Pacelle, the executive director for the Humane Society of the United States of America. The other was Tony Dungy, former head coach of the Indianapolis Colts and Tampa Bay Buccaneers.

Vick and the Humane Society

Wayne Pacelle of the Humane Society had used his stature to organize mass protests against Vick, which helped to convict him in his criminal case. In addition, the organization contributed to the hysteria by sending over 160,000 messages to Nike, imploring the company to take action against Vick. The organization also pressured the NFL to punish Vick. Both obliged. But now, Vick saw in Pacelle an important piece of the puzzle in his quest for redemption. Vick's reentry into the NFL would have to mean a public display of regret to better insulate himself and the league from public rancor. To achieve this objective, he needed to partner with an animal rights group that would attest to his worthiness as an advocate against dog fighting. Vick made overtures to PETA, the other major advocacy group that had vilified him during the scandal, but they rejected him outright. So Pacelle and the Humane Society were his best shot at redemption as an advocate. But was Vick's decision to seek out Pacelle an act of necessity or naiveté? Clearly, the Humane Society saw an opportunity to help Vick rebound with his career. But the organization also saw a greater opportunity for free publicity at the expense of Vick as they did during his demise in 2007.

Interestingly enough, upon his release from prison, the NFL and the media expected Vick to show more remorse, despite publicly apologizing for his actions before he was sentenced. Additionally, he paid $1 million for the rehabilitation of the dogs that were kept alive after Bad Newz Kennels was shut down by authorities. Vick seemed to reason that the opportunity to alter the public's view of him as the face of animal cruelty offset any feelings of being exploited by Pacelle and the Humane Society. If the partnership with Pacelle went well, it was expected to help

Vick's reputation as an animal rights' advocate. But would it be enough to secure reentry into the NFL?

To gain re-admittance, Vick needed to earn the confidence of an NFL insider. That significant someone would come in the person of Tony Dungy, who, as head coach of the Indianapolis Colts, won a Super Bowl in 2007. Although Dungy had retired as head coach of the Colts, he was still among the most respected men in NFL circles. After leaving the sidelines, he became an analyst on NBC Sports' *Sunday Night Football*, which broadcasts NFL games during the season. Dungy is also renowned off the field as a man of great substance with a strong Christian faith. The former head coach has also established charitable works around fatherhood and prison ministries. After witnessing Vick's perilous plunge, he felt compelled to help the fallen star redirect the course of his life. Dungy felt an even greater obligation, given a conversation he and Vick had years prior. In 2005, while in Japan to play an NFL exhibition game involving their respective teams, the Colts and Falcons, the two dined and discovered a mutual appreciation for fishing.

Dungy vowed that he and Vick would one day go fishing. When the Vick dog fighting scandal came to light, Dungy regretted that the two never found time for the excursion. He felt strongly that had the two gone fishing, perhaps Vick would have intimated some of his personal challenges. On the other hand, Vick could have very well benefitted from a more forthright discussion with Dungy about the NFL, one that would have reminded him of his unique privilege in being among the star quarterbacks in the league. Such a discussion could have underscored the historical pangs associated with being seen as a black quarterback. For his part, Dungy is well aware of the perils, pitfalls, and pathologies associated with being labeled a black quarterback in the NFL. As an NFL coach, he was renowned as a defensive specialist, although he was actually a quarterback by trade out of the University of Minnesota. Moreover, like many African-Americans before and after him, structural racism necessitated a position change to one other than quarterback in the NFL. He could have told Vick about the racial discrimination faced by black quarterbacks of the 1950s, such as Willie Thrower and George Taliaferro, for whose book Dungy wrote the foreword. He knew all too well the stories of Marlin Briscoe, Elridge Dickey, and Joe Gilliam, all of whom were victimized by racial discrimination as black quarterbacks in the NFL. Dungy could have also spoken to Vick about the harm of fulfilling low expectations on and off the field. On the other hand, these important conversations could have been held without the benefit of a fishing trip. Despite the missed opportunity, both Vick and Dungy realized all was not lost. With fifteen days to go before his release from prison, Vick knew his heart-to-heart discussion with the former head coach might be just what the doctor ordered. The two met, and both came away pleased about the visit.[113]

Dungy would emerge proclaiming good reviews about the beleaguered former superstar. He pronounced Vick relatively fit physically, and described his mood as bright and positive. More importantly, Dungy announced that he believed Vick was a changed person. He described being convinced that Vick felt bad about his mistakes and would do his best to atone for them. Thus, Dungy set the stage for Vick's plea for penance in society and the NFL. Dungy offered reassurances that included his unequivocal endorsement, which was meaningful given his impeccable reputation in the NFL. Upon Vick's release from prison in 2009, Dungy did not stop there. He was so intent on helping Vick gain reentry to the league that he called several NFL owners and lobbied for the quarterback to get a second chance.

Second Chance in Life and the NFL

Upon his release from prison in 2009, Michael Vick was intent on making the most of his second chance in life. Success going forward would have to involve effectively balancing faith and family. If Vick could achieve such symmetry, then his plans

---

113 Retrieved from http://sports.espn.go.com/nfl/news/story?id=4164165. "Dungy: Vick wants second chance." May 13, 2009.

to return to the NFL might be more attainable. But before he could walk out of the Leavenworth Federal Prison into a new day, Vick would soon realize that in two years the contempt for him had not totally waned. While the majority of the 27,000 letters he received in prison were favorable, death threats streamed in as his release date approached. Consequently, officials at Leavenworth decided to release him early, without divulging the time. After being released from prison, Vick sought to get back to the simple things in life. He and his fiancée Kijafa alternated driving duties in the long drive from Kansas to their home in Hampton, Virginia. Vick noted that he ate at McDonald's and Dairy Queen along the way. But most importantly, he was committed to rebuilding important relationships with his family, which was torn apart during his imprisonment. This also meant rebuilding trust with his children, including his youngest daughter, London, who was a newborn when he went to prison.

After arriving home to everyone's excitement, Vick had to digest the difficulty of being a stranger to his two-year-old daughter, who, unlike the rest of America, did not know her famous father. The stranger anxiety she felt in his presence was especially difficult for Vick and his fiancée. Although Vick may have been a stranger to his baby daughter, he was no stranger to a cynical and sinister public. No sooner could he establish himself as an animal rights advocate with the Humane Society than a ghost from the past came back to haunt him.

In April 2009, Rush Limbaugh recorded a public service announcement for the Humane Society, one month before Vick was to be released from prison.[114] Limbaugh knew of Vick's stated plans to work with the Humane Society, so his interest in recording a spot was a deliberate attempt to undermine their alliance. The divisive radio commentator, perhaps still smarting over losing his dream job as an NFL analyst on ESPN after making racially divisive remarks about black quarterbacks, blindsided Vick. Limbaugh typecast street fighters of dogs as

---

114 Retrieved from http://www.humanesociety.org/news/press_releases/2009/04/ rush_limbaugh_records_audio. *Rush Limbaugh Records Audio Spots for the HSUS.*

"people like Michael Vick." With Vick seeking to be de-labeled as a dog fighter, supposedly with the help of the Humane Society, Limbaugh beat him to the punch in relabeling Vick as just that. For Vick, having Limbaugh taking a swing at him was one concern, but a sucker punch to the gut by the Humane Society was unexpected. I suppose the remarks would have been easier to digest had Limbaugh lambasted him from his radio show. Instead, he denigrated Vick with the help of the Humane Society and his self-described "friend," Wayne Pacelle. Why would Pacelle agree to work with Vick to repair his image by advocating against dog fighting, only to give Limbaugh a platform to re-label him as a dog fighter? The decision by Pacelle and the Humane Society to partner with Limbaugh prior to working with Vick reinforced the view that they cared less about Vick and more about gaining publicity at his expense. Still, in his book, Vick referred to Pacelle as his *friend*. This sort of reference to someone who double-crossed him underscores how naïve and exploitable Michael Vick can be. Unfortunately, this tendency to be too trusting of people like Pacelle is similar to his trust for unscrupulous *friends* from his neighborhood. Another individual who Vick referred to as his *friend*, whose motives were also questionable in the quarterback's quest for redemption, is NFL Commissioner Roger Goodell.

How Good of a Friend is Goodell?

While Vick identified Goodell as a friend, the NFL commissioner never reciprocated with such a reference to him. If there is any truth to the axiom actions speak louder than words, then Goodell's actions made it clear—Vick was not a friend of his. Instead, his actions toward the quarterback were very much consistent with the commissioner's signature phrase: "It's all about the shield." The shield, of course, is the NFL logo or insignia that is the league's official icon. Of the thousands of letters Vick received in prison, none came from Roger Goodell. In anticipation of his meeting with Commissioner Goodell to discuss being reinstated in 2009, Vick recalled not speaking to him while he was away. According to Vick, he had rehearsed what he planned to say, including offering a sincere apology to the commissioner for lying about his involvement in dog fighting. But, Goodell told him the past was the past, and it was time to move forward (Vick, p. 192). On the other hand, when it came to his public persona, Goodell sounded a different theme. Rather than emphasizing the past is the past and that it was time to move forward, Goodell stated publicly that Vick needed to show more remorse before the *larger community*. The *larger community* seemed to be a veiled reference to Vick's need to placate angry whites who were still seething over his crimes. After all, African-Americans had forgiven Vick, and most did not want to see him imprisoned. As noted previously, Goodell never required Ben Roethlisberger to show remorse to the *larger community* as a condition for reinstatement after two incidents involving accusations of sexual assault involving two different women in two states.

In 2007, when Vick's involvement in dog fighting came to light, Goodell condemned it publicly. To date, he has never condemned China for its atrocities against dogs. For all of Goodell's friendship that Vick was claiming, actions spoke differently. At the height of public anger against Vick, NFL.com posted a caption of a protester holding a sign that read "Kick Vick." In addition, while the media was pummeling Vick with a one-sided onslaught, Goodell essentially forbade any NFL player to say anything in support of the besieged quarterback. If that were not enough, the league informed Deion Sanders and his hometown newspaper, the *News-Press* of Fort Meyers, Florida, that he could not write any articles expressing support for Vick (Neus, 2007).[115] Then in 2009, despite serving nearly two years in prison and having publicly apologized before a throng of media, in addition to paying a king's ransom for the rehabilitation of the dogs, Goodell told him he needed to show more remorse.

Given the reticence of the commissioner to publicly pronounce Vick fit, as he would do with Ben Roethlisberger, none

---

115 http://usatoday.printthis.clickability.com/cpt?action=cpt&title=NFL+Network+intercept.

of the NFL teams expressed an interest in acquiring him. While Vick claimed a number of people as his friends, a real friend emerged at just the right time. Donovan McNabb, the All-Pro Super Bowl quarterback of the Philadelphia Eagles, persuaded his team to sign Vick. The two became friends when McNabb hosted Vick during his recruitment trip to Syracuse University. McNabb had also been one of the NFL players who wished Vick well in 2007 when his dog fighting crimes were a major story. Now in 2009, he used his influence within the Eagles organization to get Vick an audience with the Eagles front office. The Eagles executives, including team owner Jeff Lurie, met with Vick, and with the endorsement of Dungy and others, offered him a one-year contract with an option. After all that he endured, Michael Vick was back in the NFL.

Vick is Back in the NFL

Although Vick achieved an important goal on his road to redemption, he would start at the bottom of the team's quarterback depth chart. At third string, he backed up the franchise leader Donovan McNabb and his anointed successor, Kevin Kolb. Because most third-string quarterbacks rarely see game action, and generally have a short shelf life in the NFL, there was not much expected from Vick. As preparations for the season were underway, he was given permission to participate in preseason games. But the commissioner was non-committal on reinstating him for the regular season. As Goodell pondered his decision as to whether to reinstate Vick, it was still unclear what criteria the NFL commissioner would use. The idea of Vick needing to show remorse was certainly noted as a condition for reentry. Part of that remorse was demonstrated by his commitment to work with the Humane Society, which the league found acceptable. But which factor would ultimately influence Goodell's final decision? It became rather clear that the commissioner was primarily concerned about Vick's impact on the NFL's ability to make money off his return.

Despite being noncommittal on Vick's reinstatement, the NFL Pro Shop was advertising Michael Vick's Philadelphia Eagles jersey for sale on the Internet. When objective reporters questioned Goodell's principles in selling Vick's jerseys before officially reinstating him, the NFL pulled the advertisement from its website's cover page. Although not before Jeff Schultz of the *Atlanta Constitutional Journal* opined, "But how can a league not be ready to accept a player back with open arms and yet, be ready to open the cash drawer right away?"[116] Goodell seemed to be testing whether Vick was still a viable commodity who could generate revenue for the league and its teams. But as Schultz observed, the unfortunate message being sent was that the NFL was not ready for Vick to become a *face of the league*, but was ready for him to become a face on the NFL's financial ledger. At the height of his success, Vick's jersey in Atlanta was one of the top sellers. Goodell wanted the NFL to regain such revenue from Vick, which enriches all thirty-two teams, as proceeds from merchandise are shared league-wide. Other indicators suggest that Vick's revenue-generating potential was a factor in his decision to sign with Philadelphia.

In 2011, Vick made a stunning admission when he expressed appreciation, for the NFL commissioner who encouraged him to go to Philadelphia rather than Buffalo or Cincinnati. Why would the commissioner direct Vick to Philadelphia over Buffalo and Cincinnati? It is rather obvious: Philadelphia is not only a perennial playoff team, but the city is a major wealth market of the NFL. Perhaps this also helps to explain why the NFL was marketing and selling his Eagles jersey before he was cleared to play and despite the fact he was third string. Moreover, the NFC East is the wealthiest division in the NFL. The Eagles, along with the Dallas Cowboys, the New York Giants, and the Washington Redskins, are among the wealthiest teams in the NFL. By contrast, the Buffalo Bills and the Cincinnati Bengals

---

116 Retrieved from http://blogs.ajc.com/jeff-schultz-blog/2009/08/16/if-goodell-is-so-principled-why-is-he-selling-Vick-s-jersey? August, 16, 2009.

are small-market teams who have been critical of the growing revenue disparities being driven by wealthier teams. In fact, Bills owner Ralph C. Wilson and Bengals owner Mike Brown both voted against the 2006 collective bargaining agreement between the owners and the players union. It was also widely known that when NFL owners were picking a successor to NFL Commissioner Paul Tagliabue, the wealthier owners favored Goodell from the beginning. So is it unfathomable that Goodell would steer Vick away from two small-market teams who are not perennial contenders?

Furthermore, Vick playing in the NFC East would be more impactful league-wide, and especially in the large television markets. The inter-divisional games between NFC East teams are often nationally televised, which contributes to higher ratings. In the NFL, greater ratings equal greater revenues. Apparently, the league had a hunch that if Vick ever returned to his high level of play, it would pay dividends given competitive matchups between these divisional rivals. Perhaps not so ironically, Vick's best game as a pro occurred against the division rival Washington Redskins on *Monday Night Football* in 2010. Although Vick initially stated that the commissioner suggested that he sign with Philadelphia, he later said it was ultimately his decision.

It appears as though Vick revised his statement, because left alone, the comments showed the NFL commissioner being partial to the Eagles franchise with a free agent signing. The idea of Vick going to Philadelphia on his own volition was questionable, given that his goal at the time was to be a starter. Both Buffalo and Cincinnati needed a quarterback badly. In Philadelphia, Vick was the third-string quarterback. In his book, Vick framed the scenario a bit differently. He observed that in going to Buffalo he would have been asked to play sooner than he was actually ready to (p. 194). Perhaps he felt that way in hindsight. But if Vick was genuinely interested in going to Philadelphia, why, after one season, was he seeking to be traded? In the 2010 offseason, it was expected that Philly would make a trade with a quarterback. Vick reported to camp in what may have been the best shape of his career. Furthermore, he used the team's offseason training regimen to reestablish himself as a quarter-backing talent, rather than a situational wildcat option. Vick's camp performance must have been remarkable. Without any indication that he might compete for the starting job, the team's assistant head coach and offensive coordinator Marty Mornhin-weg declared of Vick, "He's back!" Although most of the NFL's public proceeded without much afterthought, Mornhinweg's comments were a harbinger of things to come.

In April 2010, the Philadelphia Eagles decided to trade Donovan McNabb, the quarterback who was the face of the franchise for eleven years. As bittersweet as the moment had to be for Vick, he helped himself by being in excellent shape. He also improved his value by publicly expressing a desire to be traded. But after the Eagles picked up the option on the one-year deal with Vick, the McNabb trade elevated him from third to second string on the quarterback depth chart. Moreover, with Kevin Kolb being an unproven commodity, there was a greater need for Vick to be ready to perform. Vick's value was enhanced by his status as a three-time Pro Bowler in Atlanta, where he was also a two-time playoff quarterback. But before he could appreciate his growing value, Vick would find out how tenuous his return to the NFL could be.

A Birthday Party to Forget

In June 2010, Vick's tendency to compromise his better judgment in the interest of others came back to haunt him again. Those same tendencies that cost him his freedom and financial security would resurface just as he had earned the organization's confidence. During what was supposed to be his thirtieth birthday party at a night club in Virginia Beach, Vick's NFL comeback nearly came to an end. On the evening in question, Quanis Phillips, one of Vick's co-defendants in the dog fighting case, showed up at the party that was, inexplica-bly, open to the public. Because both Vick and Phillips were convicted felons who were on probation, they were forbidden to be in one another's presence. To say Vick was courting disaster would be an understatement. Vick and Phillips came face to face and had to be separated. Sensing a potential problem, Vick left the party, but Phillips remained and got into a fight and was shot. But because it was at a birthday party in Vick's name, the event drew national headlines in the wrong way. Most of the sports reporting media, which would have preferred to not see Vick return to the NFL anyway, were clamoring for the Eagles to release him.

The media pressed for the commissioner to discipline him. There were suggestions the Eagles would release him. Even the investigating officers were being prodded to name him as a suspect. Although Virginia Beach police spokesman Adam Bernstein never named Vick as a suspect, he did indicate that it was the media that kept using his name (Mihoces, 2010). Video surveillance showed Vick leaving the club before Phillips was shot. Even so, it was obvious the media wanted the birthday fiasco to be the final straw for Vick. After ultimately being cleared of any wrongdoing, Vick was asked by a reporter if he felt "railroaded" by the media following the shooting. Ever mindful of being burned by the media, Vick indicated that he was not. In truth, the media not only tried to railroad him, but were equally intent to derail his comeback. For Vick, this lapse in judgment nearly spelled the end of his road to redemption in the NFL. Once more, his tendency to be exploited by trying to help others nearly cost him his second chance in the NFL.

According to Vick, his mother and his fiancée planned to host a private party for him that would have included family and close friends. Such a controlled environment made more sense. Instead, Vick decided to go with a plan hatched by his brother Marcus Vick, who suggested opening it up to the public with a cover charge (Vick, p. 208). By opening it up to the public, it opened Vick up to risks of the unknown, which should have occurred to him. Vick stated that he agreed to the idea to help his brother Marcus, who was due to make money from the party. This error in judgment magnified the microscope Vick was under. But once it was established that he was not a suspect and the league and

Eagles were satisfied with their inquiry, Vick remained on the team's roster for the 2010 season as an insurance policy.

2010: A Season to Remember for Vick

Although the Eagles offensive coordinator Marty Morn-hinweg had pronounced that Vick was "back," as in having regained his skill set, he remained an afterthought as the season began. The 2010 opener against the Green Bay Packers was to be the long-awaited coronation of the Kevin Kolb era in Phila-delphia. Oddly enough, before the game, Vick's former high school football coach Tommy Reamon told him that this game would change his life. Vick had a hard time believing something significant would happen while serving as the team's backup. But an interesting development occurred on the day of Kolb's coming-out party. With the team struggling in its season opener, and behind 20-3, Kolb suffered a concussion and was unable to finish. Enter Michael Vick. With the Eagles on the verge of a blowout, Vick entered the game without much practice time dur-ing the week. But despite being admittedly nervous, he nearly rallied the Eagles to victory in the second half. Although the Packers would hold on to win 27-20, Vick showed that he could still compete against the NFL's best.

In one half of football, he nearly engineered a come from behind win. Vick went 16-24 for 175 yards and added eleven rushes for 103 yards in roughly two quarters. With less than a full week's practice, Vick had sparked the Eagles offense in accounting for 278 of the team's 320 yards of total offense. After the game, an excited Vick proffered innocently enough that had he played the entire game, the Eagles would have won. Typi-cally, the sports reporting media would respect such a comment from a quarterback as simply being competitive. But the media, still skeptical about Vick, questioned whether he was slighting Kolb with his comments. Vick indicated that he was not. In an attempt to placate the media, he stated that Kevin Kolb was the starter and "our leader." But since the NFL had implemented new tests to determine if a player had sufficiently recovered from a concussion, Kolb needed to be cleared by the team doctor. After administering baseline tests, it was determined he was not able to return, which meant Vick would start in the next game. In a pivotal matchup against a young upstart Detroit Lions team, Vick had an opportunity to not only show the Eagles what he could do, but the entire NFL as well. With one week of preparation as the starter, Vick showed the near comeback win against Green Bay was no fluke. He led the Eagles to a tough 35-32 win, going twenty-one of thirty-four for 284 yards and two touchdowns and no interceptions. When you include his thirty-seven yards on eight rushes, Vick accounted for 321 of the team's 410 total yards. In what amounted to six quarters of football, Vick amassed 599 of the team's 730 total yards, with three touchdowns and no turnovers. Still, the media pundits were unimpressed. Vick's play in week two was dismissed.

According to the media, it happened against Detroit, which was renowned for losing. After the game, while Vick was no doubt excited about his resurgent performance, he continued to tow the company line that Kolb would resume his role as starter when he was healthy. To remove any doubt that Kolb would be the starter, Eagles head coach Andy Reid told the press the same thing. But something unforeseen happened in the week leading up to the team's next game against the Jacksonville Jaguars. According to Vick, Reid informed him that he would be the team's starting quarterback. While Vick felt bad about Kolb's injury costing him his job, he was re-signed by the Eagles for this very reason. He was expected to become leader of the team if necessary, since he had playoff success in his career. In a stunning reaffirmation that he was capable of leading the Philadelphia Eagles, the team rallied around Vick in a thoroughly dominating 28-3 win over the Jacksonville Jaguars. In his most complete performance yet, Vick went seventeen of thirty-one passing, for 291 yards and three touchdowns with no interceptions. For good measure, he ran another four times for an additional thirty yards rushing. Thus, Vick accounted for 321 of the team's 373 total yards. Such production was indeed an indicator that Michael Vick was fit to lead the Eagles. Furthermore, he removed any doubt as to whether he was back as a dominating quarterback in the NFL. But just as he was demonstrating his worthiness with the Eagles, a critical matchup against his good friend Donovan McNabb and the division rival Washington Redskins would deal Vick a setback. He suffered cracked ribs that would sideline him for the next three weeks. The change of fortunes put Kevin Kolb back in the starting role, where the team went 2-1 in Vick's absence. Would Reid stay with Kolb, who had also demonstrated an ability to lead the team, or put Vick back in the lineup? Because Kolb had played relatively well, the pressure was on Eagles head coach Andy Reid to decide who deserved to play more. Apparently sensing something special developing with Vick at the helm, Reid reinserted him in the lineup. Vick was now challenged to show he could recapture the success that he demonstrated before he got hurt.

The Eagles next opponent was the Indianapolis Colts, who were led by future Hall of Fame quarterback Peyton Manning. In a meaningful contest, Vick prevailed by once again being the best player and quarterback on the field. He completed seventeen of twenty-nine passes for 218 yards, while rushing ten times for another seventy-four yards. The win was important, not only because it moved the Eagles to 5-3 on the season, but because the game featured a quarterback duel between Vick and Manning which drew 27.8 million viewers. It was one of the highest-rated NFL games in the 2010 season.[117] Clearly, the nation was taking notice that Vick was reestablishing himself as a superior talent at quarterback. He was NFC Player of the Month in September, with some of the most productive numbers of any player in the NFL. But the next game would put Vick on the national stage in primetime against the Washington Redskins and would demonstrate that he was not just back, but better than ever. In what was easily the greatest performance of his career and in the annals of *Monday Night Football,* Vick single-handedly dismantled the Washington Redskins en route to a 59-28 rout.

---

117 Retrieved from http://content.usatoday.com/communities/thehuddle/post/2010/11/Michael-vick-win.

In a game that *ESPN The Magazine* dubbed "The Game of the Century," Vick was twenty of twenty-eight, in passing for 333 yards and four touchdowns, including an eighty-eight-yard strike on the game's first play from scrimmage. He also contributed another eighty yards rushing on eight carries and two touchdowns. When taken as a whole, Vick accounted for 413 total yards and six touchdowns in a game that was played in the rain. His performance of at least 300 yards passing with at least four touchdown passes, and at least fifty yards rushing, with another two touchdowns on the ground, were firsts for a quarterback in NFL history (Vick, p. 227). While Vick's outstanding game against the Redskins was the single most memorable performance of his career and the 2010 season, there was more to come. The win over the Redskins was a part of a pivotal stretch as the Eagles won five of their next six games. But to win the NFC East there was more football to be played, including a late-season matchup on the road against the New York Giants on December 19.

After being dominated by the Giants in the first thirty minutes, the Eagles were down 24-3 at halftime. But in a tale of two halves, Vick, who seems to thrive on second chances, led the Eagles in a second half surge, where they outscored the Giants 35-7, including twenty-eight points in the decisive fourth quarter to win the game. For his part, Vick reassured his NFC East divisional foes and the NFL that he was indeed a force to be reckoned with. In pulling out the fourth quarter comeback victory, he was twenty-one of thirty-five passing for 242 yards, with three touchdowns and one interception. He also ran for 130 yards and one touchdown. The game's outcome reminded Giants fans about the infamous *Miracle at the Meadowlands* of 1978, a game the Eagles won 19-17, in the final seconds after a fumbled exchange between Giants quarterback Joe Pisarcik and fullback Larry Csonka. Eagles defensive back Herman Edwards alertly scooped up the ball and returned the fumble for the game-winning touchdown. But the "New Miracle at the New Meadowlands," as the game would be called, was led by Vick's strong performance, which elevated his team. This was especially apparent when Eagles wide receiver DeSean Jackson returned a punt for a touchdown late in the fourth quarter that gave the Eagles a 38-31 victory. The huge win not only catapulted the Eagles to the playoffs, it encapsulated the great comeback season of Michael Vick. But it would be the team's last victory of the season. The Eagles would lose their last two regular season games and bow out to the Green Bay Packers, the eventual Super Bowl champions, in the wild card round of the playoffs. Yet 2010 was certainly a breakout year for Michael Vick that won him a newfound level of respect.

From Commissioner Goodell, who suspended him, to Judge Henry Hudson, who sent Vick to prison, to President Barack Obama, who commended him, the accolades streamed in over his improbable season. He was runner-up to Tom Brady for NFL MVP, which is no insult. Vick was named NFL Comeback Player of the Year and was voted to his fourth Pro Bowl after garnering the most votes in the NFC. Although he had achieved a greater measure of respect, his 2010 season was especially impressive since the media coverage seemed intent on undermining him. Vick's redemptive season was not only remarkable in recasting him in the limelight as an NFL superstar, but it occurred in the shadows of his dog fighting past.

The Press Keeps Pressing Vick

While he was available for questions about dog fighting when he was reinstated in 2009, most media types ignored him because he was third string. But during his incredible return to glory in 2010, the media revisited questions about the dog fighting scandal. Whether it was ESPN's Chris Berman or NBC's Bob Costas, the dog fighting crimes were constantly infused into discussions about his phenomenal year. Other indicators of media disdain for Vick kept cropping up. For example, after a nationally televised game in which the Eagles beat the Dallas Cowboys, Tashard Choice, an opposing player, asked Vick to autograph a glove for his nephew. He obliged, but because NBC cameras filmed the scene, it became a national news story.[118] Even Cowboys head coach Jason Garrett was asked for comment on the matter. As the accolades continued to pour in for Vick following his triumphant return to NFL stardom, so too did the animus.

This was never more apparent than when Tucker Carlson of Fox News suggested that Vick should be "executed" for his crimes against dogs. Carlson issued his rancorous retort in response to President Barack Obama's commending Eagles owner Jeff Lurie for giving Michael Vick a second chance. This gesture on the part of the president should not have evoked such media outcry as it did. After all, Philadelphia is the city where the Declaration of Independence was signed. In fact, there was a bit of presidential irony as well. At the time of the exchange between the Eagles owner and President Obama, the nation was in its worst economic crisis since the Great Depression. But it was during the Great Depression when President Franklin D. Roosevelt called on the nation to find ways to symbolize pride in America. The Philadelphia franchise, which was then owned by future NFL Commissioner Bert Bell, became the "Eagles." This name was adopted from the "Blue Eagle" insignia of the National Recovery Act, which became the manifesto of Roosevelt's New Deal. President Obama extolling Lurie for giving Vick a second chance should have been lauded for reflecting the spirit of recovery and redemption in America. While the media attempted to sack Vick, others like Tucker Carlson attacked him, without anyone speaking up for him.

What Are Friends For?

Carlson's parasitic paroxysm should have been decried. Wayne Pacelle, who was supposed to be Vick's partner in advocating against dog fighting, never uttered a word of support. Pacelle was also silent when Mark Buehrle, a pitcher for the Chicago White Sox, indicated that he and his wife were animal

---

118 Retrieved from http://sports.espn.go.com/dallas/nfl/news/story/id=5914095.

lovers who had hoped Vick might get hurt during his 2010 season. Oddly enough, Buehrle added that members of his family were hunters. By contrast, he noted dog fighting was never a sport. Again, Pacelle missed an opportunity to educate the public and show that he cared about Vick as a person and not just as an advocate for their cause. Pacelle should have noted that before it became illegal, dog fighting was considered a sport. The results of dog fights were reported in the local sports sections of newspapers. Furthermore, that Buehrle's family hunted animals should have evoked comment from Pacelle, especially since his organization condemns hunting animals except for subsistence. Pacelle's selective agitation over animal cruelty goes far and wide. Mike Silver, of Yahoo! Sports, reported on the hypocrisy in the public's reaction to Vick's mistreatment of animals.[119]

He noted that Peyton Manning is an avid hunter who openly admitted to shooting animals as a release after playing football, and especially after a tough loss. Yet Pacelle never chastised Manning for hunting animals for sport. Manning, being a multi-millionaire, hardly needs to hunt animals to subsist. On the other hand, that Manning loves to hunt may help to explain why he sent Vick his best in the midst of his dog fighting duress in 2007. While Vick's 2010 season culminated in his redemptive return to Hawaii for the NFL Pro Bowl, he maintains that his ultimate goal is to be a Super Bowl-winning quarterback. After coming off his great 2010 season, Vick got a sample of how hectic Super Bowl week can be, especially if you become a media story.

Super Ballyhoo

While Vick is no stranger to negative media coverage, he soon realized that despite his sensational Pro Bowl season in 2010, the press was still gunning for him. During Super Bowl week, several incidents touched off controversies involving

---

119 Retrieved from http://sports.yahoo.com/nfl/news;_yItAiHhhiMRcNsLYHvZz WyyNXGr0op4? Michael Silver, August13, 2007. *Society of Hypocrites.*

Vick, even though he was not playing in the game. Although this championship game was being played in Dallas Cowboys Stadium, the crown jewel of NFL stadiums, and that it involved two storied franchises in the Green Bay Packers and the Pittsburgh Steelers, stories about Michael Vick dominated. First there was the report that a Super Bowl party was being held in his name, something he flatly denied. But not before the press asked NFL Commissioner Roger Goodell for comment after he gave his annual State of the League address. Goodell responded that he had reviewed Vick's schedule with him before he arrived in Dallas and that a party in his name was not on the list. While the commissioner felt it was important to know what Vick's schedule was during Super Bowl week, he was less concerned about Ben Roethlisberger's. As previously noted, TMZ had broadcast video that showed Roethlisberger and his offensive lineman running up an estimated $800 bar tab. Not only was this amount staggering given the impending Super Bowl, but Roethlisberger was in the same element that brought about allegations of sexual assault against him in Georgia less than a year earlier. Yet the media did not ask the NFL commissioner to comment on Roethlisberger drinking in a bar, despite Roethlisberger also being on a redemptive path. That Goodell did not comment on Roethlisberger's questionable conduct is notable since he did not play particularly well in a Super Bowl that the Steelers would lose. Still the public relations hits on Vick kept coming in. The mayor pro tem of the Dallas City Council presented Vick with a key to the city, for which he was ripped by his colleagues in government. Then there was the story of a dog owner who reportedly adopted one of Vick's rehabilitated dogs, who claimed the quarterback ignored his attempts to speak with him. The media criticized Vick for it, which was terribly unfair. These same reporters chose to ignore that Vick's life is threatened continuously by so-called animal lovers. Many of the threats come from fringe personalities in the animal rights sector who can be extreme and potentially dangerous. Since Vick is often heckled by so-called dog lovers, his decision to avoid a potentially cantankerous exchange was actually good judgment. Yet he was criticized anyway. Throughout Vick's career, some in the media have loved him while others have hated him. But after the dog fighting debacle, the media has perpetuated more hate. Since being reinstated in 2009, Vick has consistently ranked high among the most hated players in sports.

His quest for redemption is far from done. While Vick realizes that there are many people in America that will never forgive him, he remains committed to rectifying the wrongs he committed against animals. He continues to seek personal atonement by demonstrating his commitment to advocating for animals rather than simply talking about it. As a sign of his sincerity, Vick has given more than twenty speeches condemning dog fighting. Some of his most meaningful advocacy against animal combat has been his lobbying efforts before Congress.

Vick the Lobbyist

Vick's commitment to advocacy for tougher laws against animal cruelty has included lobbying on Capitol Hill with the Humane Society. Those efforts have involved pushing Congress to pass legislation making it a misdemeanor to even attend a dog fight or a cockfight. In July 2011, Vick was back on Capitol Hill, along with Wayne Pacelle, to lobby Congress for tougher penalties for defendants who finance dog fighting. In addition, he lobbied for legislation making it a felony to take children to a dog fight. In April of 2012, Vick took his advocacy to the state level. He urged lawmakers in the state of Alabama to pass tougher penalties against cockfighting.[120] While his ability to address concerns about animal fighting at the state and federal level is meaningful, his lobbying efforts in Washington, D.C. amount to a significant turn of events.

Only four years prior, Vick was indicted on federal dog fighting charges with the AWA passed by Congress. In addi-

---

120 Retrieved from http://usatoday30.usatoday.com/sports/football/nfl/eagles/story/2012-04-17/Michael-Vick.

tion, lawmakers on Capitol Hill increased the prison sentence for dog fighting from three years to five in the wake of his criminal investigation and indictment. As much as Vick's lobbying efforts on Capitol Hill are important indicators of his commitment to change, he is still at risk for being exploited, especially since entities like the Humane Society and Congress helped to convict him. In addition, these entities greatly skewed the discussion of animal cruelty to street fighters of dogs, a significant number of whom are African-Americans. Such a narrow focus has seemingly exacerbated the plague of selective enforcement by race, which has led to an unequal distribution of laws in America. These sorts of inequities have increased the racial disparities in the rate of imprisonment for groups like African-Americans. While Vick's advocacy for tougher penalties associated with dog fighting is important, there are other forms of animal cruelty that warrant attention, such as hoarding, abuse, neglect, and bestiality.

It is worth reiterating, bestiality (humans having carnal relations with animals) is illegal in only twenty-nine states. Of those, only fifteen punish it as a felony. By contrast, the federal government made dog fighting a felony in all fifty states, yet, there are no federal laws against bestiality. Moreover, recent developments on Capitol Hill suggest that the preoccupation with dog fighting means bestiality is less likely to be punished as a crime. In November 2011, the U.S. Senate repealed Article 125 of the U.S. Military Justice Code, which lifted the prohibition against bestiality among military personnel.[121] Neither the Humane Society nor PETA had anything to say about this development. Bestiality, which involves a measure of brutality, is perhaps the worst form of animal cruelty.

According to the sexually polymorphous theory, bestiality and aggression become mutually inclusive. Moreover, individuals who engage in bestiality have a higher propensity of

---

121 Retrieved from http://cnsnews.com/news/article/senate-approves-bill-legalizes-sodomy-and-bestiality-us. Pete Winn, December 1, 2011. *Senate Approves Bill that Legalizes Sodomy and Bestiality in U.S. Military.*

committing acts of interpersonal violence, including sexually assaulting women and in some cases children. Therefore, if part of the reason the Humane Society and Congress sought tougher laws against dog fighting was because street fighters engage in other acts of crime, what explains the lack of concern over bestiality? If Vick is to be successful in rooting out problems of animal cruelty, he should broaden his perspective on animal cruelty beyond dog fighting. Aside from the greater concern over selective enforcement by race, bestiality is extremely harmful to animals and potentially to human beings. Since zoophiles (individuals who engage in bestiality) believe that animals can give consent, the failure of state and federal lawmakers to pass laws that criminalize bestiality provides consent by default.

"Watch Them Dogs"

An emerging concern over Vick's advocacy with the Humane Society lies in his attempts to stem the growth of the blood sport in urban communities. Since his release from prison, Vick has spoken at scores of city high schools about the harm associated with dog fighting. Most of the student bodies have been predominantly African-American. But who benefits more from these discussions? Is it Vick, the students, or the Humane Society? It is helpful for Vick to speak with students about this problem, because he made a commitment to do it. However, his speaking to students who are predominantly African-Americans only perpetuates the myth that dog fighting is a social problem unique to inner cities. It should not be lost on Vick that the Humane Society used his downfall to frame dog fighting exclusively as an inner-city problem. Actually, dog fighting has been a greater phenomenon in rural communities populated by whites. Why didn't the Humane Society have Vick speak at predominantly white high schools in suburban and rural communities where professional dog fighters flourish? Another latent consequence of Vick speaking before young blacks is that law enforcement efforts against dog fighting has focused more on the inner cities. This of course leads to an unequal distribution of the law and selective enforcement by race, which gives suburban and rural whites who engage in dog fighting greater cover. An analysis in this work shows that racial disparities in dog fighting arrests between African-Americans and whites widened in the wake of Vick's criminal investigation and conviction. The other concern about Vick's discussions with urban students is that an inordinate amount of attention is accorded to what he did wrong, often obscuring what he did right.

One of the most important achievements in Michael Vick's life is that he graduated from high school. This accomplishment is especially noteworthy since fifty percent of high school students in fifty of the nation's largest cities drop out. Therefore, the students Vick has been addressing are at greater risk of dropping out of high school than becoming dog fighters. Evidence that these high school students would rather hear about Vick's success and quest for redemption became clearer in 2011. In one of the most remarkable developments in his life since being released from prison, Vick was chosen as the commencement speaker at a high school graduation for at-risk students in Philadelphia.[122] The students chose him based on his extraordinary story of succeeding with a second chance. During his commencement address, he encouraged the students to make the most of life's opportunities. He also provided scholarship assistance to at least two high school students who were graduating. In future addresses to high school students, Vick should highlight other character-building achievements that helped define him. He has a host of charitable works that give back to the less fortunate. Vick should also encourage his sponsors to contribute to scholarship funds for at-risk high school students.

The Humane Society has had its banner emblazoned in the foreground whenever Vick has spoken to students on its behalf. Why can't it contribute to a scholarship drive for at-risk students? Since the NFL has committed to helping Vick on his

---

122 Retrieved from http://content.usatoday.com/communities/thehuddle/post/2011/ 05/nfl-michael-vick. Arin Karimian, May, 5, 2011. *Michael Vick to serve as commencement speaker for Philly school.*

quest to redemption, why not have the NFL contribute to needy urban school districts that are traditionally underfunded? Why can't Nike work with Vick to offer greater financial assistance to urban high school students, especially since Nike contributed to the popularity of dog fighting in 2003 with a commercial that inferred a dog fighting match? In response to complaints about the commercial, a company spokesman indicated the dog fighting scene was designed to keep Nike in touch with its urban consumer base.

In 2011, Nike re-signed Vick as an endorser of its brand after the shoe giant abandoned him at the height of the dog fighting scandal. Nike's actions were questionable, since it never acknowledged its own contributions to the popularity of dog fighting. On the other hand, Nike did not drop quarterback Ben Roethlisberger despite two allegations of rape. While Vick eventually pled guilty, Nike suspended its sponsorship deal *before* he entered his plea (Sandomir, 2007). Although there are corporations that have shown an interest in Michael Vick endorsing their brands, he must not become gullible given his renewed value in the NFL.

Despite the ups, downs, and dualities, perhaps the most outstanding indicator that Vick achieved a significant measure of redemption was the 2011 contract extension that the Eagles rewarded him with after a stellar 2010 season. The contract, although not fully guaranteed, was worth an estimated $100 million, which gave Vick yet another twosome in his life. He became the first player in NFL history to sign two contracts worth more than $100 million in one career. Even Vick's Eagles jersey, which the NFL began, selling prematurely in 2009, was reportedly a top seller in 2010. Despite these indicators of progress and greater social acceptance, Vick remains an enigma in the eyes of most. He must remain ever conscious that most of the media that covers him would rather not have anything good to say. Their stories of him only changed for the better because his performance dictated it. He must continue to tread with caution. His life has been a testament of the notion "expect the unexpected." His fall and subsequent rise has only made him an easier target for critics and cynics alike, especially those looking to exploit his unique story. This became apparent after *ESPN The Magazine* enlisted Vick's consent to dedicate its entire September 5, 2011 issue to him. While it may have sounded good on the surface, Vick would soon learn that everything that glitters is not gold.

ESPN Sacks Vick Again

In 2011, someone at *ESPN The Magazine* came up with the idea of making Michael Vick the sole subject of its entire September issue. For *The Magazine* it marked the first time the publication had ever featured one sports figure for a whole issue. The idea seemed a great way to capitalize on his resurgence. The mere thought bolstered the high expectations for the 2011 season after he was named the 2010 NFL Comeback Player of the Year. Not so coincidentally, the September issue was timed with the start of the NFL season. Perhaps Vick and his advisors believed the unique opportunity would do more to improve his public image, or so it appeared. ESPN's decision to solely spotlight him underscores how compelling Vick's life as a sports figure remains. On the other hand, depending on how the stories cast Vick, there were considerable risks. Would this issue amount to another sign of Vick's road to redemption, or would the magazine simply exploit the Vick narrative for publicity and profit? Unfortunately for Vick, the sports issue had an ominous tone with unsavory themes in abundance. The momentum Vick created in 2010 was totally overshadowed by a host of denigrating diatribes, which relabeled him as a villainous dog fighter.

The cover shot alone was an indicator that the idea would be problematic for Vick in his attempts to improve his public image. In the photo, Vick is seen as this shadowy figure, with his arms folded across his chest, making him appear defensive, distant, and opaquely dark. His face, while expressionless, was hardheartedly tense, and seemed to convey more contempt than the contrition Vick was carefully cultivating publicly. How could such imagery have helped the public's perception that Vick had changed for the better? Although it has been said that a picture is worth a thousand words, ESPN left nothing to chance. A projector beamed a host of distasteful descriptors that were supposed to define Vick. In fact, *The Magazine* was so intent on shaping the view of Vick that the top of the cover page read "Michael Vick Defined." In one single issue, ESPN took the harmful effects of negative labeling to heights uncharted.

Color Vick Bad

David Fleming, who writes for *The Magazine*, gave the impression that the terms used were balanced with good and bad concepts like: *Monstrous, Humble, Criminal,* and *Gifted.* Yet the terms that actually appear in the foreground of the cover were excessively acerbic and did much to nullify Vick's attempts to rehabilitate his name and persona. Among the more notorious notions, which were quite visible, were terms like *Sins, Criminal, Banned, Spoiled, Monstrous, Cursed, Shame, Appalling,* etc. These villainous expressions were projected against a wall, which Vick stood in front of, causing the words to be reflected across his entire body. ESPN was intent on ensuring that no matter how Vick attempted to redefine himself in better terms, these disparaging words would burn fiercer in the public's view. Fleming makes it clear the magazine intended to brand Vick negatively when he observed that each word "burns its way into the contours of his face and body."[123] *Burns its way into the contours of his face and body...?* Lest Fleming and ESPN forget, blacks were burned about their faces and bodies as slaves upon their arrival in the Western Hemisphere before they were sold off. Where is the racial sensibility filter system at ESPN? Even more shocking than the content of the articles is that there was no outrage over these indices of deprecation being masked as journalism. Vick was not only branded like a chattel slave, but he was relabeled as a deviant and resold to the public as a menace. Despite his attempts to move

---

123 Retrieved from http://espn.go.com/nfl/story/_/id/6885774/nfl-michael-vick-makes-neutrality-impossibility. David Fleming, August 26, 2011.

beyond the shadows of his unfortunate past, ESPN's magazine made his painful plunge front page news all over again.

Upon being released from prison, he vowed to never return. Still, the unpleasant characteristics of him on the magazine's cover appeared like prison stripes, confining him to his past. Whether intentional or not, *ESPN The Magazine* contributed to the view that Vick would be forever imprisoned by his perilous path of perdition. No matter how much money Vick might make or the number of speeches he may give against dog fighting, this issue painted an indelible picture of him as an incorrigible rogue. To further underscore how repugnant *The Magazine's* idea was, Vick came to the photo shoot with his children.

As Vick stood with these pejorative concepts burnished across his body, his children saw it all. ESPN noted that upon seeing the awful words illuminated against a darkened wall, Vick was unfazed. Fleming was apparently desensitized to the potential harm such ideations could have on Vick's children. The decision to proceed with such unpleasant characterizations not only reflected poorly upon ESPN, but Vick as well. He should have raised a concern about his children, who were devastated enough about the scandal and were still learning to appreciate their father. Perhaps *The Magazine* expected Vick to object. He did not. Fleming observed, "Not even when he glances off-camera and sees his children staring at the constellations of the world's wildly conflicting opinions of their father" (p. 1). But to which *world* of conflicting opinions was Fleming referring to? Apparently, he was referring to ESPN, the so-called *Worldwide Leader in Sports*, which has also been a leader in denigrating black quarterbacks. This is why Vick ultimately had the responsibility to tell ESPN that the distasteful suggestions were not a good idea, especially since he was committed to improving his public image.

According to the magazine, Vick saw the terms and said *he* was all of them (p. 2). Although those expressions may have reflected Vick's life prior to his imprisonment, were there not more appropriate descriptors that define Michael Vick today? On the other hand, *The Magazine* cover shot was just the beginning. There was an article titled "Zero-sum game: Michael Vick mishandled his money and went bankrupt. Unfortunately, he won't be the last NFL player to do so."[124] The article, written by Elena Bergeron, rehashed how Vick went broke, which perpetuated the idea that black athletes squander their wealth. But white athletes, including quarterbacks who retire from professional sports, file for bankruptcy as well. Former NFL quarterbacks who are white, such as Bernie Kosar and Mark Brunell, filed for bankruptcy despite making considerable wealth, as have other white athletes, none of which was noted by Bergeron. Here was an opportunity to offset the perception that only blacks encounter financial problems once their careers end. Rather than dissuading this inaccurate perception, Bergeron and ESPN preferred to perpetuate it. Still another article written by Fleming ("The dog in the room") resurrected the animus of animal rights groups that will never forgive Michael Vick.[125]

In the article, Vick laments that he was told by everybody that if he played well and had success on the field, then his past transgressions would be forgotten. Incredibly, it did not occur to him that features like the stories in ESPN's magazine undermined his attempts to be seen in a different light. To rehash so many overstated discussion points that have been hashed out previously was revolting. As much as these negatively conceived stories were retreaded themes, there was one perspective in the issue that was unprecedented, but no less absurd.

The most insulting article was one that asked if Vick were white, would it have kept him from engaging in dog fighting.[126] The poorly conceived article was also poorly researched. It was written by culture critic Touré, who failed to adequately note that whites have been the primary purveyors of dog fighting in America historically, and to a far greater extent than blacks. So the hypothetical question of whether Vick being white would

---

124 Retrieved from http://espn.go.com/nfl/story/_/id/6895017/nfl-michael-vick-typifies. Elena Bergeron, August 25, 2011.

125 Retrieved from http://espn.go.com/espn/commentary/story/_/id/6889579/espn-magazine. David Fleming, August 25, 2011.

126 Retrieved from http://espn.go.com/espn/commentary/story/_/id/6894586/imagining-michael-vick-white. Touré, August 25, 2011.

have lessened his potential of becoming involved in dog fighting is a gross distortion of reality. Such a fallacy did more to perpetuate the misinformed notion, promulgated by the mainstream media, that dog fighting is a problem unique to blacks in poor neighborhoods. The reality is that dog fighting has been more pronounced in white communities, particularly in the South. Historically and even presently whites are heavily involved in dog fighting. This book has highlighted the research of Evans, Gauthier, and Forsyth (1998), from the University of Louisiana at Lafayette, who studied a dog fighting subculture in the South and found that ninety percent of the participants were working-class whites. Additionally, the researchers examined this phenomenon as a "symbolic expression of...white masculinity" in the American South. But for Touré and ESPN, it was not enough for the feature to probe the hypothetical question of Vick being white. Instead, the publication converted the special issue on Vick into a coloring book that included an illustration of Michael Vick as white.

Color Vick White

Shamelessly, *The Magazine* defended its decision to make a mockery of Vick and the issue of race. A more relevant question on race, without the white face, would have been whether a white quarterback would have gone to prison for dog fighting. Touré could have addressed this meaningful question but demurred, noting that "...white privilege would not have been enough to rescue a white NFL star caught killing dogs" (p. 2). Somehow it was lost on Touré that a white NFL star, Ben Roethlisberger, benefitted from some measure of privilege, it seems. He was never arrested despite two allegations of forcible rape, by two different women in two different states, nine months apart. By contrast, Vick served nearly two years of a federal prison sentence for his crimes against dogs. But on the question of whether a white NFL star would have avoided prosecution for harming dogs, clearly, one doesn't have to be an NFL star: merely being white is sufficient. ESPN could have probed how race may have been a factor in the decision of the federal government to charge Vick despite him already facing state charges. Yet no one questioned why the federal government never charged Floyd Boudreaux and his son Guy for dog fighting, even though they were also facing state charges in Louisiana. Not surprisingly, the two were acquitted on all charges while Vick was still in prison. Touré and ESPN should have explored the question of why white males who have been arrested for dog fighting have often pled guilty to lesser crimes and in some cases received lesser sentences than Vick.

Since ESPN and Touré seemed to appreciate caricatures, a more interesting feature would have been a discussion of how dog fighting had been considered a sport in America histori- cally. Remember, the results of dog fighting matches used to be published in the sports section of newspapers. Furthermore, given that *ESPN The Magazine* is owned by the network, which touts itself as the "Worldwide Leader in Sports," why not ques- tion the use of the bulldog mascot by nearly 300 interscholastic and intercollegiate learning institutions in America? This would have been a fascinating perspective for the issue on Vick, given the parent culture of dog fighting that began with the bulldog. It is noteworthy that the bulldog, which is celebrated in sports culture, was bred for the expressed purposes of animal combat. Furthermore, the pit bull terrier, which Michael Vick used for dog fighting, has a lineage that is traceable to the bulldog.

No Bull on the Bulldog

ESPN could have informed readers that the nexus between dog fighting and sports long ago preceded Michael Vick. Such a refreshing view would have been meaningful in revealing the hypocrisy of sports culture. We vilified Vick for harming dogs. Yet as he speaks to high school students about the blood sport, no attention is accorded to the fact that a significant number of high schools in America use the bulldog as their mascot. This is especially noteworthy, since the bulldog earned its reputation as a ferocious fighter in the course of animal combat. Such factual material should be considered valuable in cultivating critical thinking among high school students. If young people could discuss and debate such matters, might they have a greater interest in learning? Additionally, some of the most prestigious institutions of higher learning, many of which appear on ESPN, such as Yale University, the University of Georgia, Mississippi State, Gonzaga, and James Madison University, among others, use the bulldog as their mascot. *The Magazine* could have broached the irony of Georgetown University, a Catholic institution, having *Jack the Bulldog* as a mascot. This phenomenon is not as ironic as it may appear. Historically, churches in Europe would host dog fighting matches as fundraisers. ESPN could have noted that among nicknames for major NCAA Division I-A institutions, "Bulldogs" is second only to "Tigers." While the tiger is an animal who earned its reputation in wildlife, the bulldog earned its reputation through dog fighting.

As noted, the bulldog, with its large head and wide-spanning jaws, was bred for the express purpose of taking down large animals and human beings in England. Readers would have been captivated to learn that the English bred the bulldog specifically to fight bulls, hence its name. Moreover, the English were so impressed with the bulldog's fighting prowess that the dog became their national symbol. The bulldog's symbolism gained popularity in America in the late nineteenth and early twentieth centuries. This long-standing tradition of interspersing the bulldog and sports is not relegated to high schools and colleges in America. One of the more dominant teams in the history of the National Football League was the Canton Bulldogs.

ESPN would have illuminated its readers by highlighting the historical significance of the Bulldogs, who still hold the NFL record for twenty-five consecutive wins, between the years 1921 and 1923. In an interesting aside, ESPN broadcasts the annual induction ceremony of the Pro Football Hall of Fame, which is located in Canton, Ohio. The media attributes the Hall of Fame's location in Canton to the NFL being formed there. It is less often noted that the Canton Bulldogs' dominance also influenced the town's selection as the site for pro football's greatest shrine. Why couldn't the self-proclaimed *Worldwide Leader in Sports* have provided such a leading perspective? Even more egregious, the September issue on Vick was but another in a litany of low blows the network delivered against blacks as quarterbacks in the NFL.

ESPN: No Shame in Their Game

As previously stated, ESPN's decision to hire Rush Limbaugh was ranked number eight by *GQ Magazine* among the twenty-eight worst decisions ever made in television.[127] While working for the network in 2003, Limbaugh asserted that the media was desirous to see a black quarterback succeed in the NFL out of social concern. Apparently those comments were still echoing at the network in 2007 with Michael Vick under investigation for dog fighting. In the midst of growing public rancor, ESPN's *Outside the Lines* did a feature on the developing story. But the content of the segment completely disavowed the idea of any media-harbored social concern for black quarterbacks. During the broadcast, the network used a so-called confidential informant who implicated Vick as a *heavyweight* in dog fighting, although ESPN never established for viewers what made this individual a reliable informant.

The story also featured John Goodwin, a campaign manager for the Humane Society, who discussed the implications of Vick's involvement in dog fighting. Oddly enough, ESPN perched Goodwin before the public as if he were a reliable expert on dog fighting. But the network failed to tell viewers, that only months prior to his appearance, a judge in Wisconsin would not allow him to testify as an expert witness in a dog fighting case. This was after Goodwin conceded during a pre-trial hearing that he had only read books about dog fighting. Nor did ESPN tell viewers that Goodwin had been arrested for radicalism, including vandalizing businesses and supporting economic sabotage of fur retailers. Were Goodwin and the Humane Society angling to engage in the economic sabotage of Michael Vick?

---

127 GQ Magazine. (2012). *The XVIII Worst Decisions in Sports History*. pp. 194-196.

Apparently so, since the Humane Society placed over 150,000 calls to Nike, imploring the shoe giant to drop Vick, which they did. The Humane Society also pressured the NFL to end its relationship with Vick. The league obliged by suspending Vick, which ultimately drove him to bankruptcy. As if that were not enough, ESPN also allowed Goodwin to state, without qualification or evidence, that there was a "roster" of professional athletes who are involved in dog fighting. The general public seemed to take notice, and so too did the law. After ESPN aired its feature on Vick's involvement in dog fighting, public animus increased, and the federal government began its own investigation of him. Ultimately he was indicted, convicted, and sentenced to a federal penitentiary. But the undermining of Vick would not end with ESPN's *Outside the Lines* feature. Subsequent to his release from prison in 2009 and renaissance season of 2010, *ESPN The Magazine* sent Vick tumbling backward with its 2011 exclusive issue on him. When compared to other salacious scandals, involving high-profile NFL figures, differential treatment by race seems to have been a factor.

Why didn't *The Magazine* dedicate an entire issue to Bill Belichick and color him black and question if he would have gotten off so lightly for the "Spygate scandal" had he been a black head coach? Why not dedicate an entire issue to Ben Roethlisberger, color him black, and ask if he were black would he have gotten away with two allegations of rape from two different women in nine months? Instead, ESPN chose to reduce Vick to an incorrigible deviant, while the scandals of white males like the above were swept under the rug. Even more undeserving, the ESPN issue on Vick obscured a lot of good he had done both before and after his downfall. Not enough was said about his charitableness, including financial contributions to the victims of Hurricane Katrina. In 2012, Vick once again showed his compassionate side when he contributed $50,000 to the victims of Hurricane Sandy, despite being in the throes of bankruptcy. Once more, he responded with aid to Americans in need faster than the federal government, which imprisoned him for harming dogs. How about focusing more on his successful lobbying on Capitol Hill for tougher laws against animal fighting? How come *The Magazine* did not focus more on his commitment to working with inner-city youth? Sadly, after all of Vick's hard work to rehabilitate his persona, including his incredible riposte in 2010, *ESPN The Magazine* expunged it.

The magazine issue, which thoroughly maligned him, became a harbinger of things to come. Following its publication in 2011, the season of promise for the Philadelphia Eagles went unfilled. While the NFL labor dispute with its players union disrupted the offseason, it seemed to adversely affect the continuity and chemistry of the Eagles even more. With an assortment of free agent signings in the offseason, there was great optimism that the team could make a run at the Super Bowl. But after a slow start in which the Eagles lost four of their first five games, Vick suffered broken ribs. The injury limited his effectiveness and the Eagles did not qualify for the playoffs. In 2012, the injury bug, which has plagued Vick throughout his illustrious career, resurfaced again.

During back-to-back preseason games, he sustained injuries to his hand and ribs. These events had the media questioning whether he was worth the money the Eagles had invested in him. Realizing that the Eagles' aspirations for competing for a championship rested on his availability, Vick was held out of the remaining preseason games. His lack of action seemed to contribute to his rocky start in the 2012 season. He was plagued by turnovers and was roundly criticized in the press, despite leading the team to a share of the NFC East through the first four weeks of the season at 3-1. Somehow lost in the media-induced subterfuge were the three game-winning drives he engineered in the first four games. But rather than appreciate the good start, which included victories against the New York Giants and the Baltimore Ravens, the defending and eventual Super Bowl champions, the media magnified Vick's turnovers. So although the team was 3-1, sports journalists portrayed the team as if they were 1-3 or 0-4. Had Vick been white, it is unlikely that his mistakes would have overshadowed his game-winning drives. Rather, we would have heard classical sports axioms, like

"Great players are not always great, just great when they have to be." As a case in point, in 2011 when Tim Tebow became the starting quarterback of the Denver Broncos, he struggled mightily through much of his games. But when he rallied to win games in the waning moments, the media raved, calling it "Tebow Time." Such differential treatment by race by the media is problematic and does not get criticized enough.

But for Vick and the Eagles, the 2012 season ended disappointingly as the team once again failed to make the playoffs, finishing 4-12. Afterward, Eagles owner Jeff Lurie fired long-time head coach Andy Reid, who had been one of Vick's biggest supporters. Following a topsy-turvy head coaching search in 2013, the team finally hired Chip Kelly, who had been the head coach at the University of Oregon. Kelly, who the team targeted, comes to the Eagles with a reputation for building high-scoring offenses at the collegiate level. His system, which has been emulated by several NFL teams, relies on speed and athleticism, particularly at quarterback. Therefore, the rumors of Vick's demise in Philadelphia seem a bit premature. The media had discussed February 6 as a referendum on Vick's future with the team; if he was still on the roster by this date, the team would owe him $3 million. But the date passed without any change in his status. It was reported that he met with Coach Kelly, and the team's plans for 2013 have Vick in mind. Although Vick initially declined the organization's overture to restructure his contract in 2012, he eventually did in 2013. The newly restructured deal is reportedly a three-year contract, with an opportunity to earn up to $10 million in year one. Apparently excited, Vick stated, "I look forward to playing for Coach Kelly, (owner) Jeff Lurie and the entire Eagles organization, the city of Philadelphia, and the fans."[128] He added that he was training hard and readying for the upcoming season, where the goal is to win. Such an optimistic tone is reminiscent of his preparations for 2010, when he unexpectedly reestablished himself as one of

---

128 Retrieved from http://www.usatoday.com/story/sports/nfl/eagles/2013/02/11/ michael-vick-one-year-contract.

the most dominant players in the game. As he looks forward to the 2013 season, Vick will be challenged to not only prove he is still a great player on the field, but an even better human being off of it. No matter if the season goes good or bad, he can expect greater media scrutiny for anything he does. For example, in March of 2013, it was widely reported that Vick canceled his book tour that was to promote his biography, *Michael Vick: Finally Free*, after his life was threatened, along with members of his family and employees of Barnes & Noble Booksellers.

Then in June, at the conclusion of the NFL's OTA's (Organized Team Activities), the embattled quarterback faced another media controversy, when he expressed the view that his rookie head coach should pick a starting quarterback before training camp. Of course, most national news sources conveniently omitted the fact that Vick was merely answering a question posed to him that way. They also ignored his central premise, which is to avoid a potential distraction with daily questions on the quarterback competition. But if Vick's comments about the starting quarterback, reflected some degree of righteous indignation, was it not warranted? The idea of a competition between himself, Nick Foles, and Matt Barkley, for starting quarterback, was beyond a fallacy, it became an insult. Vick is a seasoned veteran and four-time NFL All-Pro, whose record as a starting quarterback is an impressive 56-44-1. He has led two NFL franchises to divisional titles, and remains one of the most feared and respected players in the game. Yet, Vick's detractors in the media would prefer to eulogize his NFL career as if his demise is imminent. Their pessimism has only grown in the last two years when his team struggled. By contrast, other veteran quarterbacks have seen their teams falter in the last two years, like Carson Palmer, Jay Cutler, Tony Romo, Philip Rivers, and Ben Roethlisberger-all of who are white, but none of whom faced competition at quarterback on their teams—nor the same level of critical scrutiny in the media. To further underscore Vick's peculiar situation in Philly, three of the aforementioned quarterbacks also have new head coaches. For Vick, the tumultuous last two years in Philadelphia was largely the result of

Andy Reid's doing or undoing for that matter. Reid presided over an unmitigated disaster due to his bad decisions as head coach. None worse than the inexplicable blunder of switching his offensive line coach—one of the most important roles on the team, especially when it comes to offensive continuity, and the comfort level of the quarterback—to defensive coordinator. Is it any wonder that Vick struggled with protection issues, which also impacted his ability to protect the ball, and avoid injuries. Reid only exacerbated those problems when his new offensive line coach feuded with another offensive assistant throughout the 2012 season. Despite that Reid authored this disastrous dilemma, Vick took the weight for his head coach mishandling such important decisions. That Vick is still in Philly, while Reid was let go is an indicator that the organization felt at least partly the same.

But the Eagles Nation should be encouraged. The real story-line on Vick is that he thrives on second chances. The last time Michael Vick made such a public pronouncement of concern about his status on the Eagles depth chart was the offseason in 2010. Then, he publicly asked to be traded feeling his future in Philadelphia was too uncertain. Now in 2013, he finds himself once again facing questions about his place on the depth charts. We all know what happened in 2010; we witnessed "Michael Vick 2.0" and the Eagles resumed their status as a playoff participant capturing the NFC East. Well in 2013, Vick is prepared to release, "Michael Vick 3.0", and if Chip Kelly and the rest of the Eagles Nation are serious about soaring now, then they would put the quarterback competition to rest. Perhaps, that is what Michael Vick was really trying to say.

In his book *Finally Free*, Vick made reference to how unique it is that since his college days, his teams' mascots have all been birds. At Virginia Tech, he was a Hokie. In 2001, Atlanta drafted him to be a Falcon. In 2007, he became an unsavory bird of sorts. Following the dog fighting debacle and prison term, Vick became, by his own admission, a caged bird. Then, upon being released from prison in 2009, he became a Philadelphia Eagle. In what appears to be a measure of poetic justice, the eagle is a symbol of America's commitment to freedom, prosperity, and redemption. Vick's realization that he was once a caged bird should remain ever-present in his mind, if for no other reason than to reflect on the important lesson of what the caged bird signifies. Given the duality that has punctuated Michael Vick's life, the story of the two caged birds might prove enlightening.

As the story goes, from their perch, two caged birds saw a flock of birds go flying by. One turned to the other and said, "Huh! Too bad they don't have a cage like us!" When I share this fabled story with high school students, not unlike the ones Vick speaks to, I ask them, "Which birds are in the best condition, the ones in the cage or the ones flying free?" Most of them get it right. It remains to be seen if Michael Vick will too.

Conclusion

For Michael Vick, his journey from the apex of NFL stardom to the abyss has been an interesting tale of two lives enmeshed in one. His fall and rise is an epic story of success, failure, and the importance of second chances. But what makes this story so extraordinary is that the Michael Vick narrative is far from complete. The 2012 season was expected to be a pivotal year for Vick as the quarterback of the Philadelphia Eagles, and for Vick the man, on his continuing road to redemption. Moreover, 2013 will be even more challenging as he will face newer questions of whether he can recapture the magic of 2010 when he struck a good balance between passing and running in leading the Eagles to a NFC East divisional title and the playoffs. The biggest test facing him off the field will be how well he balances his priorities. Can he maintain his focus on faith and family? Will he be able to avoid being exploited by others who care more about Michael Vick the product than Michael Vick the person? Under Chip Kelly, will he continue to fly like an eagle, or will he be abruptly grounded? These are the outstanding questions surrounding Michael Vick. The stage is set, and how he responds to these newer challenges will go a long way in determining his legacy in the NFL, and more importantly, in life.

Afterword

At its height, the Michael Vick dog fighting scandal was the biggest sports controversy in years. As a consequence, Vick faced both informal and formal sanctions that were harsh and punitive. The informal sanctions were imposed by the strong public reaction to his crimes against dogs. Among the groups leading the charge were the Humane Society and PETA. Other informal sanctions came from the media, which criticized Vick vehemently for his dog fighting crimes. These informal sanctions led to formal sanctions from corporate sponsors Nike and Rawlings, which dropped him as an endorser of their brands. The sanction that cost Vick the most, socially and financially, was the NFL's suspension. As a consequence of violating the NFL's conduct policy, Vick was suspended for the entire 2007 season and for four games in 2009. The strongest formal sanctions against Vick were the state and federal dog fighting charges, which led to a near two-year prison sentence. The clamor over his involvement in dog fighting notwithstanding, no real explanation emerged about which factors influenced his behavior. After being released from prison in 2009, Vick intimated in a revealing interview on CBS's *60 Minutes* that his involvement in dog fighting was influenced by a *so-called culture*. For all of the attention accorded to his dilemma, no one examined and analyzed this so-called culture until this work you are reading.

My research demonstrated that this culture that Vick referenced was actually a parent culture of dog fighting violence that is traceable to ancient Europe. It evolved and was transplanted to America in the nineteenth century. This culture spread throughout the South during the twentieth century and came to the attention of a young Michael Vick at the age of eight. Vick's involvement in dog fighting developed as a subcultural phenomenon, which expanded over the course of his life as socially learned behavior. I argue that Vick's participation in the blood sport is explicable by the subculture of violence theory. The perspective holds that the violence exhibited by blacks is only partly different from the parent culture of violence. In addition, the connection between this identifiable parent culture of dog fighting and its succeeding subculture is evincible through translucent conduct norms, which include gambling, baiting, and killing underperforming dogs. Although such behaviors are centuries-old, they were also demonstrated by Vick.

In addition, *Vick-tim* outlined other indices of this parent culture that influenced Vick's conduct as a subcultural phenomenon. Research in this work shows that dog fighting organizations such as the United Kennel Club and the American Pit Bull Terrier Association preceded Vick's Bad Newz Kennels. That these organizations predate Vick's own and reflected the same *conduct norms* are additional indicators of a parent culture influencing a succeeding subculture. It should be noted the subculture of violence theory is not offered to absolve Vick of responsibility for his dog fighting crimes. Rather, it provides a meaningful counterview of why it happened.

Beyond providing a broader perspective on why Michael Vick became involved in dog fighting, the historical and theoretical analyses in this work seeks to better educate society about this social problem and provide policy implications. The more informed our nation becomes about the history of dog fighting, the greater the potential of stemming the tide of this serious problem in America and the world. As noted, the subculture of violence theory was developed in part from a study of inner-city blacks in Philadelphia by Dr. Marvin Wolfgang. The theory and supporting research could have aided Vick's defense, since he had no prior criminal record.

Wolfgang's 1967 book, *The Subculture of Violence*, published with Franco Ferracuti, found that most first-time criminal offenders were less likely to become recidivists (p.286). So for Michael Vick, he may have desisted from dog fighting after the one conviction without having to go to prison. That Vick was sent to prison, despite no prior arrests or convictions, was undoubtedly linked to the view of African-Americans as criminally deviant. Some would also argue that his celebrity, wealth, and race were also factors. On the other hand, that Vick has not been charged with a crime since being released from prison in 2009 gives added credence to Wolfgang's perspective.

Vick-tim also employed the *labeling theory*, which examines the role of powerful groups and organizations who will label others as they see fit. In the Michael Vick narrative, organizations such as the media, the NFL, and the politics of the state all contributed to the negative tagging. Not surprisingly, each of the aforementioned has a history of perpetuating pejorative labels against African-Americans. The vestiges of such derogatory descriptors resurfaced over the course of Vick's NFL career and seemed to shape his self-identity. They included negative notions of him as a *black quarterback*, *running quarterback*, and *athlete,* all of which were perpetuated by the media. These unsavory suggestions reflected historical attitudes within the NFL's sports culture that have persisted. The sports reporting media often referred to Vick as *dangerous* given his style of play. Furthermore, he was treated as an *outsider* among NFL quarterbacks by virtue of his race and the occupational dominance held by whites at the coveted position. Consequently, once *outside* the ranks of the NFL, Vick participated in the *dangerous* and deviant culture of dog fighting. Another uncomplimentary form of labeling, that adversely affected Vick was his hometown of Newport News being labeled as *Bad News*.

That Vick named his dog fighting enterprise "Bad Newz Kennels" is another indicator of his tendency to be influenced by negative notions. *Vick-tim* argues that the cumulative effects of such pejorative labeling, including descriptors of him as *dangerous*, a *black quarterback*, along with his hometown being derided as *Bad News,* overtook Vick. This tagging by powerful social forces, including the media, not only shaped his self-identity but contributed to his fatalistic downfall over dog fighting. W.I. Thomas, the noted sociologist, observed that if you believe a situation is real, then it is real in its consequences.

These factors contributed to the fall of Michael Vick and seemed to shape the differential treatment he suffered at the hands of the media and the NFL. This is even more evident when compared to other high profile scandals involving whites like quarterback Ben Roethlisberger and head coach Bill Belichick, neither of whom garnered the same level of public rancor as Vick's misdeeds. Because the labeling perspective examines how certain groups like African-Americans are typecast as deviant, it provides a useful framework for addressing selective enforcement by race by dog fighting arrests. Data analysis in *Vick-tim* shows that in the five years that followed Vick's property being raided, African-Americans accounted for seventy-four percent of all arrests for dog fighting, while whites arrested were twenty-three percent. On the other hand, in the five years preceding Vick's bust, African-Americans were fifty-five percent of all defendants arrested for dog fighting, while whites were thirty-seven percent. The ten year differential shows the number of blacks arrested for dog fighting increased by nineteen percent after Vick's criminal case, while the number of whites arrested decreased by fourteen percent. Another significant factor in the negative labeling of Vick that may have impacted the arrest rates of blacks were comments made by Rush Limbaugh.

While the conservative, controversial talk show personality used his perch as an ESPN studio analyst to resurrect the racist relic of a black quarterback in 2003, he further contributed negative labeling in 2009. One month before Vick was released from prison, Limbaugh recorded a public service announcement for the Humane Society. In the recording he referred to street fighters of dogs as "people like Michael Vick." In the years that followed Limbaugh's PSA, the number of African-Americans arrested for dog fighting skyrocketed. Of the 306 blacks arrested in the five years that followed Vick's home being raided, nearly seventy percent occurred after Limbaugh recorded his PSA for the Humane Society. By contrast, the number of whites arrested in the five years that followed Vick's bust was more than 200 percent less (at ninety-four overall). Of these arrest incidents, sixty-eight occurred after Limbaugh recorded his PSA. Additionally, in the five years that followed Vick's dog fighting being exposed, the conviction rate for blacks increased by nine percent while the conviction rates for whites decreased by twelve percent.

In furtherance of the latter point, particular attention was accorded to the dog fighting charges against Floyd Boudreaux and his son Guy, who were acquitted on nearly fifty counts of dog fighting in 2008. Unlike in the case of Vick, who faced both state and federal dog fighting charges, Boudreaux and his son were only tried by the state of Louisiana, despite that Congress passed the Animal Fighting Prohibition Enforcement Act of 2007. Although there are a host of questions to pose about the actions of other individuals and groups that impacted Michael Vick, ultimately his fall rested on his shoulders.

In the end, Vick's dog fighting dilemma was primarily an issue of poor decision making. His attempts to live a double life eventually caught up to him in the worst way. As difficult as his fall from grace was, his subsequent rise has been more remarkable. Still, no matter how successful Vick is as an NFL player, his redemption will be best measured by his ability to avoid trouble with the law and his ongoing advocacy for animal rights. As he continues his advocacy for animal rights, Vick must control his own voice and message, which should include expanding the discussion of animal cruelty beyond dogs. He must also be wary of animal rights advocates who have used his dog fighting debacle to place an inordinate amount of attention on street fighters.

Recommendations

For all of the billions of dollars in licensing fees paid to the NFL by television networks such as ESPN, CBS, NBC, and Fox, there needs to be an investment in diversity training to improve the media coverage of African-Americans. The NFL and its media partners ought to mandate professional development initiatives to improve the cultural competencies of sports journalists covering the game. Other measures should include hiring more African-Americans to cover the NFL, where roughly two-thirds of players are black. It was predictable, since Michael Vick was not the first African-American athlete to suffer adverse media coverage on his path to redemption, that he would not be the last. This became apparent during the week of Super Bowl XLVII. Ray Lewis, the outgoing All-Pro middle linebacker of the Baltimore Ravens, was bombarded by questions of his involvement in a double homicide thirteen years earlier. That Lewis was absolved of double murder charges in the case mattered little to the throng of media. Nor was it enough that he had pled guilty to a misdemeanor count of obstruction of justice in the case. He even testified against his co-defendants at trial, who were later acquitted. Yet the white male-dominated media questioned Lewis about his involvement nonetheless. So while the U.S. Constitution protects citizens against double jeopardy in the court of law, the media sought to implicate Lewis once more in the court of public opinion. The harm associated with resurrecting the double murders is that it relabeled Lewis as a criminal deviant. If that were not enough, he was also besieged with questions about a *Sports Illustrated* story which suggested he used a banned substance in his recovery from a biceps injury earlier in the year. Although Lewis denied using the so-called deer antler spray, the *SI* article quoted a researcher who stated there was no evidence the substance even worked on humans. Not one reporter among the multitude covering the Super Bowl, including many African-Americans, stated as much for the record. In another oddity, the *SI* story quoted former NFL player and current NFL Network analyst Heath Evans, a league employee, who conceded in the same article that he uses the substances currently. Yet no one questioned it. Not surprisingly, Evans is white. But more evidence of racialism is notable.

When Bill Belichick appeared in the 2007 Super Bowl, U.S. Senator Arlen Specter raised the specter of Spygate, and the media ripped him for it. They said it was a bad time to bring it up and that Senator Specter should find something else to do. Again, the scandals involving Belichick and Ben Roethlisberger, which were chronicled at length in this book, offer good examples of differential treatment by race. Neither of them had to relive or contend with persistent questions about their scandals during their respective Super Bowl appearances, in 2010 and 2011, that immediately preceded Lewis's in 2012.

These case studies underscore the dire need for more diversity among sports journalists, particularly African-Americans, covering the NFL. Such additions are especially desirable given the tendencies of broadcasters to use racially-tinged language in reference to African-Americans playing quarterback. The streams of sneering references to such players during broadcasts as *running quarterbacks* and *athletes* have become euphemisms for *black quarterbacks*. Moreover, there is an awful history of disparate media coverage that has had an adverse effect on African-Americans at quarterback in the NFL. These tendencies reveal that over time very little has changed in how the press perceives so-called *black quarterbacks* in the NFL. But because the NFL and the media are purveyors of this problem, they are unlikely to initiate any structural changes on their own. Hence, Congress needs to intervene to ensure that needed reforms are implemented.

Such action is well within the purview of Congress, which has regulatory authority over the NFL and the major television networks that purchase broadcast rights. Congress passed the

1961 Sports Broadcasting Act, which allows the NFL to negotiate television contracts with the networks as one single entity
(rather than individual teams creating their own deals). Moreover, in 1967, Congress gave the league a limited exemption
from anti-trust laws, which allowed the NFL and AFL to merge
into one football league. Because Congress has played such a
pivotal role in the development of these powerful institutions
and their business relationships, the members have an obligation
to address these important questions of differential treatment by
race.

The Michael Vick dog fighting scandal brought to light the
hazards of the NFL and the sports reporting media failing to
fully acknowledge their respective histories of structural racism
toward blacks as quarterbacks. It has been well documented that
league owners were reluctant to play them as starters historically
and have rarely used them as backups. Although many African-
Americans have had success at quarterback more recently,
they are still woefully underrepresented as starters in the NFL.
Despite their greater propensity to lead teams to the playoffs,
blacks are roughly two of every ten starting quarterbacks in the
NFL. Part of the reason this paucity remains is the perpetual
plague of unconstructive media reporting. Vick's dog fighting
dilemma is simply a case in point.

Throughout his NFL career, Vick has been burdened by
media coverage. Descriptions of his style of play as dangerous and even reckless along with questions of whether he is a
legitimate quarterback have persisted. Additionally, concerns
have been raised about his level of intellectual acuity to play
the position. Hence *Vick-tim* argued that such uncomplimentary media coverage had a negative effect on Vick's self-identity,
which was manifested in his ill-fated conduct. Independent of
his criminally deviant behavior, the disparate media coverage
of him that preceded and followed his downfall reflected a new
era in the hierarchy of naming (i.e., running quarterback, black
quarterback, etc.). This *linguistic vehicle*, as it is described, benefits white quarterbacks to the detriment of black quarterbacks
in the NFL. Because white quarterbacks were considered the

norm, black quarterbacks were despised as the odd men out, the effect of which has enabled white quarterbacks to maintain a level of occupational dominance. Not surprisingly, in the aftermath of Vick's dog fighting demise, media types, most of whom were white males, suggested that he never be allowed to play in the NFL again, and certainly not at quarterback.

Furthermore, the Vick calamity suggests the NFL needs to create mentoring programs for blacks playing quarterback, especially given the level of structural racism that has plagued them historically and presently. Such programming might enable these players to better respond to the added pressure of their unique status as black quarterbacks, including their interactions with the press. For example, Cam Newton of the Carolina Panthers was mentored by Warren Moon, a Hall of Fame quarterback who is also an African-American. In his rookie season, Newton, who was the first overall pick of the 2011 draft, set several passing and rushing records for a rookie quarterback. Consequently, he was named NFL Rookie of the Year and made All-Pro, despite the media types who questioned his readiness and worthiness to be drafted in the first round. Although Moon's relationship with Newton is independent of the NFL, the league could make greater use of former NFL quarterbacks who are African-Americans, such as Doug Williams, Randall Cunningham, Rodney Peete, Donovan McNabb, Marlin Briscoe, and Moon, among others. A mentoring program of some sort involving these former quarterbacks could have helped Michael Vick avoid his misfortune. In fact, it was McNabb's advocacy for Vick that allowed him to be signed by the Philadelphia Eagles. Still, the above mentioned quarterbacks all had to contend with the effects of negative labeling, racism, and biting cynicism from the sports reporting media during their careers.

Congress should be concerned about the NFL's strong influence over the television networks that partners with it; their largely uncritical coverage of the league is especially problematic. Television networks that purchase the license to broadcast NFL games are wary of criticizing the league for fear of hurting their ability to negotiate for future broadcast rights. Consequently, the networks become propaganda machines for the NFL's manufactured message that portrays the league as infallible. The prevailing view of the NFL as a lamb without spots is perpetuated by television networks that purchase broadcast rights and is a gross distortion of reality. On the contrary, the NFL's sordid history of racial discrimination and penchant for strong-arm tactics, especially when negotiating television contracts, suggest the league is closer to a wolf in sheep's clothing than a lamb.

Other concerns that need congressional attention are the dictatorial powers of NFL Commissioner Roger Goodell that have been unequally distributed at times. His treatment of the Vick scandal was far different than that of Ben Roethlisberger and Bill Belichick. These individuals and their scandals have been cited as cases in point to underscore the differential treatment by race that is rampant throughout the NFL. Belichick was not suspended despite his Spygate scandal amounting to cheating to gain an unfair competitive advantage in complete defiance of NFL rules. While others would argue that Vick lied to Goodell, Belichick was not totally forthcoming either. The $500,000 fine he received from the NFL was a pittance compared to what Vick lost in income and personal reputation.

Additional indicators of unequal justice by Commissioner Goodell include the differential treatments accorded to Michael Vick and Ben Roethlisberger. Goodell ordered Roethlisberger to undergo behavioral counseling, which helped to de-label him. By contrast, Vick received no such counseling at the behest of the league's front office, despite the tumultuous history of racism against African-American quarterbacks and the unsavory labeling at the hands of the media covering the NFL. Congress should also be concerned about its own differential reaction to these scandals in the NFL over the last six years. Vick's disgraceful conduct wrought a much stronger punitive response and included an amendment to the federal Animal Welfare Act, which increased the prison sentence from three to five years. By contrast, Congress did not respond at all to the scurrilous behaviors attributed to Roethlisberger or Belichick.

The only comment from a member of Capitol Hill against Roethlisberger came from Congressman Tom Rooney (R-FL), who referred to Roethlisberger as an *idiot*. That Congressman Rooney departed from the conspicuous silence on Capitol Hill was owing to his family's ownership of the Pittsburgh Steelers franchise, which employs the quarterback. On the other hand, there were no retributive remarks from other members enjoining Commissioner Goodell to act against Roethlisberger as they did Vick. The differential reaction sent the unfortunate message that members of Congress were more concerned with how a black quarterback treated dogs versus how a white quarterback reportedly treated women. The idea that Roethlisberger was never charged with a crime does not suffice for the relative silence from Capitol Hill. There is no disputing that there were chargeable actions such as serving alcohol to minors. Roethlisberger never denied remarking, "All you bitches take my shots." The sordid allegations against Roethlisberger include sexual assault and the unquestionable facts of his taking a young college student into a bathroom stall, purportedly for sex, with sizeable bodyguards, including off-duty state troopers, guarding the door. None of these acts prompted Congress to lambaste Roethlisberger. In Vick's case, congressmen began speaking out and imploring the commissioner to act before Vick was adjudicated. So the stillness in the midst of swirling allegations against Roethlisberger reflected a double standard by race by members of Congress.

As for Belichick, while U.S Senator Arlen Specter called for hearings on his Spygate scandal, his colleagues in the Senate demurred and an inquest was never held. His conduct may have risen to the level of federal wire fraud and conspiracy, in violation of federal anti-trust laws. Moreover, Commissioner Goodell's decision to destroy the Spygate tapes in the face of a congressman's growing inquiry could have amounted to obstruction of justice. Since Vick is black while Roethlisberger, Belichick, and Goodell are all white means that Congress sent the wrong message about equal protection of the law and selective enforcement by race. Moreover, the differential treatment by race only perpetuated the view that blacks are more deviant than whites. Therefore, it is suggested that Congress set up an independent committee of diverse members (i.e., black, white, Latino, men, women, etc.) which will closely monitor diversity-oriented issues in sports organizations that it regulates, like the NFL. Such a committee would augment the role of the House's Oversight and Government Reform Committee, which tends to hear concerns over sports organizations like the NFL. It might strengthen Congress's regulatory authority over the likes of the NFL and help ensure that policies and procedures are enforced unilaterally to avoid disparities in treatment by race.

Congress should also review its own ethical standards that allow NFL owners to make contributions to federal lawmakers. The results suggest that lawmakers are selective in questioning the actions of NFL players and coaches by race. The questions of unequal distribution of the law by race are not all relegated to Vick versus other NFL personnel.

In the case of white males like Floyd Boudreaux, the federal government never got involved in prosecuting the case, even though the U.S. Department of Homeland Security participated in the Boudreaux investigation, given his international sale of puppies. The highly prized litters were believed to stem from his infamous bloodline of fighting dogs. But the Boudreauxs were acquitted and federal charges were never lodged, which raises additional questions of equal protection of the law, pursuant to the Fifth Amendment and its provisions of due process. Congress needs to remain vigilant in ensuring that federal dog fighting laws are equally enforced, as opposed to selectively. Beyond questions of animal cruelty in America, concerns about mistreatment of dogs abroad are also warranted.

Congress should have the NFL open up its books on their peculiar business relationship with China, especially since China has no laws against animal cruelty and kills dogs with impunity. Furthermore, the NFL condemned Vick's mistreatment against dogs but has said nothing about China's massive culling of dogs. Even more disconcerting, China reportedly views dogs as a bourgeois affectation. That is, dogs are a reflection of Western culture and the economic system of capitalism in America. If the NFL were truly America's game, it would break its silence and condemn the mistreatment of dogs by the Chinese government as it did with Vick. On the other hand, Congress should hold the NFL to the standard of responsibility it held Vick given his mistreatment of dogs. Congress needs to question why television networks in America pay the NFL to broadcast its games while the NFL pays China to broadcast its programming overseas. While CCTV being state controlled is certainly a factor, Congress needs to question the NFL for continuing to pay China to broadcast its programming given its wretched abuse of dogs, when it refused Vick's services for his acts of animal cruelty. A Congressional probe is especially apropos since the NFL's business relationship with China should be regulated as foreign commerce.

Lastly, Congress should be concerned about the question of equal protection of the law as it pertains to the arrests and convictions of defendants over dog fighting. The data in this book showed that African-Americans have seen their arrest and conviction rates increase in far greater proportion than whites and Hispanics after Vick's criminal case and passage of state and federal laws on dog fighting. It appears as though the overemphasis on street fighters placed an inordinate amount of attention on African-Americans. Even Michael Vick needs to be wary of becoming a pawn for the criminal justice system and organizations such as the Humane Society. The organization seemed to use his case and animal rights advocacy to focus on inner-city street fighters, which made African-Americans greater targets. Therefore, Congress should review arrest data to ensure a more equal distribution of the law and explore ways to expand the scope of laws against animal cruelty.

These should include stronger laws for other forms of animal cruelty, such as hoarding, abuse, neglect, and bestiality. Especially in the case of the latter, since researchers have found that bestiality and aggression are mutually inclusive. Consequently zoophiles, as they are known, are more likely to engage in greater acts of interpersonal violence. The Obama Administration and

Congress should be aware of these findings, especially since the Senate repealed the ban on bestiality for military personnel in November 2011. There are several concerns associated with this shift by the federal government. On the one hand, bestiality is a form of animal cruelty that should be punished as felonious, like dog fighting. Moreover, if the argument for making dog fighting a felony was the propensity for collateral offenses associated with this criminal conduct, then bestiality should be treated the same. Furthermore, to allow military personnel to engage in this behavior is negligent given its ties to aggression and greater interpersonal violence against human beings. There have been a number of incidents of death and violence involving U.S. servicemen and women in the armed forces both at home and abroad. In 2009, an Army major stationed in Fort Hood, Texas, opened fire on the most populous U.S. military base, shooting forty-two people, thirteen of whom died. In 2012, a U.S. staff sergeant in Afghanistan killed sixteen people who were non-combatants, including children. There have also been reported incidents of sexual assaults involving U.S. military officers being victimized by comrades. In March 2013, U.S. Senator Kirsten Gillibrand (D-NY),[129] who chairs the Senate Armed Services Committee on Personnel, held hearings on sexual assaults in the military. The Defense Department estimated that upwards of 19,000 such incidents occurred in 2011, but less than ten percent were officially reported. While there is no evidence that the perpetrators involved in these incidents of violence engaged in bestiality, these occurrences are reminders of how interpersonal violence among military personnel is quite common. Therefore, prohibiting behavior such as bestiality, which could increase the potential for interpersonal violence, including sexual assaults, is the responsible approach to take. The other concern with lifting the ban on bestiality for military personnel is that it sends a mixed message to states when it comes to enforcing laws that prohibit this behavior. Moreover, since there are no federal laws

---

129 Retrieved from http://www.buffalonews.com/apps/pbcs.dll/article?AID=/ 20130314/ WORLD/130319581.

that prohibit this aberrant conduct for U.S. military personnel, it could lessen enforcement of this crime for civilians in states that have laws against it. Additionally, the repeal for military personnel provides a disincentive for the twenty-one states that have no laws that forbid this barbaric crime.

It is for these reasons that it is recommended that Michael Vick expand the range of his advocacy for animals to include lobbying for laws among states and the federal government that would punish other forms of cruelty like bestiality as felonious.

In the final analysis, *From Vick-tim to Vick-tory: The Fall and Rise of Michael Vick* is an important book given the unfortunate legacy of black athletes being extolled for their athleticism, only to be excoriated and excommunicated when they fail to appease our appetites for sports culture's glory. African-American athletes who aspire to become professionals and those who achieve it ought to study the history of the black athlete's participation in spectator sports. Such a study should include the triumphs and trials of these unique competitors to better understand the pathways laid by their sports pioneers. In addition, black athletes should examine the traditions of media coverage of spectator sports. Black athletes must learn, like Michael Vick: The same sports reporting media that will cover your rise will also prey on your fall.

About the Author

The author, Kenneth N. Robinson (a.k.a. "Zaid Bilal"), was born and raised in the Talbert Mall/Frederick Douglass Towers, a high-rise public housing project, in Buffalo, N.Y. There, in the comfy confines of his family's living room, he became an avid follower of NFL football at the impressionable age of four. Since those early formative years when he strained to understand the vastness of the gridiron game, he has since become a student of the sport and is highly regarded for his insightful

Photo by Bruce A. Fox/Buffalo State

analysis and expertise. Robinson notes, "While the tendency for most is to watch NFL football, I make it a point to study it." This sort of rationing has allowed him to produce a range of critical perspectives on the NFL. His objective commentaries have appeared on websites, in newspapers, and his analytical paper on the Michael Vick dog fighting scandal was presented at the annual meeting of the American Sociological Association, hosted in Las Vegas, in August 2011.

Robinson's ability to address social issues such as the fall and rise of Michael Vick follows from his appreciation for sports culture and his academic background in sociology and criminal justice. The advantage of such a fusion becomes more apparent when a significant event occurs, like the Vick dog fighting debacle. Rather than looking solely at the aberrant behavior, Robinson examines the various social contexts encompassing the subject's life to help explain what influenced the behavior.

Moving beyond the natural tendency to apply commonsensical reasoning, Robinson's use of social theories allows him to shed light on important issues often hidden in plain sight. Of course, this approach amounts to a departure from the typical explanations of significant events in sports culture, which are generally offered by sports journalists rather than social scientists.

Vick-tim was conceived in the tradition of sociologists who in the 1960s spearheaded a paradigmatic shift in how NFL football was viewed. Prior to this development, spectator sports were seen as an extension of physical education. Consequently, there was a prevailing sense that pro football should not be taken so seriously on issues like race. In altering this focus, sociologists began to study the NFL as a microcosm of society, given the widespread practice of racism against blacks. Incidentally, some of the worst forms of racial discrimination in the NFL have been directed against *black quarterbacks*. It is with an awareness of such history and the study of it that Robinson offered perspectives on the Vick dog fighting saga that the larger public never considered. The author can only hope that his best efforts to write a book that would fill such extraordinary voids in the literature and public discourse were satisfactory. Given the labor of love that this endeavor has wrought, the public can expect more of the same in the future.

Today Robinson resides in his hometown of Buffalo, New York. He is employed at his alma mater, Buffalo State, where he serves as an adjunct professor of sociology.

Over the last five years while writing this book, he has selectively integrated this material in classroom discussions, in sections such as: Sociology of Work (360), Sociology of Deviant Behavior (370), Analyzing Social Problems (240), and Introduction to Sociology (100). In each class, the students were challenged to consider their points of view on the subject objectively. These factors, when taken as a whole, reassured the author that writing the book *From Vick-tim to Vick-tory: The Fall and Rise of Michael Vick* was the right thing to do.

References

Chapter I

Adams, B., Larson, J. "Legislative History of the Animal Welfare Act." USDA. NAL. *Animal Welfare Information Center.* n.d.

Becker, G. (2009). *Congressional Research Service: Animal Welfare Act: Background and Selected Legislation.*

Bell, J. (2007). *NFL turned upside down by facets of Vick case.* Retrieved from http://www. usatoday.printhis.clickability.com/pt/ cpt?action=cpt&title=NFL +turned+upside+down.

Burke, B. (2007). *Once limited to the rural South, dogfighting sees a cultural shift.* Retrieved from http://hamptonroads.com/node/283641.

Burwell, B. (2007). *Vick is the latest to take rap for the rap in our culture.* Retrieved from http://www.stltoday.com/stltoday/emaf.nsf/Popup?Read Form&db=stltoday%5Csports%5C

CBS News. (2009). *Michael Vick: "I Blame Me" Expresses Remorse in 60 Minutes Interview, Vows To Help Put an End to Dogfighting.* Retrieved from http://www.cbsnews.com/stories/ 2009/08/10/60minutes/5231257.

Doster. S. (n.d.) Term Paper: *The Importation, Adaptation, and Creolization of Slave Leisure Forms in The Americas: 1600-1850.* http://discover-archive.vanderbilt.edu/bitstream/handle/ 1803/1301/Creolization%20 of%20Slave%20Leisure%20Forms.doc?sequence=1.

ESPN.com. (2007). *Apologetic Vick gets 23-month sentence on dogfighting charges.* Retrieved from http://sports.espn.go.com/nfl/news/ story?id=3148549.

Evans, R., Gauthier, D., and Forsyth, C.J. (1998). *Dogfighting: Symbolic Expression and Validation of Masculinity.* Retrieved from http://htmlimg2.scribdassets.com/5692.

Florida State University. (n.d). *Marvin Wolfgang's Subculture of Violence Theory* (n.d.) http://www.criminology.fsu.edu/crimtheory/wolfgang.htm.

Gibson, Hanna. (2005). http://www.animallaw.info/chapters/ddusdogfighting.htm#'s. Michigan State University College of Law.

Gramsci, A. (1971). *Selections from the Prison Notebooks of Antonio Gramsci.* New York: International Publishers.

Hausman, J. (2010). *Muskegon man charged with sodomizing his pit bull scheduled for trial.* http://www.mlive.com/news/muskegon/index. ssf/2010/muskegon_man_chaged_with_...

Hensley, C., Tallichet, S.E., & Singer, S.D. (2006). Exploring the possible link between childhood and adolescent bestiality and interpersonal violence. *Journal of Interpersonal Violence, 21*, 910-923.

Hijek, B. (2009). *Man accused of having sex with dog can attend culinary school*. Retrieved from http://weblogs.sun-sentinel.com/news/specials/weirdflorida/blog/2009/10/man_accused_of.

Humane Society (n.d.). *Fact Sheet, Bestiality and Other Violent Crime*.

Kalof, Linda., Taylor, Carl. (2007). The Discourse of Dogfighting. *Humanity and Society*. Vol. 31. (November: 319-333).

Kreigel, M. (2007). *Nike more about money than morals*. Retrieved from http://msn.foxsports. com/nfl/story/7038442.

Mihoces, Gary. (2009). *Steelers look to Roethlisberger to set tone, QB's to be ready*. USA Today Sports.

Naqi, K. (2007). Source: Vick one of the 'heavyweights of dogfighting.' Retrieved from http://sports.espn.go.com/nfl/news/story?id2884063.

NFL Security (n.d.) Retrieved from http://sports.espn.com news services.

Ortiz, F. (2010). Making the Dog-man Heel: Recommendations for Improving the Effectiveness of Dogfighting Laws. *Stanford Journal of Animal Law and Policy*. V. 3. (pp. 1-75).

Rogers, Dexter. (2010). *Why is Michael Vick the most hated athlete in sports?* Examiner.com.

Russell, Edmund. (2007). *A Tale of Two Smithfields*. Retrieved from http://www.virginia.edu/ topnews/facultyopinions/2007/russell.html.

Sabo, D, F., Runfola, R. (1980). Jock: Sports & Male Identity. New Jersey. Prentice Hall.

Sandomir, R. (2007). *In Endorsements, No Athlete is a Sure Thing*. Retrieved from http://www.nytimes.com/2007/08/01/sports/football/01sandomir.html?ref=football&pagewa.

Salem-News. (2009). *Police Arrest Gresham Man for Sexually Abusing his Pit Bull*. Retrieved from http://www.salem-news.com/articles/may022009/animal_sex_5-2-09.php.

USA Today. (2007). *Local dogfighting probe continues as Vick cancels camp*. Retrieved from http://usatoday.printthis.clickability.com/pt/cpt?action=cpt&title=Local+dog-fghting+pro...

United States of America v. Purnell Peace, Quanis Phillips, Tony Taylor, and Michael Vick, U.S. District Court for the Eastern Division of Virginia. 2007. pp.1-17.

Villavicencio, Monica. (2007). *A History of Dogfighting*. National Public Radio, July 19, 2007.

Whitlock, J. (2007). *Vick can evolve from hip-hop prison culture*. Retrieved from http://www. kanasascity.com/sports/columnists/jason_whitlock/story/195760.html.

WKRN News. (2009). *Youth football coach charged with bestiality.* Retrieved from http://www. WKRN.com.

Wolfgang, M. E.,& Ferracuti, F. (1967). The Subculture of Violence Theory: Towards an Integrated Theory in Criminology. California. Sage Publications.

Zirin, Dave. (2007). Email from Dave Zirin (edgeofsports@gmail.com). Subject: "Inching Toward Insanity: Why Michael Vick is Not a Fascist." As sent to Ron Stewart, Ph.D., who forwarded to Kenneth N. Robinson, August 24, 2007.

Chapter II

Ashe, A. R. Jr. (1993). *A Hard Road to Glory: The African-American Athlete in Football.* Amistad. New York.

Becker, G. (2009). *Animal Welfare Act: Background and Selected Legislation.* Congressional Research Service.

Bell, J. (2007). NFL turned upside down by facets of Vick case. Retrieved from http://usatoday. printthis.clickability.com/pt/cpt?action=cpt&title=NFL+turned+upside+down.

Borelli, S. (2011). '*Something Bad Need to Happen' to Michael Vick.* USA Today, Sports, February, 10, 2011.

Boyd, H. & Burroughs, T. (2010). *Civil Rights: Yesterday and Today.* Publications International, Ltd. Lincolnwood, Ill.

Chase, (2010). *Tucker Carlson doesn't actually think Vick should be executed.* Retrieved from http://sports.yahoo.com/nfl/blog/shutdown_corner/post/Tucker-Carlson-doesn-t-actually.

Clayton, J. (2009). Vick's career at critical stage. Retrieved from http://sports.espn.go.com/ nfl/columns/story?columnist=clayton_john&id=4339406.

Colston, C. (2007). *Vick protests dominate opener of Falcons camp.* Retrieved from www. usatoday.com/sports/football/nfl/falcons/2007-07-26-camp-scene_N.htm.

ESPN.com. (2007). *Alleged vicious dogfighting ring infuriates Senator Byrd.* Retrieved from http://www.sports.espn.go.com/espn/print?id=2942677&type=story.

ESPN.com. (2007). *Vick asks judge to allow to auction home.* Retrieved from http://sports.espn. go/nfl/news/story/?id=3813868.

ESPN.com. (2007). *Report: McNabb says black QB's under more pressure.* Retrieved from http://sports.espn.go.com/nfl/news/story?id=3035308.

Fermino, J. (2007). *Marbury expresses support for Vick.* Retrieved from http://msn.foxsports. com/nfl/story/7144402?MSNHPHCP&GT1=10347.

Fogarty, D. (2011). *Too far? Official Michael Vick Chew Toy will Unsettle Some, Rally others.* Retrieved from http://www.sportsgrid.com.

Fox Sports. (2007). *Vick to appear in court in July*. Retrieved from http://msnfoxsports.com/ nfl/story/7033680/MSNHPHMA.

Gibson, H. (2005). *Dog fighting detailed discussions*. Animal Legal and Historical Center. Michigan State University College of Law. Retrieved from www.animallaw.info.

Harris, David. 1986. *The League: The Rise and Decline of the NFL*. New York. Bantam.

Henderson, B.B., Hensley, C., & Tallichet, S.E. (2011). Childhood animal cruelty methods and their link to adult interpersonal violence. *Journal of Interpersonal Violence, 26*, 2211-2227.

Hensley, C., Tallichet, S.E., & Dutkiewicz, E.L. (2010). Childhood bestiality: A potential precursor to Adult Interpersonal Violence. *Journal of Interpersonal Violence, 25*, 557-567.

Hensley, C., Tallichet, S.E., & Singer, S.D. (2006). Exploring the possible link between childhood and adolescent bestiality and interpersonal violence. *Journal of Interpersonal Violence, 21*, 910-923.

Hijek, B. (2009). *Man accused of having sex with dog can attend culinary school*. Retrieved from http://weblogs.sun-sentinel.com/news/specials/weirdflorida/blog/2009/10/man_accused_of.

Hijek, B. (2010). *Man accused of having sex with Great Dane named Christie Brinkley*. Retrieved from http://weblogs.sun-Sentinel.com/news/specials/weirdflorida/blog/2010/07/ man_accused_of.

Humane Society. (2009). *Floridians urge lawmakers to protect animals*. Retrieved from http://www.humanesociety.org/news/press_releases/2009/04/florida_humane_lobby_day/040209.

Humane Society. (2008). *Florida Senate Committee Passes bill to Ban Sexual Abuse of Animals*. Retrieved from http://www.humanesociety.org/news/press_releases/2008/04_fla_committee_ passes-bill_41608.html.

Humane Society. (2009). *Rush Limbaugh Records Audio Spots for The HSUS*. Retrieved from http://www.humanesociety.org/news/press_releases/2009/04/rush_limbaugh_records_audio.

Humane Society. (n.d.). *Fact Sheet, Bestiality and Other Violent Crime*.

Kalof, L. & Taylor, C. (2007). The Discourse of Dogfighting. *Humanity and Society*. Vol. 31. (November: 319-333).

Kreigel, M. (2007). *Nike more about money than morals*. Retrieved from http://msn.foxsports. com/nfl/story/7038442.

Leahy, S. (2010). *Nike chief: We plan on changing the NFL jersey dramatically*. Retrieved from http://content.usatoday.com/communities/thehuddle/post/2010/10/.

Limbaugh, R. (2009). *Rush Limbaugh PSA for The Humane Society USA #2*. Retrieved from http://www.youtube.com.

Marable, M. (2002). *The Great Wells of Democracy: The Meaning of Race in American Life*. New York, NY: BasicCivitas Books.

317

Mercury News .(2009). Man sentenced for having sex with his dogs told he can't own animals for two years. Retrieved from http://www.mercurynews.com/ci_12502031.

Merrill, E. (n.d.). Animal rights activists says Vick case 'tip of the iceberg'. Retrieved from http://sports.espn.go.com/nfl/news/story?id=2941401.

Mihoces, G. (2007). *10 Questions in Vick case: 'Potentially stiffer penalties' possible factor in plea.* USA Today Sports Section C, August 21, 2007, p. 1. Cover story.

News4Jax. (2009). *Vick Chew Toy Claims to be Fundraiser for Humane Society.* Retrieved from http://www.news4jax.com/news/13832724/detail.html.

Neus, E. (2007). *NFL Network intercepts Deion's attempt to write about Vick.* Retrieved from http://usatoday.printhis.clickability.com/pt/cpt/?action=cpt&title=NFL+Network=intercept.

Oriard, Michael. (2001). *King Football: Sport Spectacle in the Golden Age of Radio & Newsreels, Movies & Magazines, The Weekly & Daily Press.* North Carolina: University of North Carolina Press.

Peterson, Robert, W. (1997). *Pigskin: The Early Years of Pro Football.* New York: Oxford University Press.

Powers, Ron. (1984). *Supertube: The Rise of Television Sports.* New York. Coward-McCann.

Rader, Benjamin. G. (1984). *In its own image: How television has changed sport.* The Free Press. New York.

Sabo, Donald, F., Runfola, Ross. (1980). *Jock: Sports & Male Identity.* New Jersey. Prentice Hall.

Sadchev, A. (2007). *Nike to pay 400 Chicago employees $7.6 million to settle discrimination suit.* Retrieved from http://targetmarketnews.com/storyid07310701.

Saigon.com. (n.d.) *NIKE-VN FACT SHEET.* Retrieved from http:www.saigon.com/~nike/fact-sheet.htm.

Salem-News. (2009). *Police Arrest Gresham Man for Sexually Abusing his Pit Bull.* Retrieved from http://www.salem-news.com/articles/may022009/animal_sex_5-2-09.php.

Sandomir, R. (2007). *In Endorsements, No Athlete Is a Sure thing.* Retrieved from http://www.nytimes.com/2007/08/01/sports/football/01sandomir.html?ref=football&pagewa.

Sandomir, R. (2009). *Football Star Is Accused, but ESPN Plays it Cautious.* Retrieved from http://www.nytimes.com/2009/07/23/sports/football/23espn.html?ref=football.

Schefter, A. (2007). *Vick might be the lead story for quite awhile.* Retrieved from http://www.nfl. com/nflnetwork/story/10266500.

Schultz, J. (2009). If Goodell is so principled, why is he selling Vick's jersey? Retrieved from http://blogs.ajc.com/jeff-schultz-blog/2009/08/16/.

Shropshire, Kenneth, L. (1996). *In Black and White: Race and Sports in America*. New York: University Press.

Sullivan, J. (2005). *Videotapes show bestiality, Enumclaw Police say.* Retrieved from http://seattletimes.nwsource.com/html/local-news/2002384648_farm16m.html.

Thompson, W. (2007). *A History of Mistrust.* Retrieved from http://sports.espn.go.com/espn/ eticket/story?page=vicksatlanta&lpos=spotlight&lid=tab2pos1.

USA Today. (2008). *Judge rules Michael Vick can keep $16.25 million in bonuses.* Retrieved from http://usatoday.com/sports/football/nfl/falcons/2008-02-04-vick-bonuses_N.htm.

USA Today. (2007). *Atlanta expected to try to recoup $22M of Vick's signing bonus.* Retrieved from http://usatoday.printthis.clickability.com/pt/cpt?action=cpt&title=Atlanta+expected+to+try.

USA Today Sports - The Huddle. (2009). *PETA says it may protest if Michael Vick isn't psychologically tested.* Retrieved from http://blogs.usatoday.com/thehuddle/2009/07/peta-says-it-may-protest-if-michael-vick-.

USA Today. (2007). *Congressman seeks strong action against Vick.* Retrieved from http:// usatoday.printthis.clickability.com/pt/cpt?action=cpt&title=Congressman+seeks+.

USA Today. (2007). *NAACP: Let Vick return to Falcons after jail sentence.* Retrieved from http://www.usa.today.com/sports/football/nfl/falcons/2007-08-22-vick-wednesday_N.htm.

USA Today. (2007). *Portis contrite for comments on Vick situation.* Retrieved from http:// usatoday.printhis.clickability.com/pt/cpt/?action=cpt&title=Portis+contrite+for+com.

USA Today. (2008). *Joey Porter on Vick: 'All it was was dogs.'* Retrieved from http://blogs. usatoday.com/the huddle/2008/11/joey-porter-on.html.

USA Today. (2007). *Atlanta expected to try to recoup $22M of Vick's signing bonus.* http:// usatoday.printhis.clickability.com/pt/cpt/?action.

USA Today. (2009). *PETA denies that it plans to do ads with Michael Vick.* Retrieved from http://www.usatoday.com/sports/football/nfl/2009-05-01-peta-denies-vick-ads.

Watkins, B. (2007). *Note to Sharpton and Simmons: Slow Your Damn Roll!!* Retrieved from http://www.blackathlete.net/artman2/publish/Commentary_1/Note_to_Sharpton_and...

Williamson, B. (2010). *Is taping incident the last straw for McDaniels?* Retrieved from ESPN.com.

Zirin, D. (2007). *Who let the dogs out on Michael Vick?* Retrieved from http://www.thenation. com/doc/200707370/southpaw.

Chapter III

Buffalo News. (2010). *Chinese Pet Spa creates dog of a different color.* June 20, 2010. Section A4.

Dancing dog blog. (2009). *China orders Dog Owners to Kill Their Dogs*. Retrieved from http:// www.dancingblog.com/2009/09/ china-culls-dogs-threatens-owners/.

Fur is Dead. (n.d.) *China's Shocking Dog and Cat Fur Trade*. Retrieved from http://www. furisdead.com/feat-dogcatfur.asp.

Gleason, B. (2009). *Gleason: Vick's chance at redemption is a fair one*. Retrieved from http:// www.buffalonews.com/sports/story/747560.

Harvard.edu. (2009). Retrieved from http://blogs.law.harvard.edu/ guorui/2009/05/23/heihe-city-government-ordered-to-kill-dog/.

Humane Society International. (2009). *HSI Condemns Government-Ordered Dog Killing in China*. Retrieved from http://www.humanesociety.org/news/press_release/2009/06/humane_ society_international.

Jiasi, Lin. (2009). Retrieved from http://www.china.globaltimes.cn/chinanews/2009-05/ 432228.html.

Jingjing, H. (2009). *NPC to consider animal abuse law*. Retrieved from http://china.globaltimes. cn/chinanews/2009-06/437186.html.

MSNBC. (2006). *Chinese country clubs to death 50,000 dogs*. Retrieved from http://www.msnbc. com/id/14139027/.

New York Times. (2007). Pro Football Grooms 3 Legs: With the Goal of a Billion Eyes. Retrieved from http://www.nytimes.com/2007/03/02/ sports/football/02kickers.ready.html?ex. =1187150400.

NFL News. (2003). *NFL & China Central TV reach partnership*. Retrieved from www.nfl.com.

Powers, Ron. (1984). *Supertube: The Rise of Television Sports*. New York. Coward-McCann.

Tagliabue, P. (2012). *In the Matter of New Orleans Saints Pay-for-Play Performance/"Bounty": Final Decision on Appeal.*

Weird Asia News. (2009). *The China Dog Massacres of 2009*. Retrieved from http://www. weirdasiannews.com/2010/02/12/ china-dog-massacres-2009/.

WFL Endangered Stream Live. (2009). *Special Report: China Dog Culling*. Retrieved from http://wflendangeredstreamlive.blog.com/2009/06/ special-report-china-dog-culling.html.

Word Press.com. Retrieve from http://isiria.wordpress.com/2009/06/16/ dog-massacre-in-china-30000-dead-and-counting/.

Zirin, D. (2007). *Inching Toward Insanity: Why Michael Vick is not a Fascist*. Retrieved from emailed professional communication from Dr. Ron Stewart who forwarded column from edgeofsports@gmail. com.

Chapter IV

Argest, J. (2003). *It's Monday Night Football: ABC should fill booth with football experts.* http:// archive.profootballweekly.com/content/archives/ features.

Ashe, A. R. Jr. (1993). *A Hard Road to Glory: The African-American Athlete in Football.* Amistad. New York.

Briscoe, Marlin. (2002).With Schaller, Bob. *The First Black Quarterback: Marlin Briscoe's Journey to Break the Color Barrier and Start in the NFL.* Nebraska: Cross Training Publishing.

Chalk, O. (1975). *Pioneers of Black Sport.* New York: Dodd, Mead & Company.

Gaughn, M. (2004). Buffalo News Sports.

GQ Magazine. (2012). *The XVIII Worst Decisions in Sports History.* p. 194-196.

Hoose, Philip., M. (1989). *Necessities: Racial Barriers in American Sports.* New York: Random House.

Humane Society (2009). *Rush Limbaugh Records Audio Spots for The HSUS.* Retrieved from http://www.humanesociety.org/news/ press_releases/2009/04/rush_limbaugh_records_audio.

Knox, Chuck, Bill Plaschke. (1988). *Hard Knox: The Life of an NFL Coach.* Florida: Harcourt Brace Jovanovich.

Loy, John, W., McELVogue, Joseph. F. (1981). *Racial segregation in American Sport.* Sport, Culture and Society: A reader on the sociology of sport. Second and Revised edition. Philadelphia: Lea & Febiger.

Martze. R. (2003). *Limbaugh fumbles the ball, and ESPN fails to recover.* Retrieved from http:// www.usatoday.com/sports/columnist/ martzke/2003-10-01-martzke_x.htm.

Mirabile, M. (2004) *Intelligence and football: Testing for Differentials in Collegiate Quarterback Passing Performance and NFL Compensation.* Retrieved from http://www. thesportjournal.org.

Mirabile, Mirable. (n.d.). *NFL Quarterback Wonderlic Test Scores.*

NFL.com. 2003. *Analyst Limbaugh resigns from ESPN job.* Retrieved from http://www.nfl.com.

NFL.com. (2009). *The NFL head coaches show to debut in September.* Retrieved from www. nfl.com/nflnetwork/story?id.

Oriard, Michael. (2001). *King Football: Sport Spectacle in the Golden Age of Radio & Newsreels, Movies & Magazines, The Weekly & Daily Press.* North Carolina: University of North Carolina Press.

Ortiz, F. (2010). Making the Dog-man Heel: Recommendations for Improving the Effectiveness of Dogfighting Laws. *Stanford Journal of Animal Law and Policy.* V. 3. (pp. 1-75).

Pittsburg Steelers (n.d.) Retrieved from www.pittsburghsteelers.co.uk/steelers/players/joe% 20gilliam.htm.

Pro Football Weekly. (2003). *Random quotes from around the NFL.* Retrieved from http:// profootballweekly.com/PFW/Features/ They+Said+It/2003/said45.htm.

Sage, George S. 1998. *Power and Ideology in American Sport: A Critical Perspective* (2nd Edition). Colorado: Human Kinetics, 1998.

Sabo, Donald, F., Messner, Michael, A., (1994). *Sex, Violence & Power in Sports: Rethinking Masculinity.* California: Crossing Press.

Spanos, Alex. (2002). *Sharing the Wealth: My Story.* Washington, D.C. Regnery Publishing, Inc.

St. Petersburg Times. (2003). *Limbaugh to join ESPN.* July 15, 2003. Retrieved from http:// www.sptimes.com/2003/07/15/Sports/Limbaugh_to_join_ESPN.shtml.

USA Today. (2009). *Bart Scott, Mathias Kiwanuka: No possibility of playing for Rush Limbaugh owned team.* Retrieved from http://content. usatoday.com/communities/thehuddle/post/2009/10/.

USA Today. (2009). *Rush Limbaugh acknowledges bid to buy St. Louis Rams.* Retrieved from http://www.usatoday.com/sports/football/nfl/ rams/2009-10-06-rush-limbaugh-rams.

Washington Post. (2009). *From Bad to Worse.* Retrieved from http://views. washingtonpost. com/theleague/panelists/2009/10/rush-limbaugh.

Chapter V

Ashe, A. R. Jr. (1993). *A Hard Road to Glory: The African-American Athlete in Football.* Amistad. New York.

Becker, H.S. (1987). Outsiders: Deviance and the Responses of Others. In Earl Rubington & Martin S. Weinberg (5th ed.) *Deviance: The Interactionist Perspective* (pp. 10-12). New York, NY: Macmillan Publishing Co.

Bell, J. (2010). *Once a 'Nervous Ned,' now all-too-dangerous qb.* Retrieved from http:// www.usatoday.com/sports/football/nfl/ eagles/2011-01-05-michael-vick-package.

Bell, J. (2009). *Goodell: Vick must show 'remorse' to play in NFL again.* Retrieved from http:// www.usatoday.com/sports/football/ nfl/2009-03-25-goodell-vick.

Benedict, J., Yaeger, D. (1998). *Pros and Cons: The Criminals who Play in the NFL.* New York: Time Warner.

Briscoe, Marlin. (2002). With Schaller, Bob. *The First Black Quarterback: Marlin Briscoe's Journey to Break the Color Barrier and Start in the NFL.* Nebraska: Cross Training Publishing.

Burke, B. (2009). *Vick as a quarterback? He's Underrated.* Retrieved from http://fifthdown. blogs.nytimes.com/2009/07/23/ vick-as-a-quarterback-hes-underrated.

Chalk, O. (1975). *Pioneers of Black Sport*. New York: Dodd, Mead & Company.

Colston, C. (2007). *Vick protests dominate opener of Falcons camp*. Retrieved from www. usatoday.com/sports/football/nfl/falcons/2007-07-26-camp-scene_N.htm.

ESPN.com news services. (2007). *NFL Security offers to help Virginia probe of Vick*. Retrieved from http://ESPN.com news services.

ESPN.com news services. (2010). *Tucker Carlson addresses Vick role*. Retrieved from http:// www.espn.comnewsservices.

Franzese, R.J. (2009). *The Sociology of Deviance: Differences, Tradition, and Stigma*. Springfield, Ill: Charles C. Thomas.

Gleason, B. (2009). *Gleason: Vick's chance at redemption is a fair one*. Retrieved from http:// www.buffalonews.com/sports/story/747560.

Hill, J. (2010). *Goodell's slippery Roethlisberger slope*. Retrieved from http://sports.espn.go. com/espn/commentary/news/story?page=hill/100326.

Kriegel, M. (2010). *Roethlisberger has earned his punish-ment*. Retrieved from http://msn. foxsports.com/nfl/story/roethlisberger-has-earned-suspension-kriegel-041210.

Lapchick, R.E. (1996). *Sport in Society: Equal Opportunity or Business as Usual?* California: Sage.

Leahy, S. (2010). Police in Ohio investigated Ben Roethlisberger Golf Foursome for alleged Public Urination. Retrieved from http://content. usatoday.com/communities/thehuddle/post/2010/ 07/police-in-ohio-inves-tigated-ben-roethlisberger-golf-foursome-for-alleged-public-urination/1.

Leahy, S. (2010). Grandson of Art Rooney calls Steelers QB Ben Roeth-lisberger 'an idiot'. Retrieved from http://content.usatoday.com/communities/thehuddle/post/2010/05/grandson-of-art-rooney.

Leahy, S. (2010). Pittsburgh Zoo removes image of Ben Roethlisberger after calls from the Public. Retrieved from http://content.usatoday.com/communities/thehuddle/post/2010/04/ pittsburgh-zoo-removes.

Marvez, A. (2009). *Vick reinstated, but not free under Goodell*. Retrieved from http://msn. foxsports.com/nfl/story/9861576/Vick-reinstated,-but-not-free-under-Goodell.

Mihoces, G. (2010). *Police: No Suspects ruled out in shooting at Michael Vick part*. Retrieved from http://www.usatoday.com/sports/football/nfl/eagles/2010-07-01._

Mihoces, G. (2010). *Steelers look to Ben Roethlisberger to set tone, QB's to be ready*. Retrieved from http://www.usatoday.com/sports/football/nfl/steelers/2010-08-01-nfl-pittsburgh-steelers (see ASA submission).

Mihoces, G. (2010). *Big doubts about Ben: Support for Roethlisberger wavering*. Retrieved from http://www.usatoday.com/sports/football/nfl/steelers/2010-03-29-benroethlisberger.

Piquero, A. R., Piquero, N.L., Gertz, M., Baker, T., Batton, J., and Barnes, J.C. (2011). Race, Punishment, and the Michael Vick Experience. Social Science Quarterly, 92: 535-551.

Pfhol, S. (1994). *Images of Deviance and Social Control: A Sociological History*. New York: McGraw-Hill.

Raissman, B. (2011). *Phil Simms provides realistic analysis of Ben Roethlisberger's progress as ESPN dodges the issue*. Retrieved from http://www.NYDailyNews.com.

Saraceno, J. (2007). If true, Vick has committed cruel acts to game and fans. Retrieved from http://www.usatoday.com/sports/columnist/saraceno/2007-07-24-Vickcolumn.

Tagliabue, P. (2012). *In the Matter of New Orleans Saints Pay-for-Play Performance/"Bounty": Final Decision on Appeal.*

Trice, H.M., Roman, P.M. (1987). De-labeling, Re-labeling, and Alcoholics Anonymous. In Earl Rubington & Martin S. Weinberg (5th ed.) *Deviance: The Interactionist Perspective* (pp. 371-376). New York, N.Y: Macmillan Publishing Co.

Vick, Michael. (2012). *Michael Vick: Finally Free*. North Carolina: Core Media.

Wilson, A. (2009). *PETA goes too far with NFL's Vick*. Retrieved from http://www.buffalonews. com/sports/story/569076.html?imw=Y.

Wilson, A. (2010). *Wilson: Bad Choices put Big Ben on hot seat*. Retrieved from http://www. buffalonews.com/sports/article40897.

Yardbarker.com. (n.d.) *PETA wants Vick off Madden Tourney*. Retrieved from http://www. yardbarker.com/nfl/articles/peta_asks_ea_sports_to_remove_michael_vick.

Chapter VI

Becker, H.S. (1987). Outsiders: Deviance and the Responses of Others. In Earl Rubington & Martin S. Weinberg (5th ed.) *Deviance: The Interactionist Perspective* (pp. 10-12). New York, NY: Macmillan Publishing Co.

Evans, R., Gauthier, D., and Forsyth, C.J. (1998). *Dogfighting: Symbolic Expression and Validation of Masculinity*. Retrieved from http://htmlimg2.scribdassets.com/5692.

Frias, C. (2007). *Vicious fight: World of dogfighting seems to be growing despite awareness of its cruel side*. Palm Beach Post, 1B, June 3, 2007.

Gibson, Hanna. (2005). http://www.animallaw.info/articles/ddusdogfighting.htm. Michigan State University College of Law.

Hutchinson, E., O. (2007). *Vick versus Boudreaux: A Tale of Hypocrisy*. Retrieved from http:// www.huffingtonpost.com/earl-ofari-hutchinson/vick-versus-boudreaux-a-t_b_61990.html.

Ortiz, F. (2010). Making the Dog-man Heel: Recommendations for Improving the Effectiveness of Dogfighting Laws. *Stanford Journal of Animal Law and Policy*. V.3. (pp. 1-75).

Pfhol, S. (1994). *Images of Deviance and Social Control: A Sociological History*. New York: McGraw-Hill.

Weir, T. (2007). *Vick's Case sheds light on dark world of dogfighting*. Retrieved from http:// usatoday30.usatoday.com/sports/football/nfl/falcons/2007-07-18-vick-cover_N.htm.

Wenger, Y. (2007). *Tant is granted parole*. Retrieved from http://www.post-andcourier.com/ article/20100908/PC1602/309089938.

Wolfgang, M. E.,& Ferracuti, F. (1967). The Subculture of Violence Theory: Towards an Integrated Theory in Criminology. California. Sage Publications.

Chapter VII

Aaronson, A. and Kimmel, M. (2012). *Sociology Now: The Essentials*. (2nd ed.) MA: Allyn & Bacon.

Alsup, D. (2013). *Michael Vick cancels book tour after threats*. Retrieved from http://www. cnn.com/2013/03/11/sport/michael-vick-threats/index.html.

Bergeron, E. (2011). *Zero-sum game: Michael Vick mishandled his money and went bankrupt. Unfortunately, he won't be the last NFL player to do so*. Retrieved from http://espn.go.com/nfl/ story/_/id/6895017/nfl-michael-vick-typifies.

ESPN.go.com. (2009). *Dungy: Vick wants second chance*. Retrieved from http://sports.espn.go. com/nfl/news/story?id=4164165.

ESPN.go.com. (2010). *Michael Vick signs Cowboys RB's glove*. Retrieved from http://sports. espn.go.com/dallas/nfl/news/story/id=5914095.

Evans, R., Gauthier, D., and Forsyth, C.J. (1998). *Dogfighting: Symbolic Expression and Validation of Masculinity*. Retrieved from http://htmlimg2.scribdassets.com/5692.

Fleming, D. (2011). *The dog in the room: A lot of people will never forgive Michael Vick. A lot of people wonder why, too*. Retrieved from http://espn.go.com/espn/commentary/story/_/id/ 6889579/espn-magazine.

Fleming, D. (2011). *There is no middle ground*. Retrieved from http://espn.go.com/nfl/story/_/id/ 6885774/nfl-michael-vick-makes-neutrality-impossibility.

Garafolo, M. (2013). *Eagles restructure Michael Vick's contract*. Retrieved from http://www. usatoday.com/story/sports/nfl/eagles/2013/02/11/michael-vick-one-year-contract.

GQ Magazine. (2012). *The XVIII Worst Decisions in Sports History*. p. 194-196.

Kenneth N. Robinson, MS

Mihoces, G. (2010). *Police: No Suspects ruled out in shooting at Michael Vick part*. Retrieved from http://www.usatoday.com/sports/football/nfl/eagles/2010-07-01.

Sandomir, R. (2007). *In Endorsements, No Athlete Is a Sure thing*. Retrieved from http://www. nytimes.com/2007/08/01/sports/football/01sandomir.html?rcf=football&pagewa.

Schultz, J. (2009). *If Goodell is so principled, why is selling Vick's jersey?* Retrieved from http:// blogs.ajc.com/jeff-schultz-blog/2009/08/16/if-goodell-is-so-principled-why-is-he-selling-Vick-s-jersey?

Touré. (2011). What if Michael Vick were white? Retrieved from http://espn.go.com/espn/ commentary/story/_/id/6894586/imagining-michael-vick-white.

Vick, Michael. (2012). *Michael Vick: Finally Free*. North Carolina: Core Media.

Zremski, J. (2013). *Victims of military sexual assault tell senators about need for justice*. Retrieved from http://www.buffalonews.com/apps/pbcs.dll/article?AID=/20130314/WORLD.

CPSIA information can be obtained
at www.ICGtesting.com
Printed in the USA
FFOW02n1850020315
11498FF